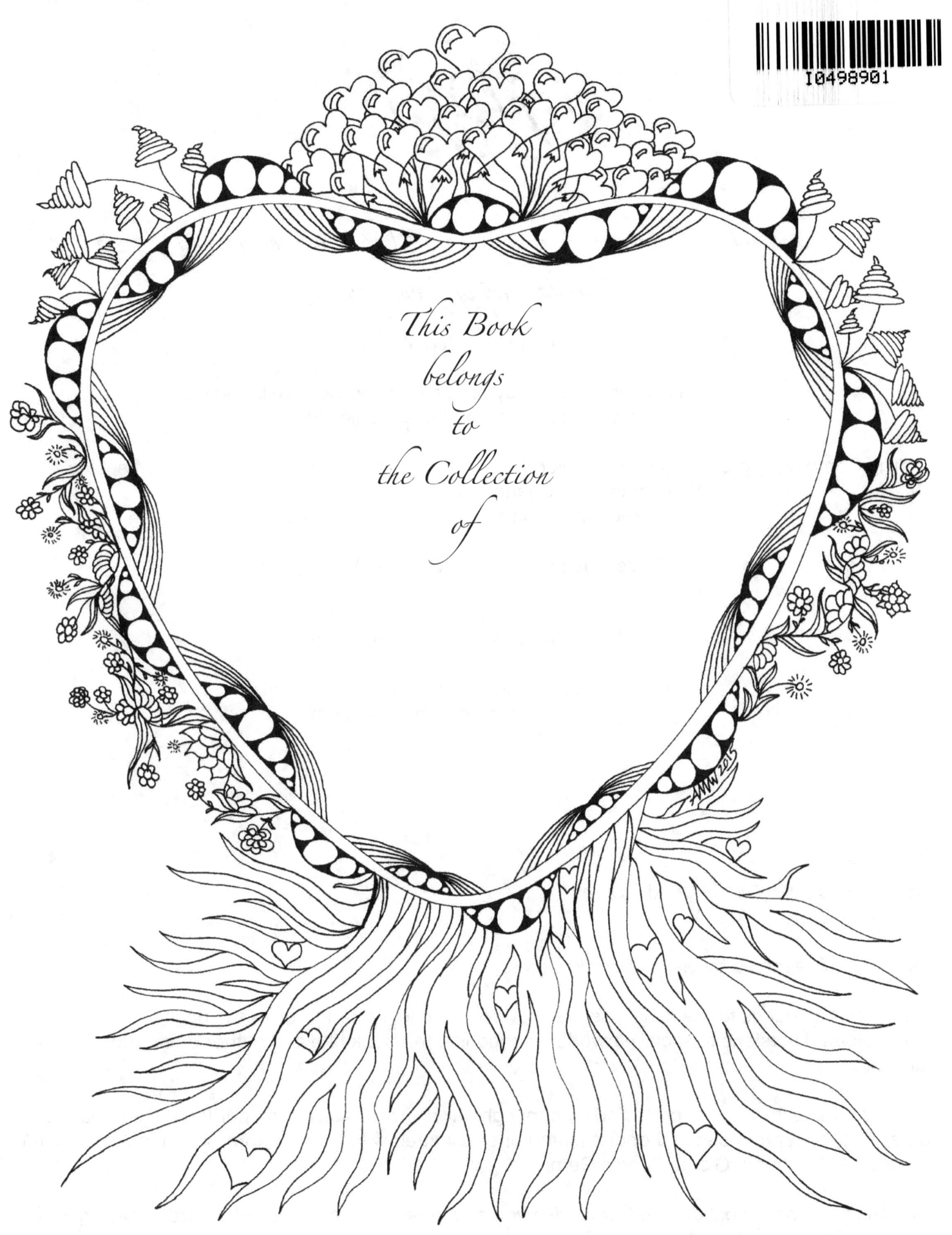

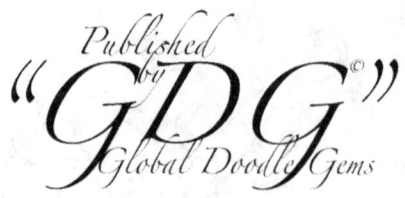

Share your colored versions with us ! We love seeing your results and hearing from you we are social !

The Official FB book page, stay on top of what we have in the works !
www.facebook.com/globaldoodlegems

The Community group, share your colored pages, meet the artists, enjoy exclusive freebies, take part in community Charity books and so much more......
www.facebook.com/groups/globaldoodlegems/

Follow us on Twitter.... @GlobalDoodlegem

We are on Instagram too
@globaldoodlegems for instagram

...and if you are not social like that we have a blog
globaldoodlegems.wordpress.com

Copyright © 2016 Global Doodle Gems

All rights are reserved by Global Doodle Gems.

Duplication of pages for personal use are allowed. You are invited to color the pages then scan/post your coloured versions to social networks, mentioning the book title and author/artist (Global Doodle Gems).

All artwork and images are protected by copyright laws. This book or any portion thereof may not, otherwise, be reproduced and/or distributed or transmitted without the express written permission of the artist/publisher of Global Doodle Gems.

All of us from the Global Doodle Gems wish you a colortastic time and look forward to seeing your wonderful color results online !

Annual Colorists Choice Collection
Volume 1 2015/16

We had a huge nomination round on our Global Doodle Gems Coloring Group,
colorists nominated their favorite drawings by submitting their colored pieces
from the Global Doodle Gems Books published from the first year July 2015 to April 2016.
Over 500 Drawings were nominated for the book.
We had a Jury of 7 Judges from the large Coloring Groups, vote on their favourites
and here is the result, We hope you will enjoy it !

The Cover was colored by Vero Pignot and the colored piece on the cover was chosen from all the nominated colored pieces... then Vero was asked to color the back with the portrait of Maria Wedel, the founder of Global Doodle Gems, in the same style.

Cover drawings are by Orbleu's and Alfred E. Villanueva.

And a few lines from each of our Judges.

Cynthia Elhorst, the owner of the biggest online Coloring for Adults community in the Netherlands. It was a pleasure to judge the collection and can't wait to see the book! Curious about us? See our website www.kleurvolwassen.nl.

Linda Op 't Eijnde, the other owner of Kleuren voor Volwassenen in the Netherlands. Together with Cynthia we allready own the website and community for allmost 2 years now. I liked the judging and can't wait for the book. You can find us at https://www.facebook.com/kleurenvoorvolwassnen/

Deb Norman, i am the owner of 50 Shades of Colouring.. i enjoyed judging the wonderful talent that has come together to make this amazing book. Can't wait to see it :)
https://www.facebook.com/groups/1639567539660887/

Angie Thompson, I am a huge coloring enthusiast! I am a HUGE GDG fan, having nearly all of the books in my collection! I love independent artists and supporting them. I can't get enough coloring books or supplies--ever!! I also help admin the group, International Coloring Club, with my best friend- Vanessa Lee.
Check our group out if you're inclined: https://www.facebook.com/groups/1399664530361770/

Jody Estabrook, I am a reviewer. I met several of the ladies here in coloring groups. I started color because a friend told me it would help with my PTSD and she was correct! I color and review a lot of coloring books and mediums as I just can't get enough!! My husband teases me all the time about having so many!! I found GDG when I bought The Who's Whos and haven't looked back!!
https://www.facebook.com/Reviews-by-Jody-284752938390956/

#cherylcolors creator of Adult Coloring Worldwide. Colorist, Artist, Line Art Critic, Coloring Book and Artist Promoter. www.facebook.com/cherylcolors

#anniecolors co-creator of Adult Coloring Worldwide and The Coloring Hangout. Colorist, coloring book and artist promoter. Find me here https://www.facebook.com/anniecolorsworldwide/

Contributing Artist
Adriana Graciela Volpe
Argentina

Global Doodle Gems Valentines Collection Volume 2

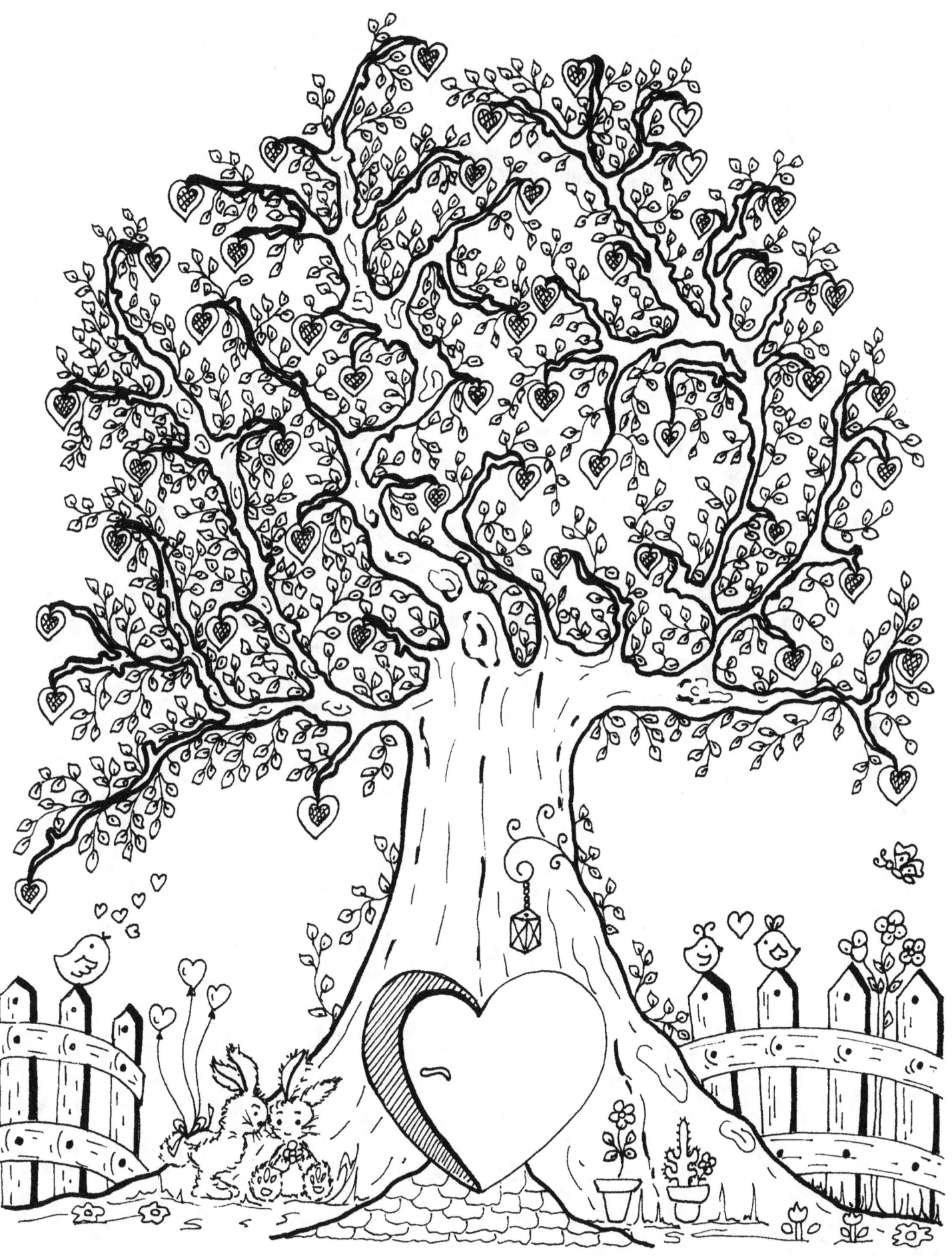

Contributing Artist
Ahmed Fouad Eid
Egypt
Facebook : Celestialarttherapy

Celestial Art

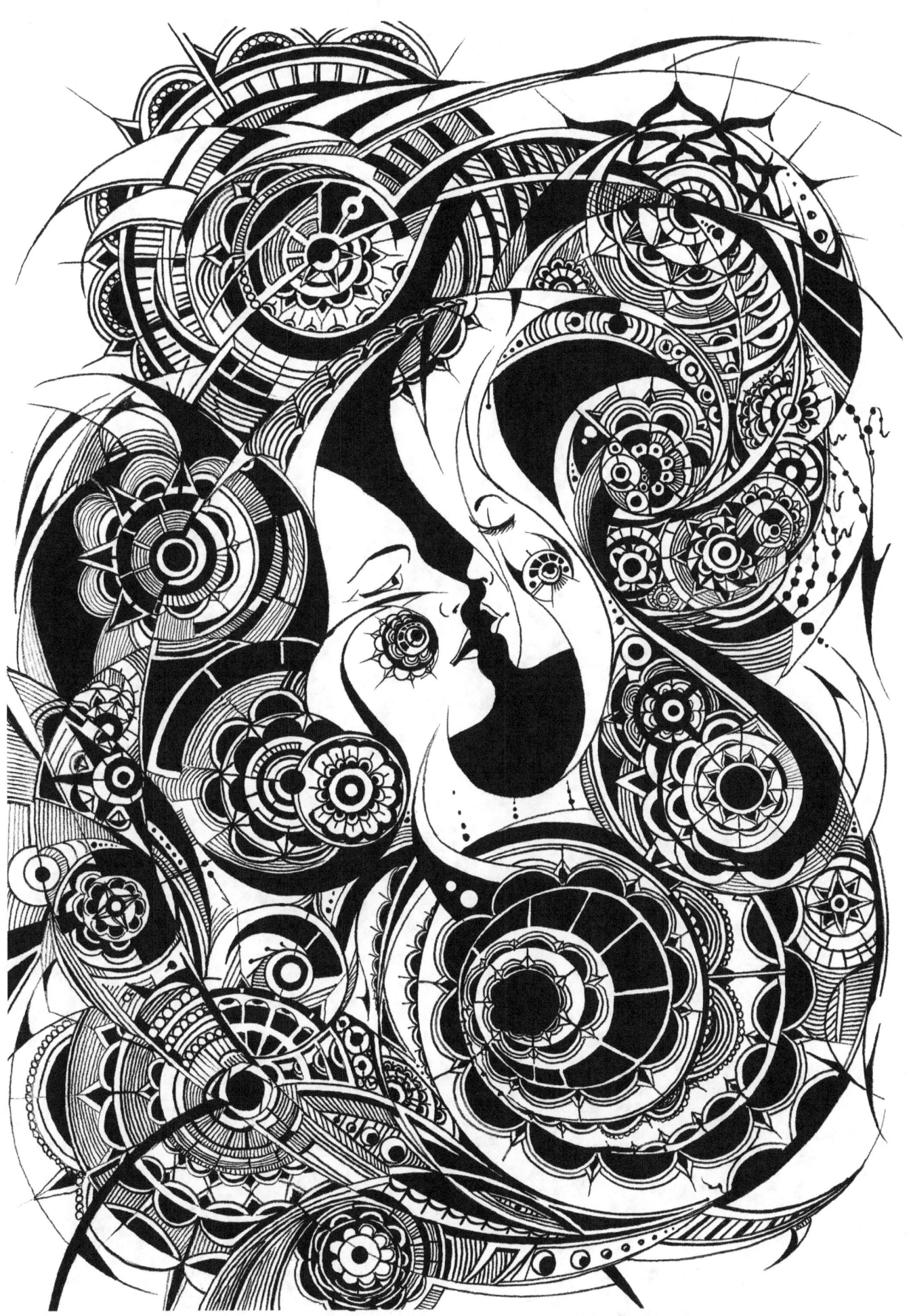

Contributing Artist
Ahmed Fouad Eid
Egypt

Facebook : Celestialarttherapy

Celestial Art

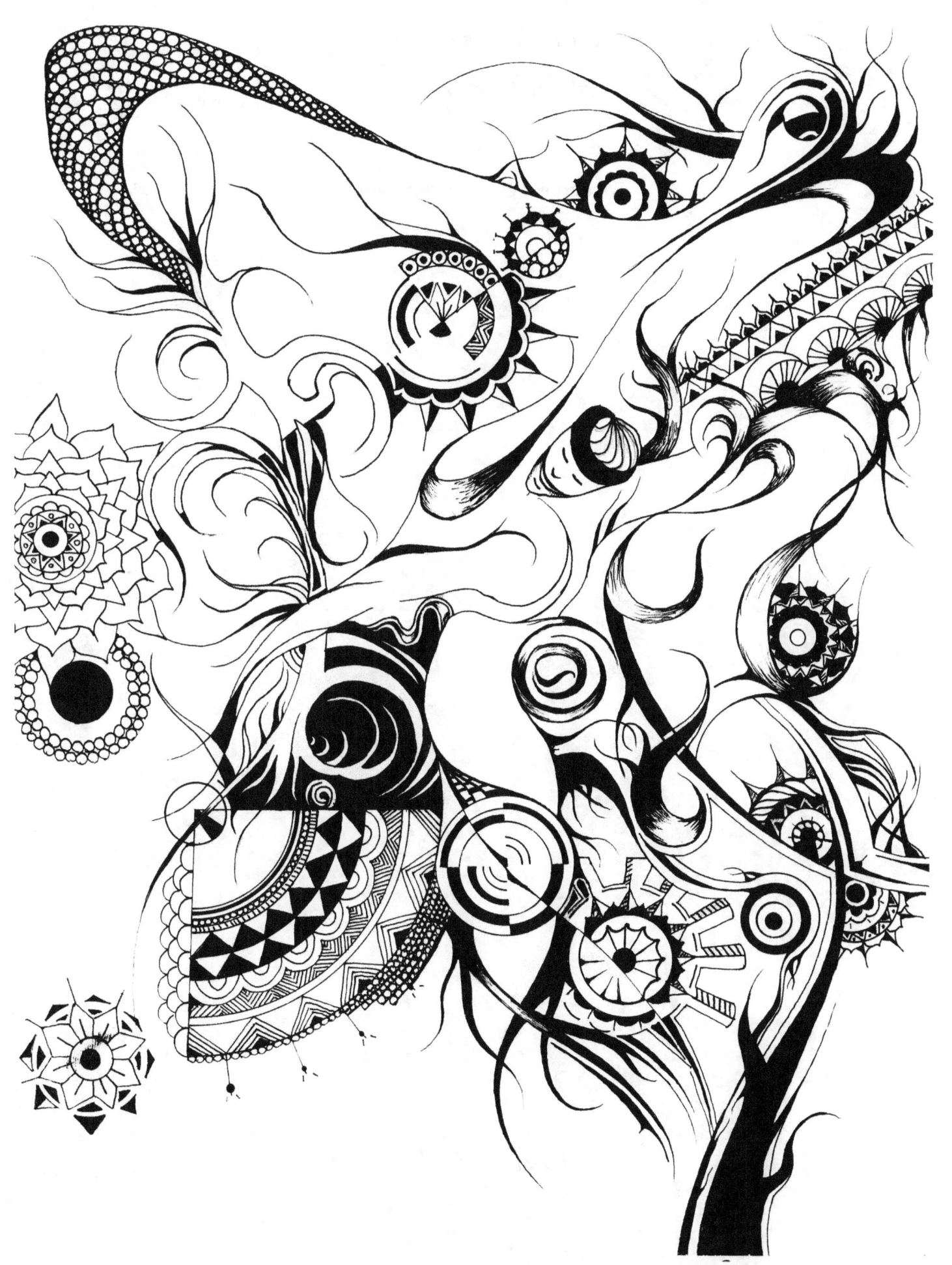

Contributing Artist
Ahmed Fouad Eid
Egypt
Facebook : Celestialarttherapy

Celestial Art

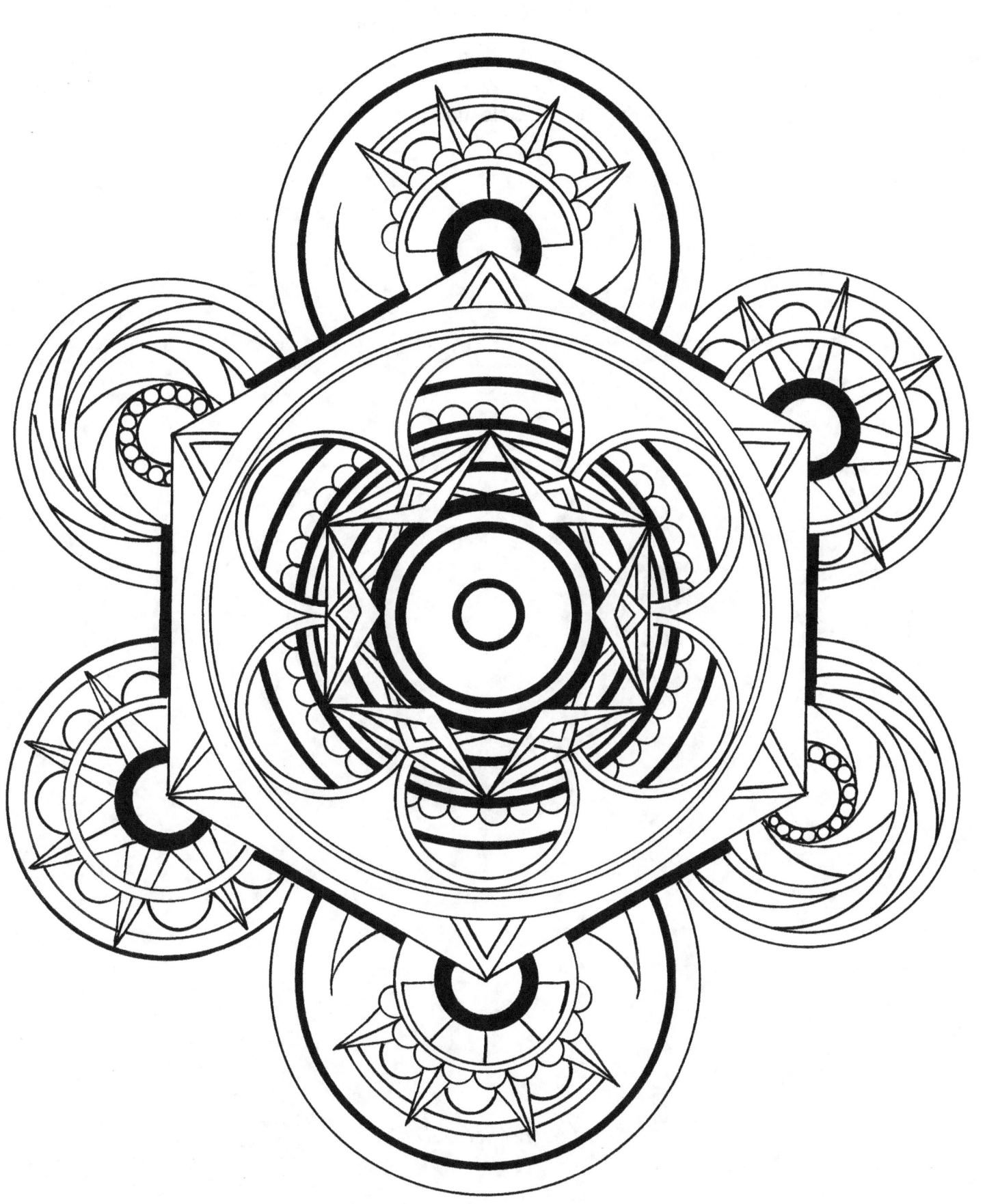

Contributing Artist
Ahmed Fouad Eid
Egypt
Facebook : Celestialarttherapy

Celestial Art

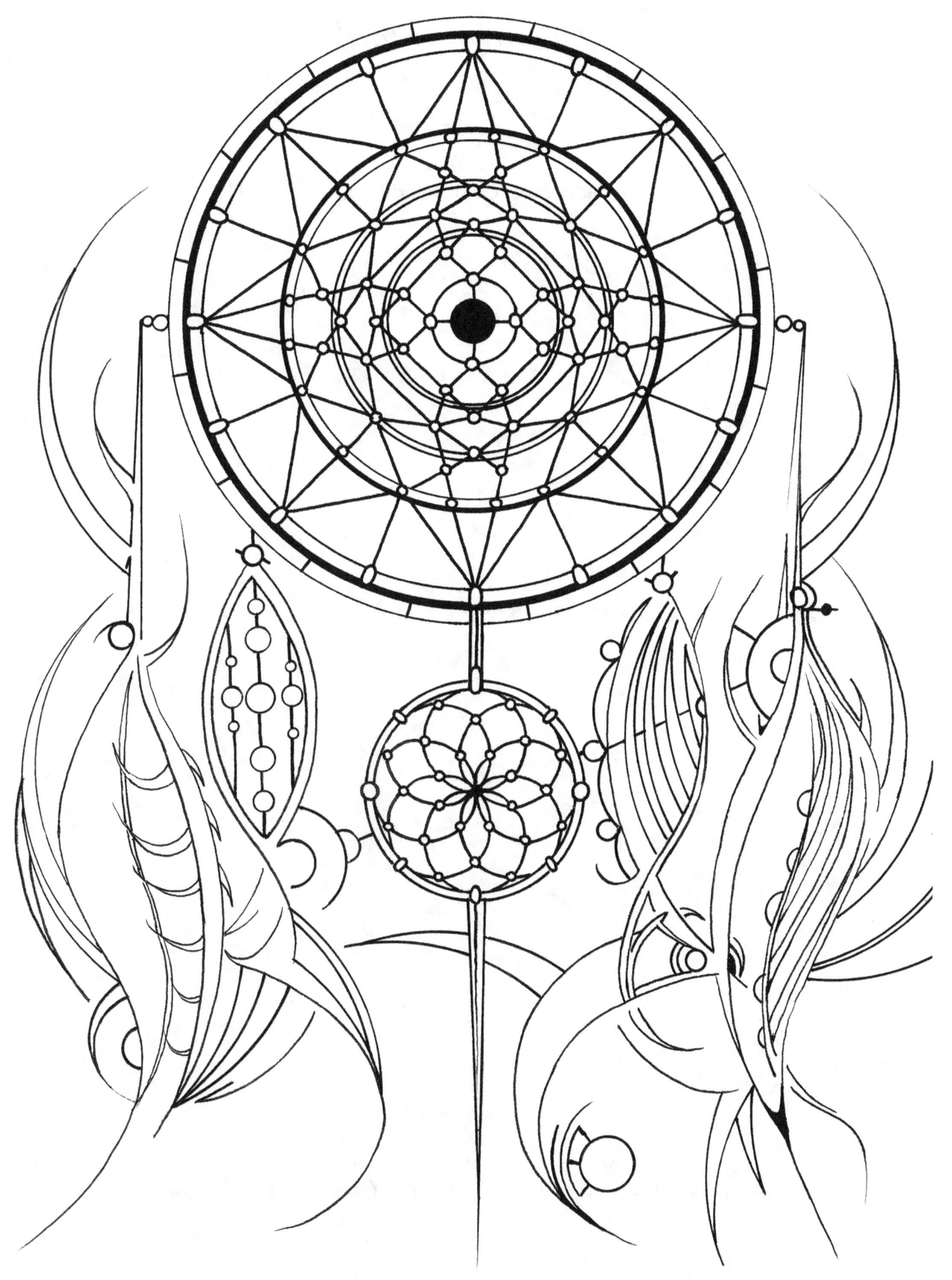

Contributing Artist
Ahmed Fouad Eid
Egypt
Facebook : Celestialarttherapy

Global Doodle Gems Mandala Collection Volume 1

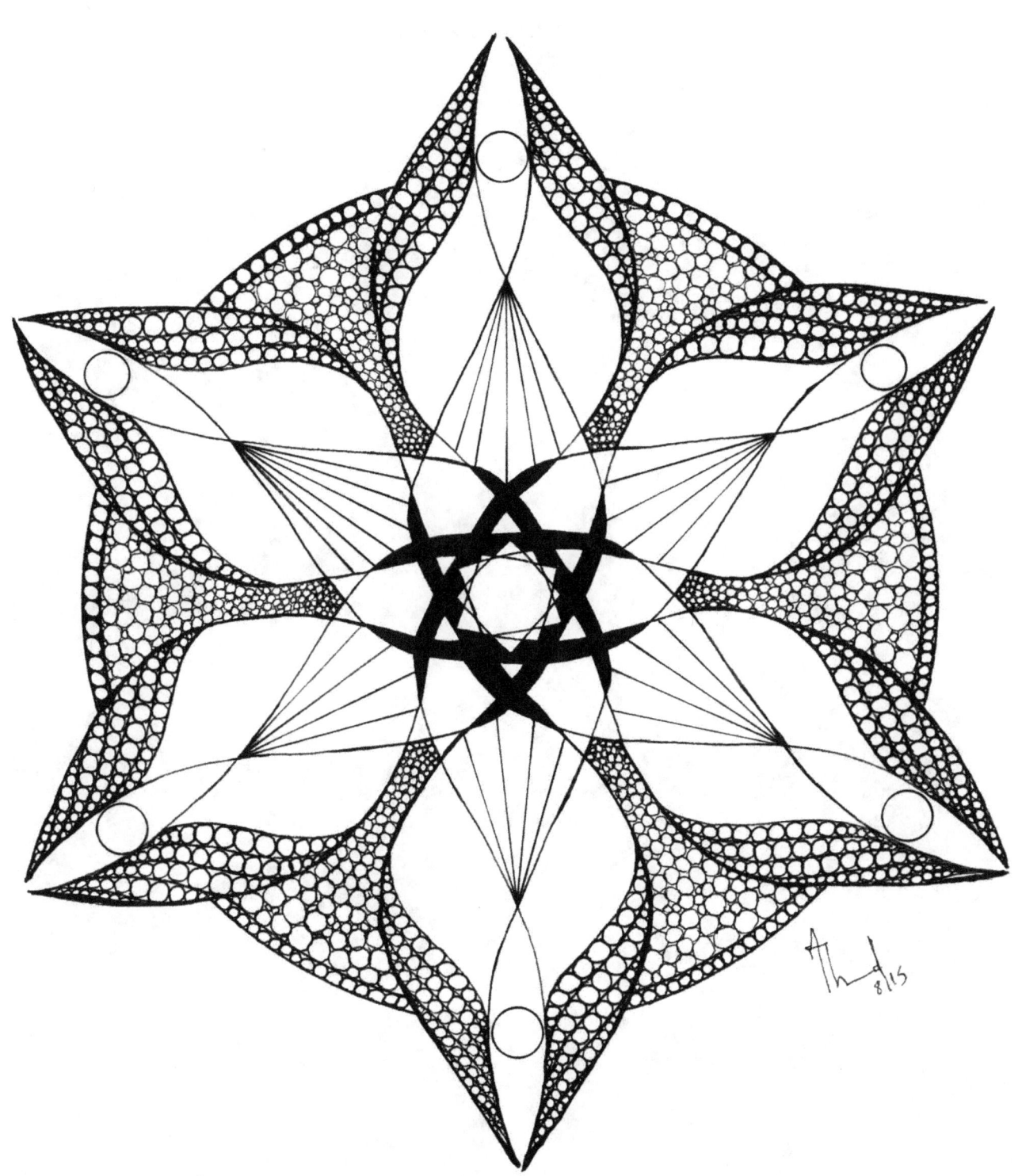

Contributing Artist
Alfred E. Villanueva
Philippines
Facebook : viworksart2015

GemInsects

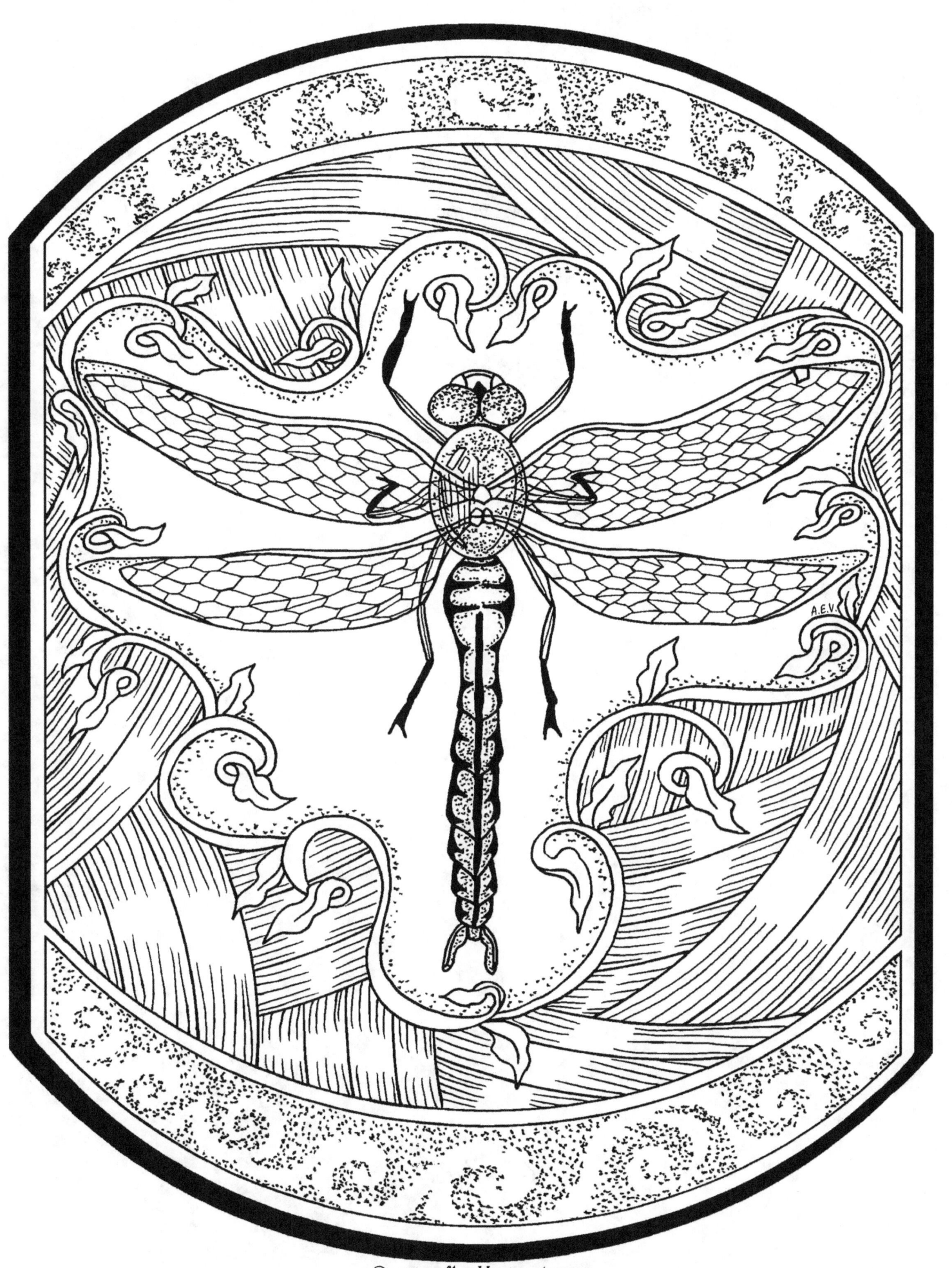

~Dragonfly Moonstone~

Contributing Artist
Alfred E. Villanueva
Philippines
Facebook : viworksart2015

GemInsects

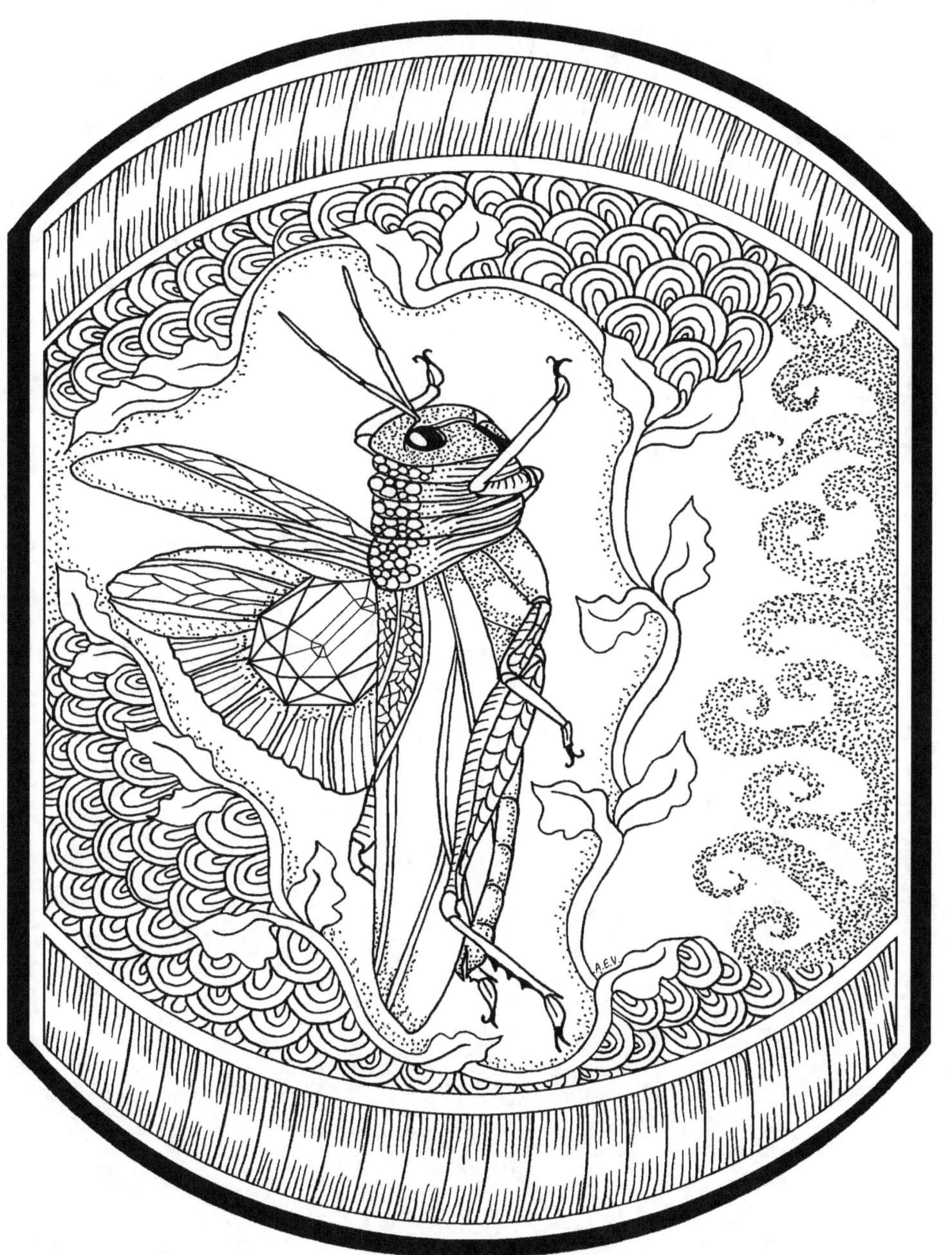

~Grasshopper Garnet~

Contributing Artist
Alfred E. Villanueva
Philippines
Facebook : viworksart2015

GemInsects

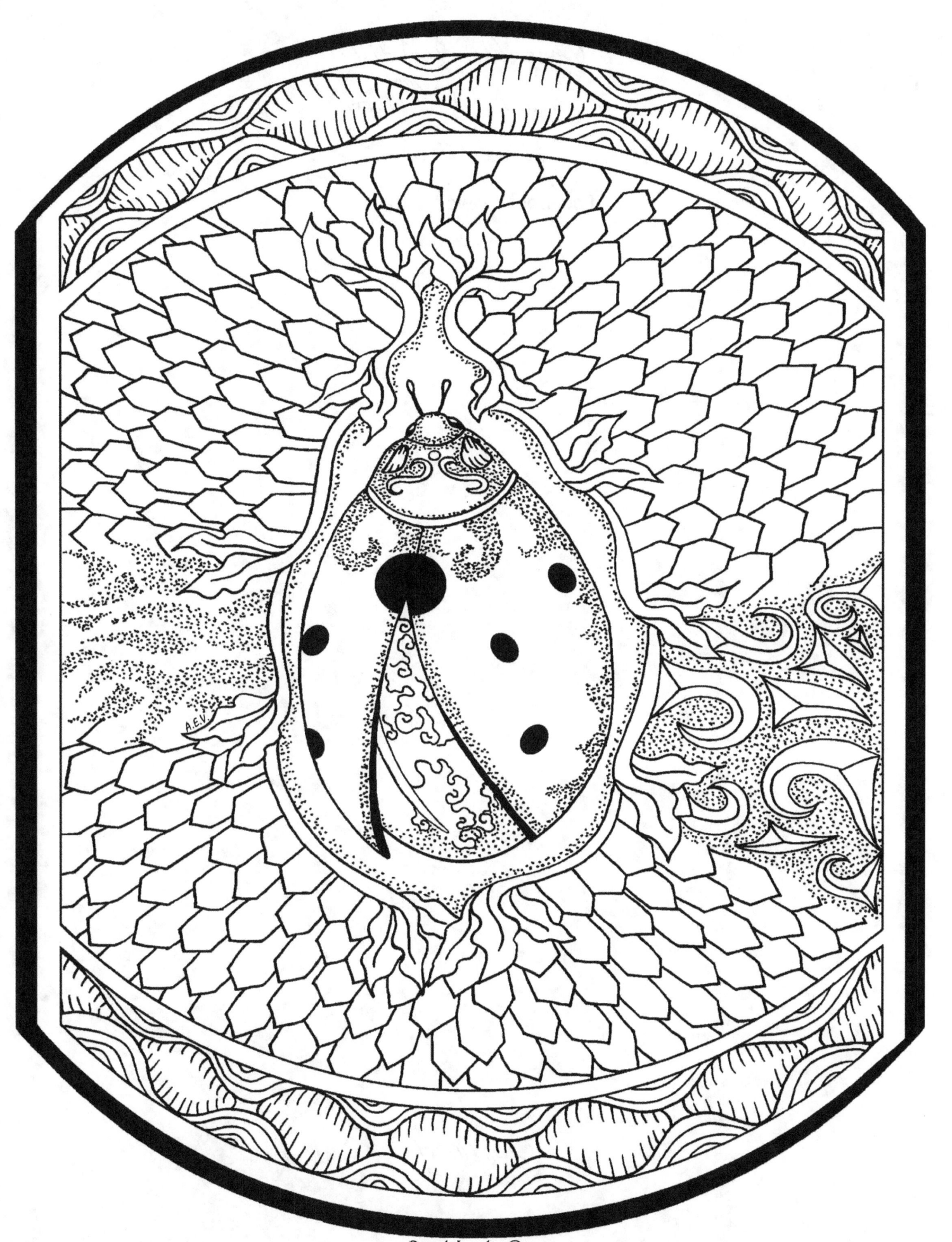

~Opal Lady Bug~

Contributing Artist
Alfred E. Villanueva
Philippines
Facebook : viworksart2015

GemInsects

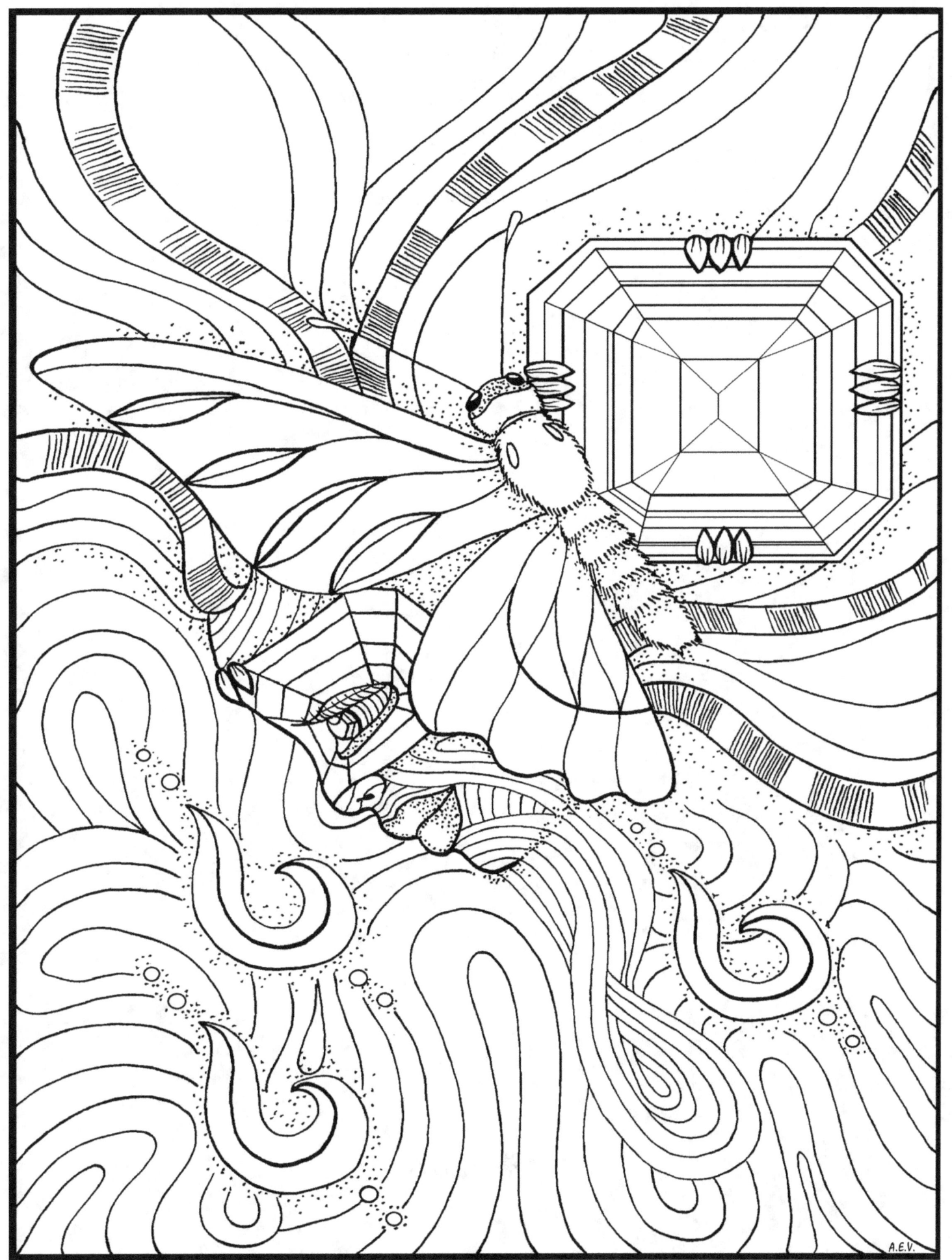

~Peridot~

Contributing Artist
Alfred E. Villanueva
Philippines
Facebook : viworksart2015

GemInsects

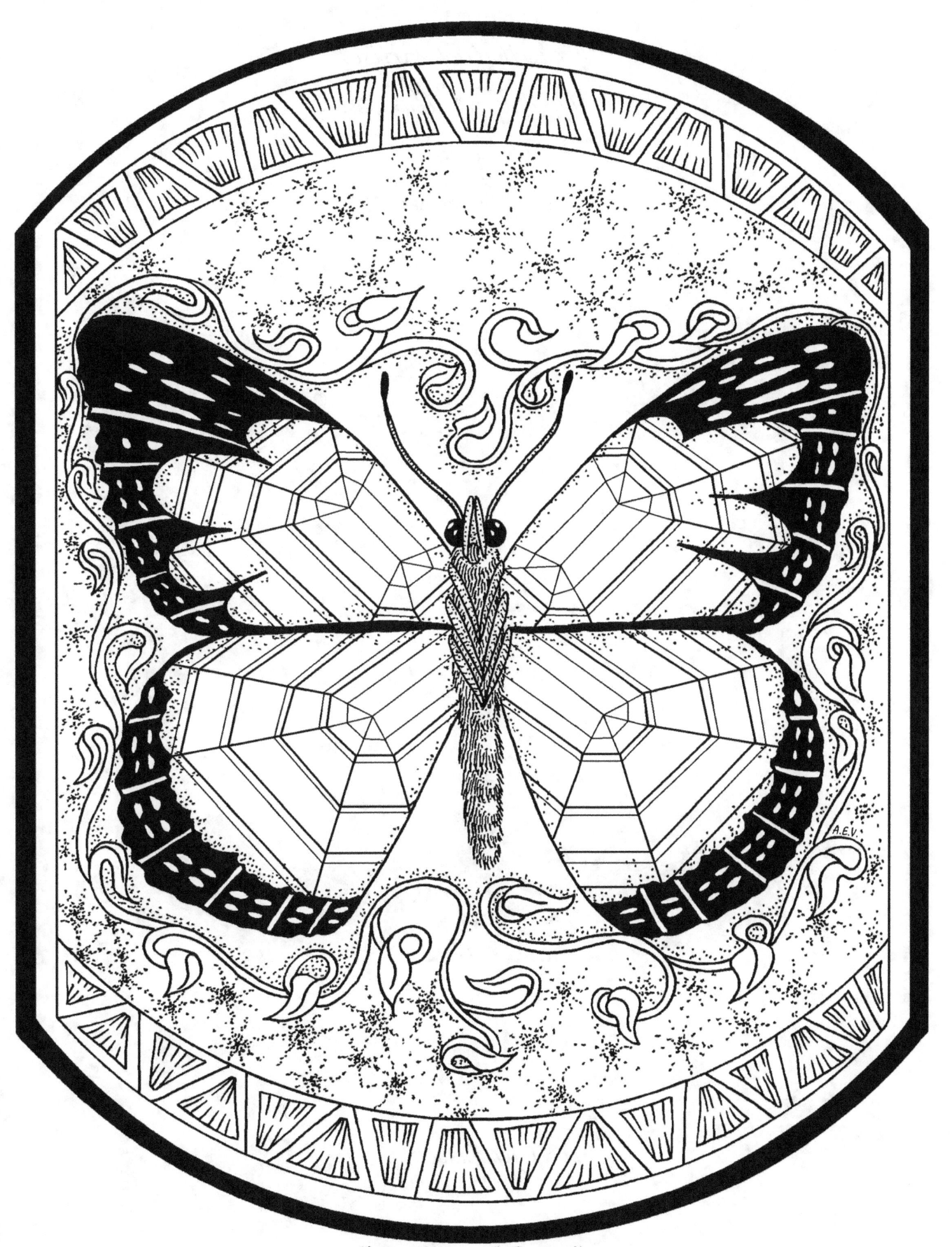

~Topaz Monarch Butterfly~

Contributing Artist
Alfred E. Villanueva
Philippines
Facebook : viworksart2015

GemInsects

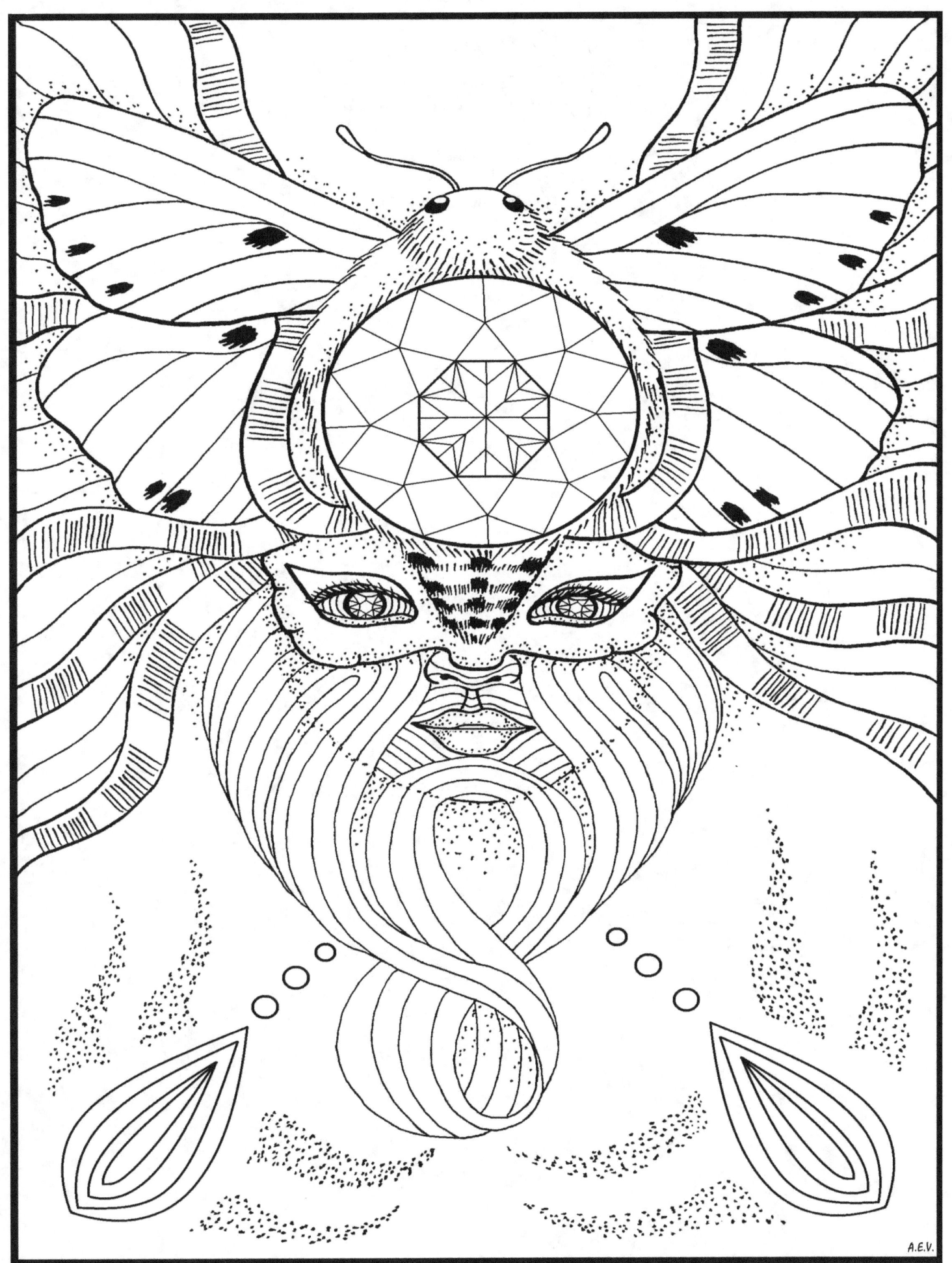

~Zircon~

Contributing Artist
Alfred E. Villanueva
Philippines
Facebook : viworksart2015

GemInsects

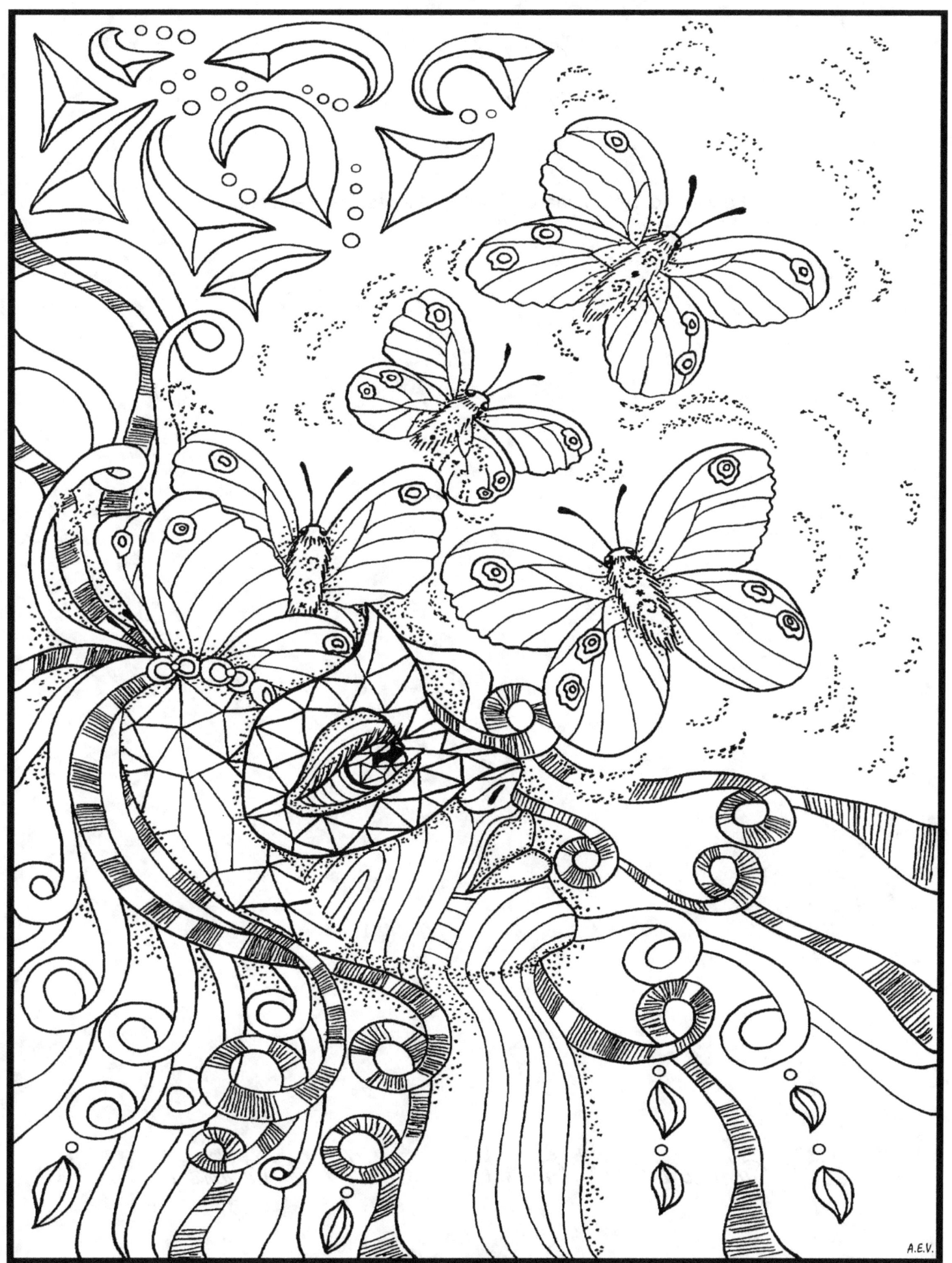
~Alexandrite~

Contributing Artist
Amandine Cyril M.L
France

Facebook : Amandine-Cyril-ML-Mes-dessins-et-coloriages

Global Doodle Gems Gems Collection Volume 1

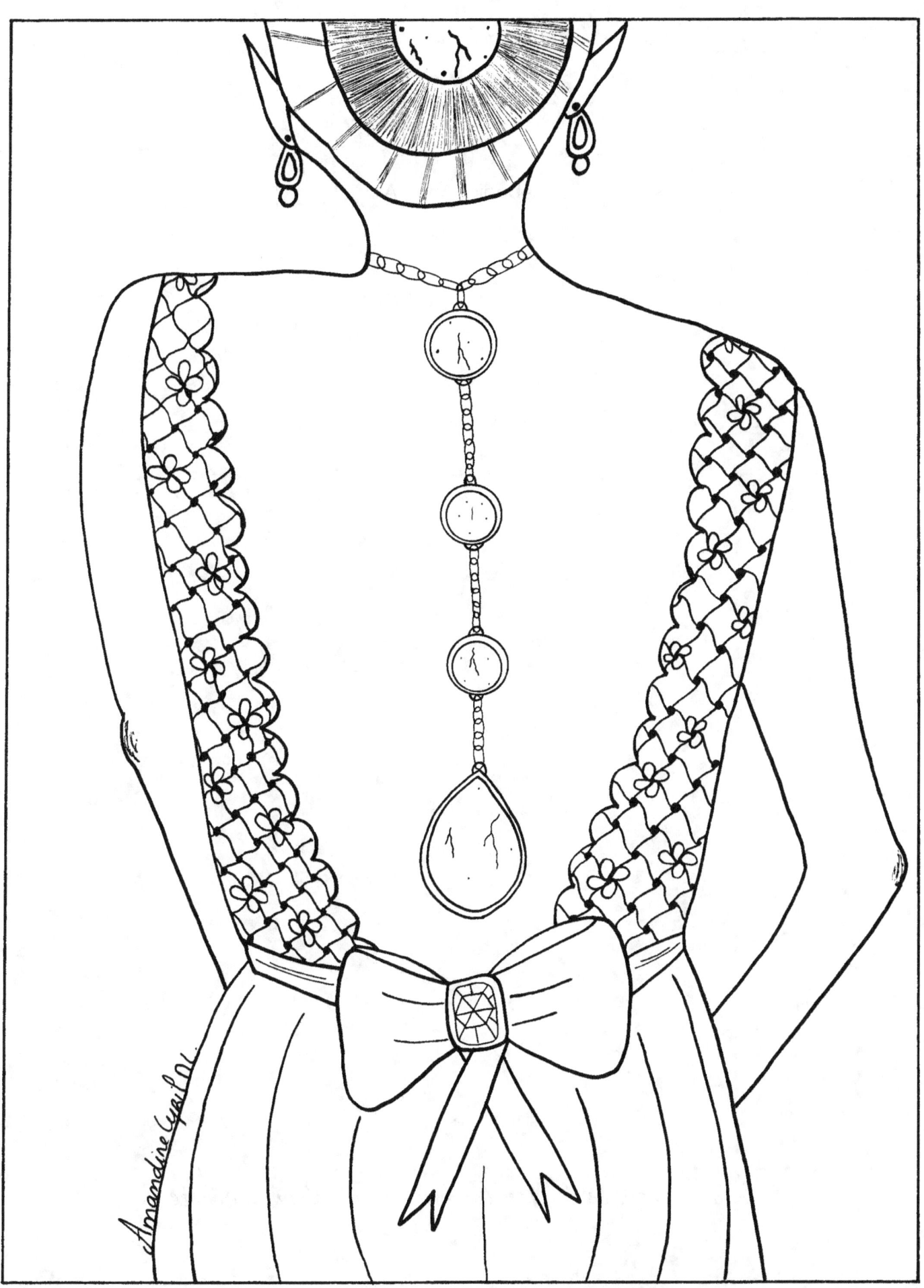

Contributing Artist
Angel Huang
Taiwan

Facebook : An99.Art

Global Doodle Gems Easter Collection Volume 1

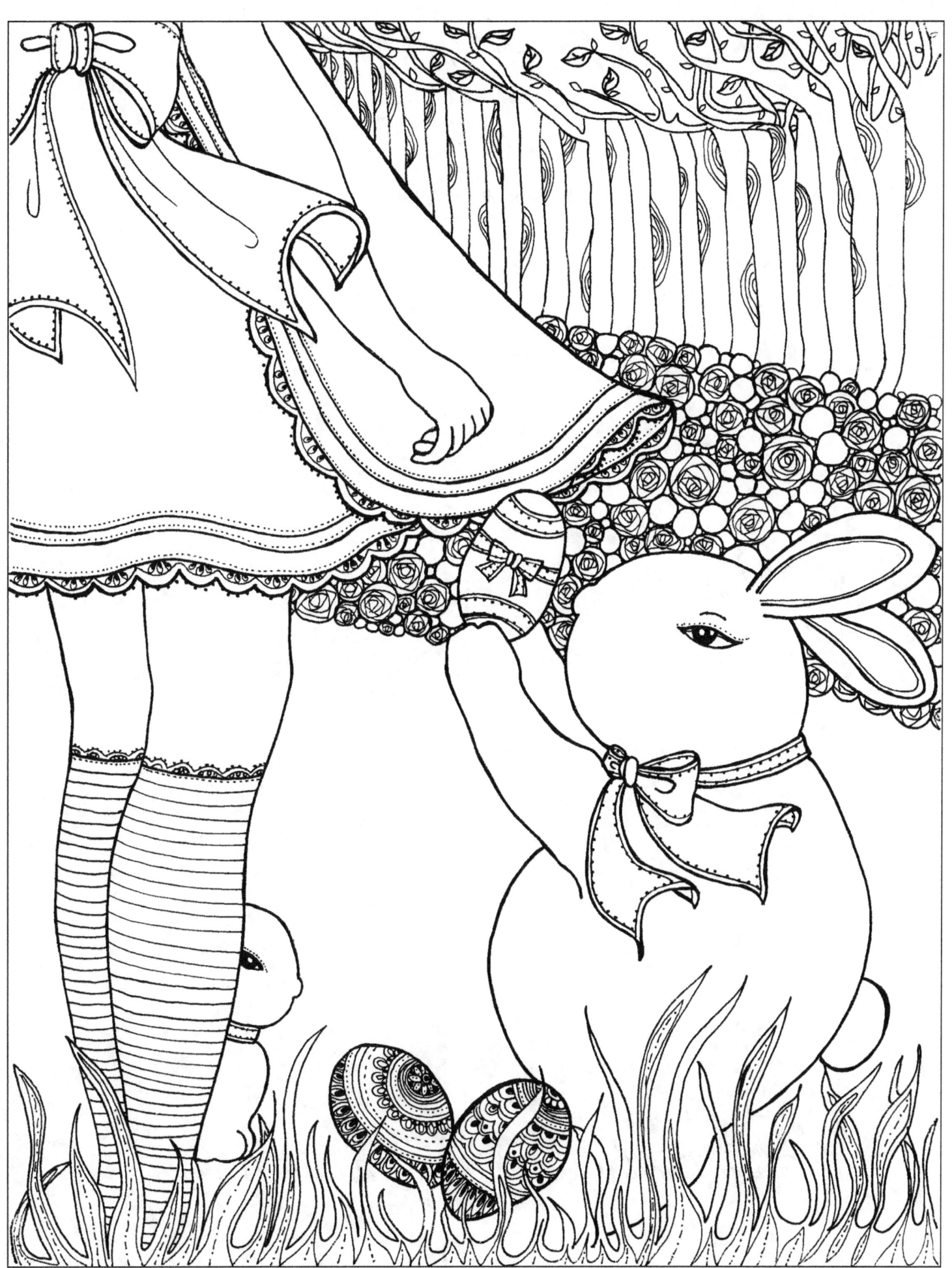

Contributing Artist
Angel Huang
Taiwan

Facebook : An99.Art

Global Doodle Gems Valentines Collection Volume 2

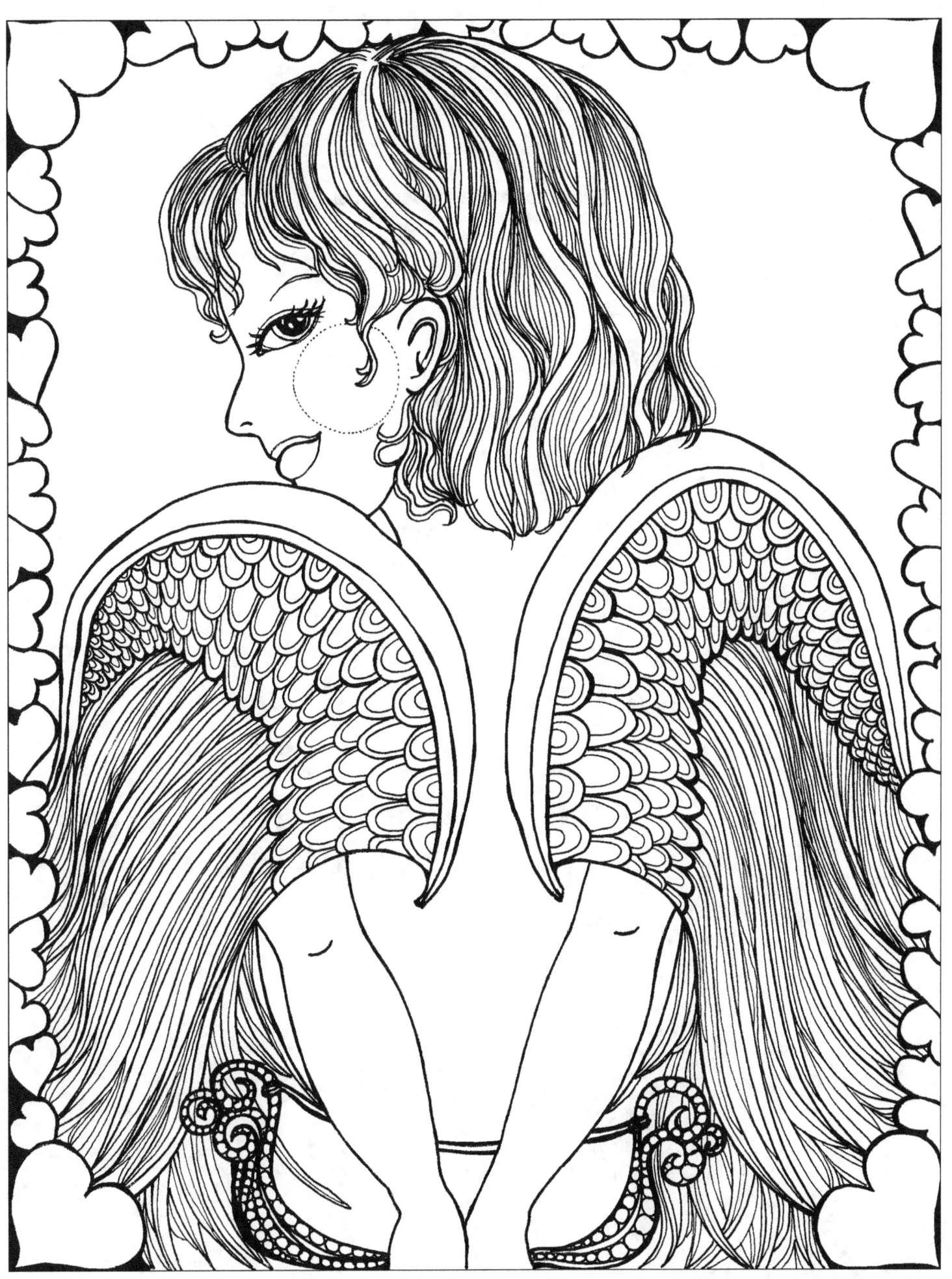

Contributing Artist
Arianne Schimmel
The Netherlands

Facebook : ArianneSchimmel

Global Doodle Gems Easter Collection Volume 1

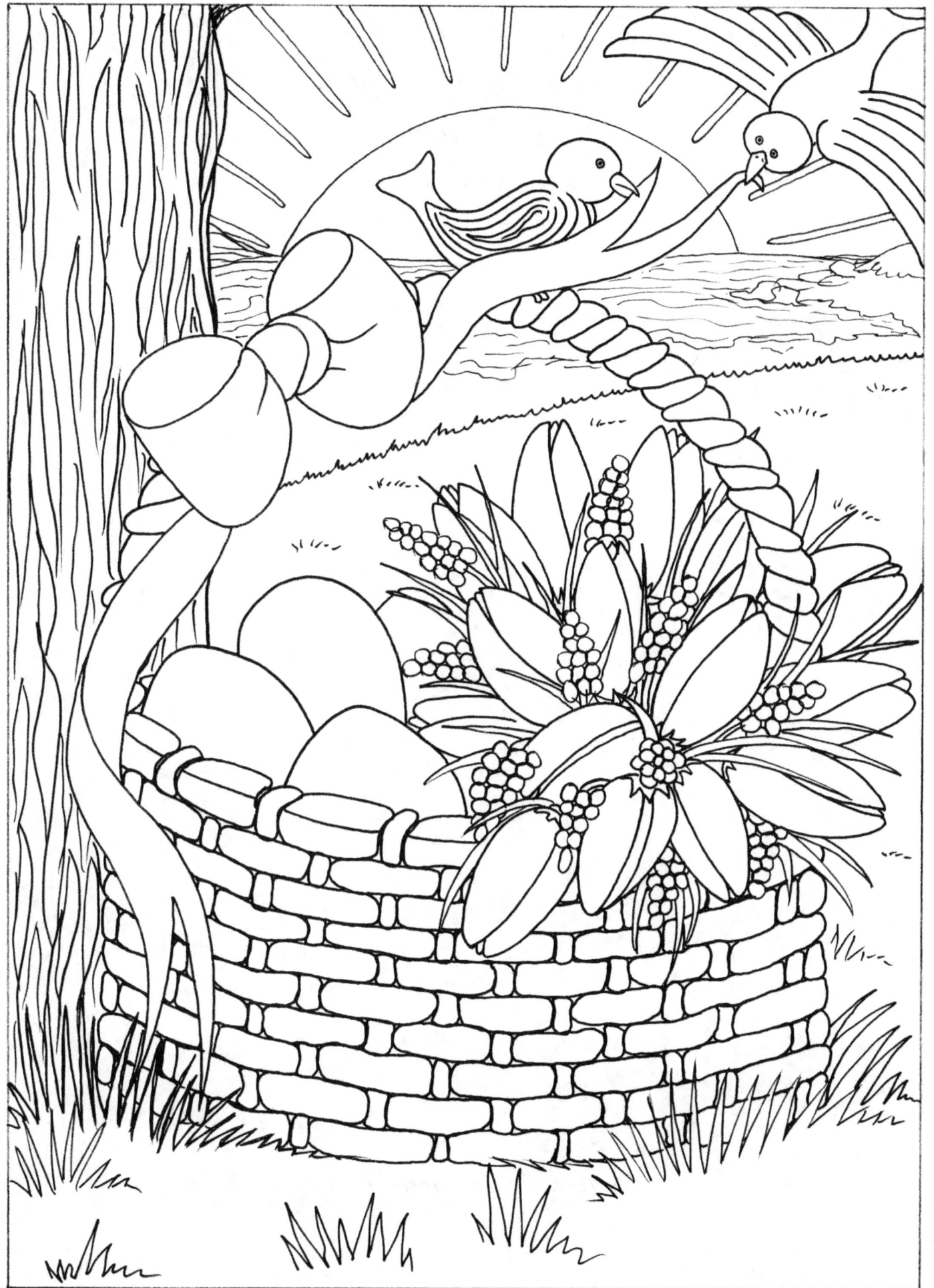

Contributing Artist
Arthur Santiago Quirat
The Philippines
Facebook : Arqui-Doodle

Global Doodle Gems Volume 6

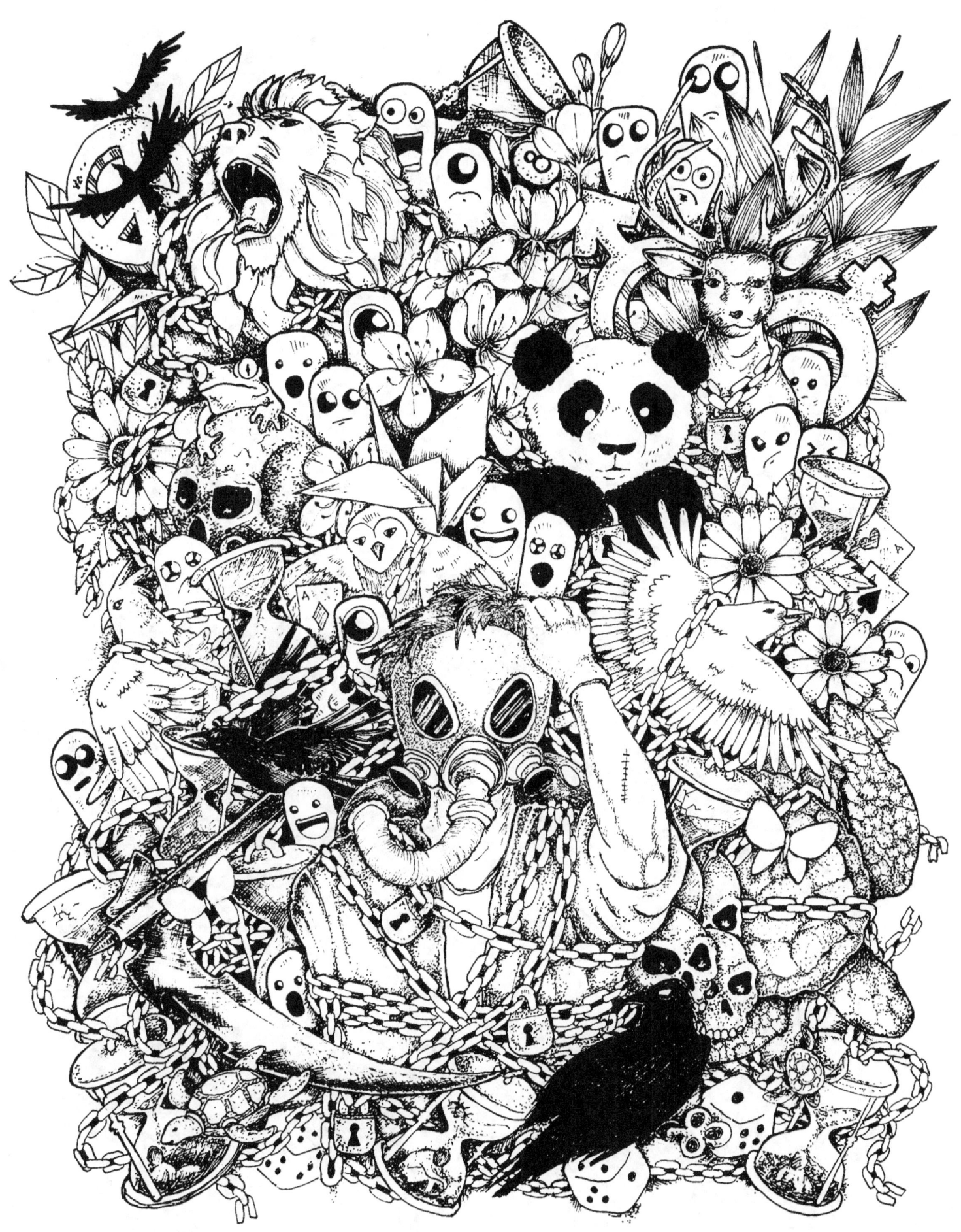

Contributing Artist
Audrey Sagh
Saskatoon, Saskatchewan Canada

Facebook : AMS-Artwork

Global Doodle Gems Flowers Collection Volume 1

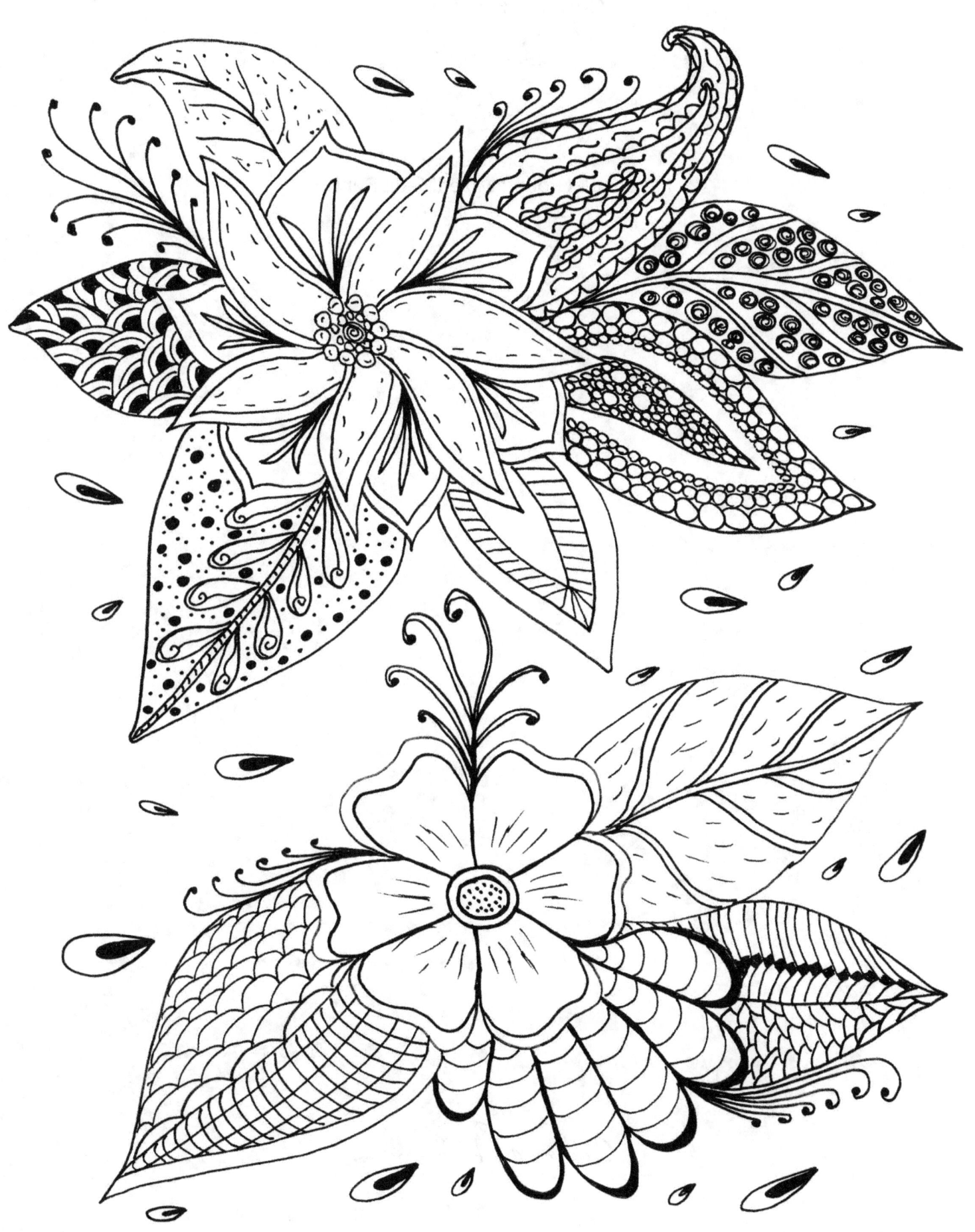

Contributing Artist
Bev Choy
USA

Facebook : bevchoyart
Facebook Group : MixedMediaSupport
Etsy : BevChoyArt

Colors of Whimsy 2

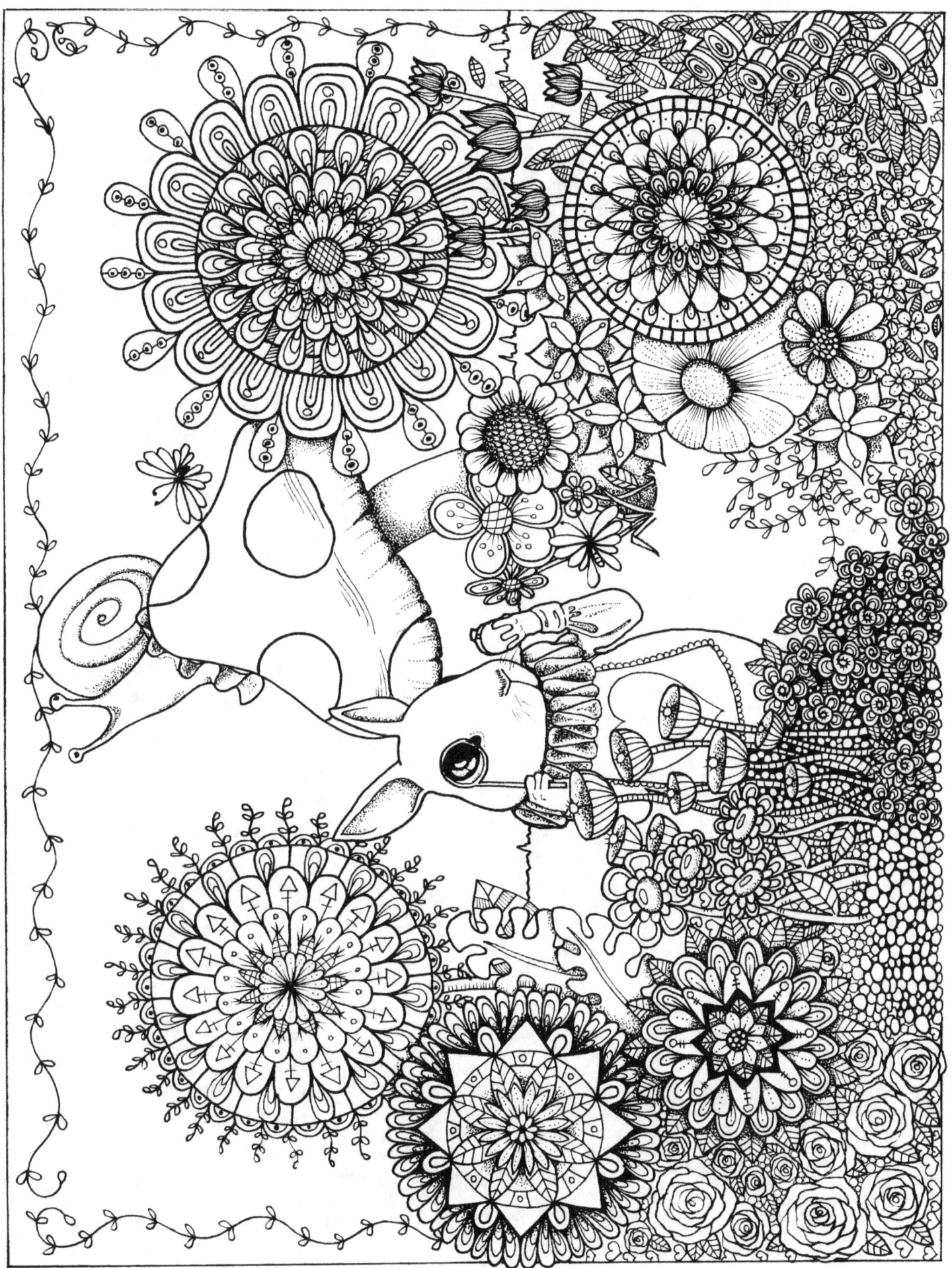

Contributing Artist
Bev Choy
USA

Facebook : bevchoyart
Facebook Group : MixedMediaSupport
Etsy : BevChoyArt

Colors of Whimsy 2

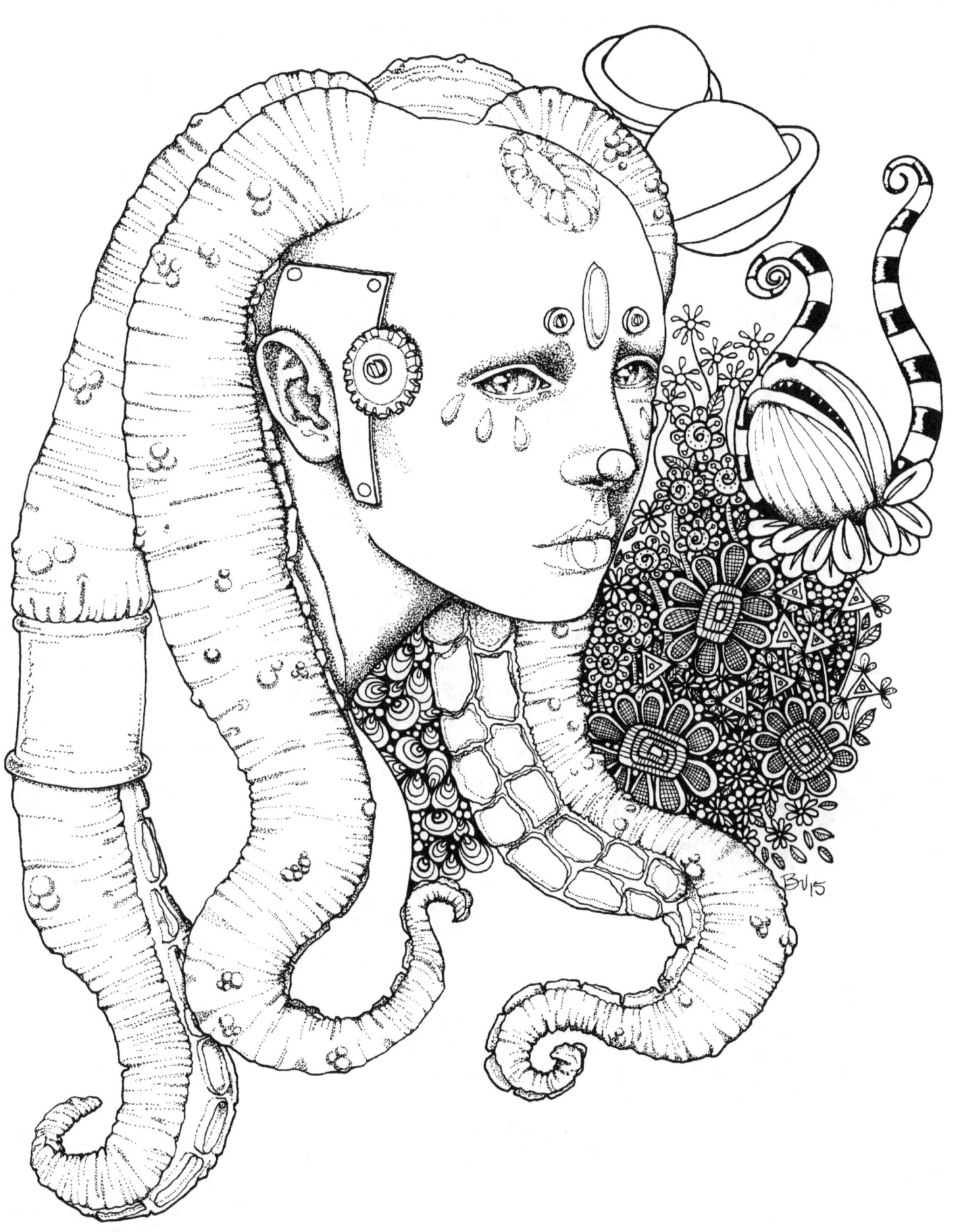

Contributing Artist
Bev Choy
USA

Facebook : bevchoyart
Facebook Group : MixedMediaSupport
Etsy : BevChoyArt

Colors of Whimsy 3

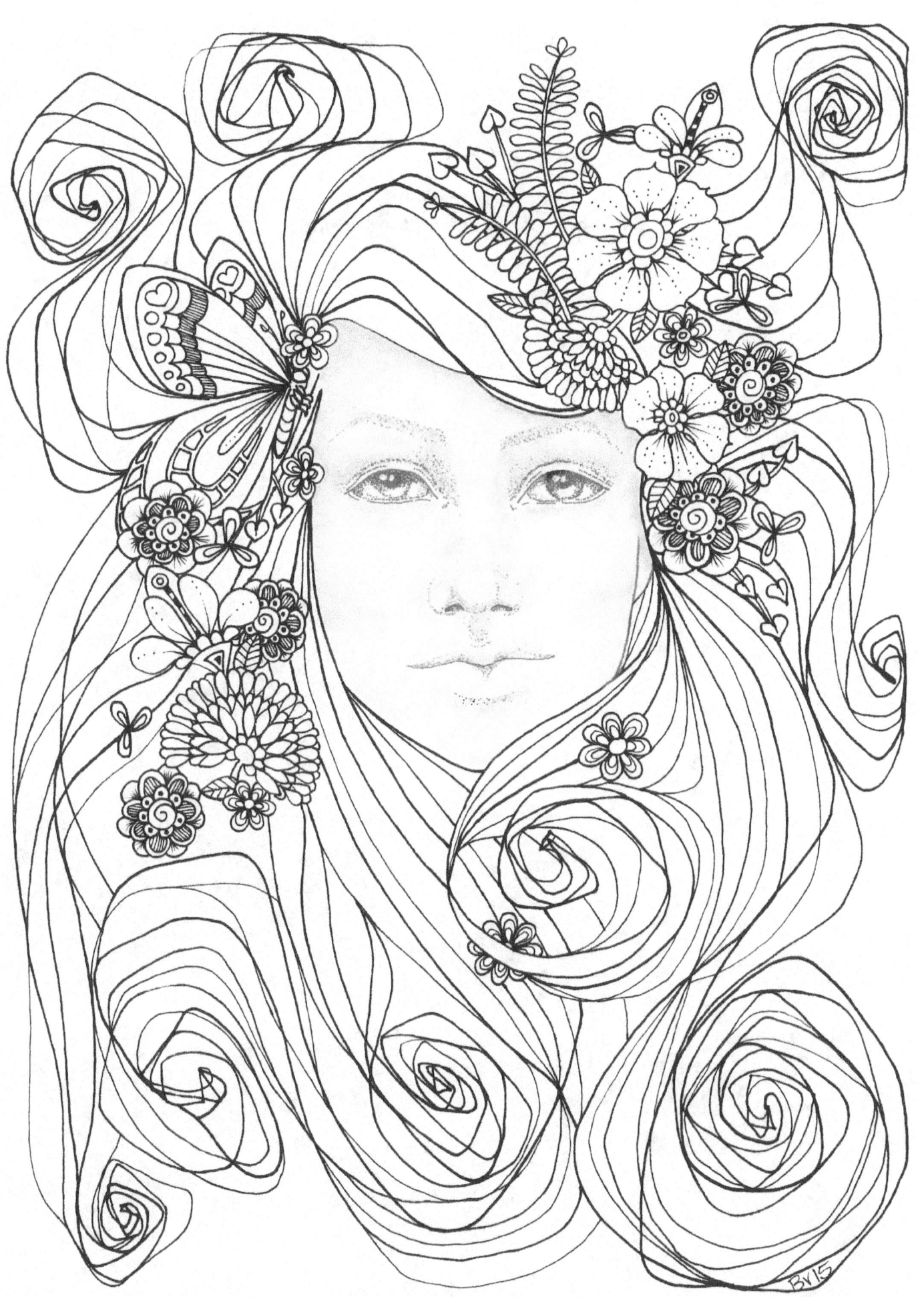

Contributing Artist
Bev Choy
USA

Facebook : bevchoyart
Facebook Group : MixedMediaSupport
Etsy : BevChoyArt

Colors of Whimsy 3

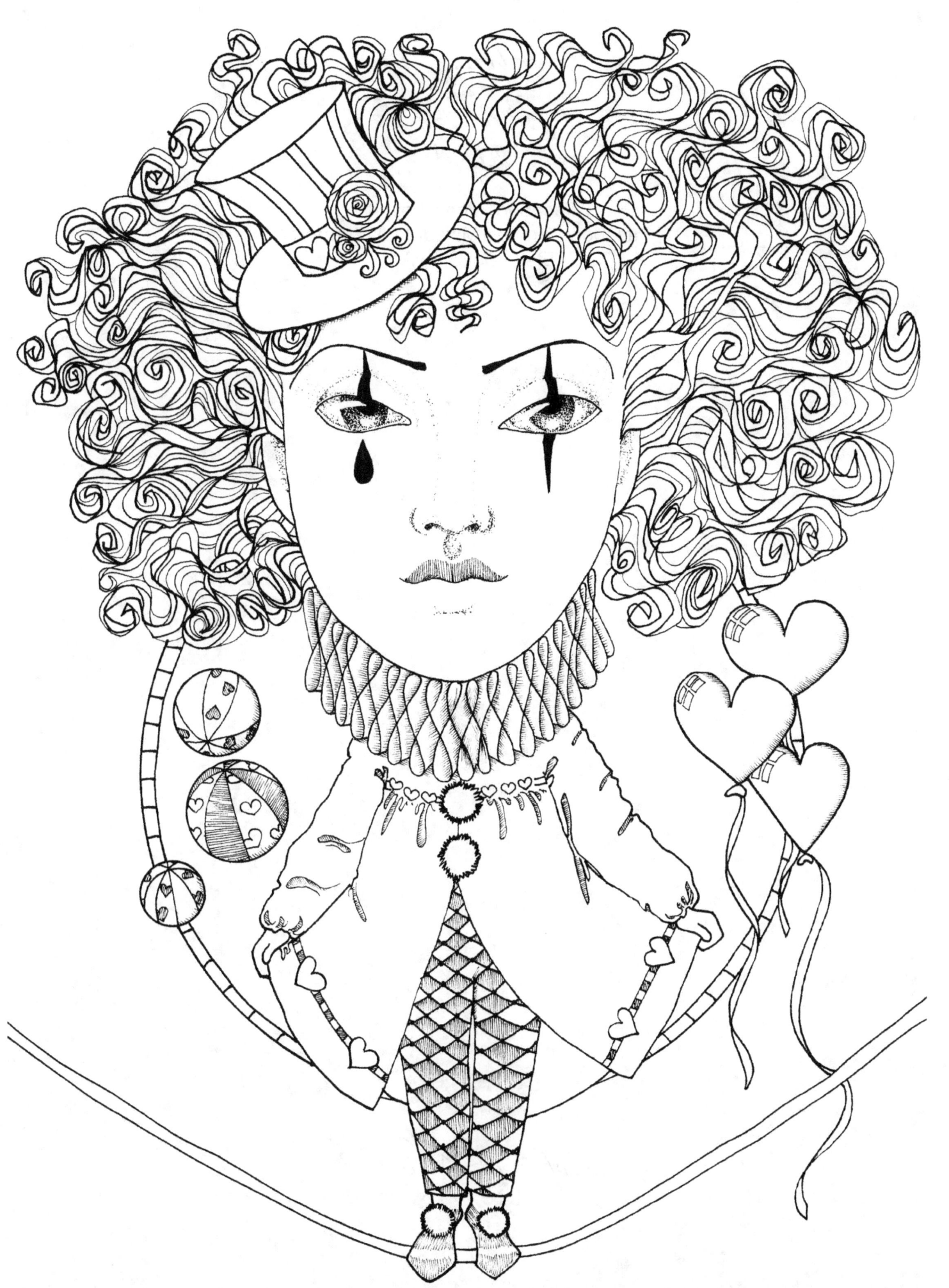

Contributing Artist
Bev Choy
USA

Facebook : bevchoyart
Facebook Group : MixedMediaSupport
Etsy : BevChoyArt

Colors of Whimsy 3

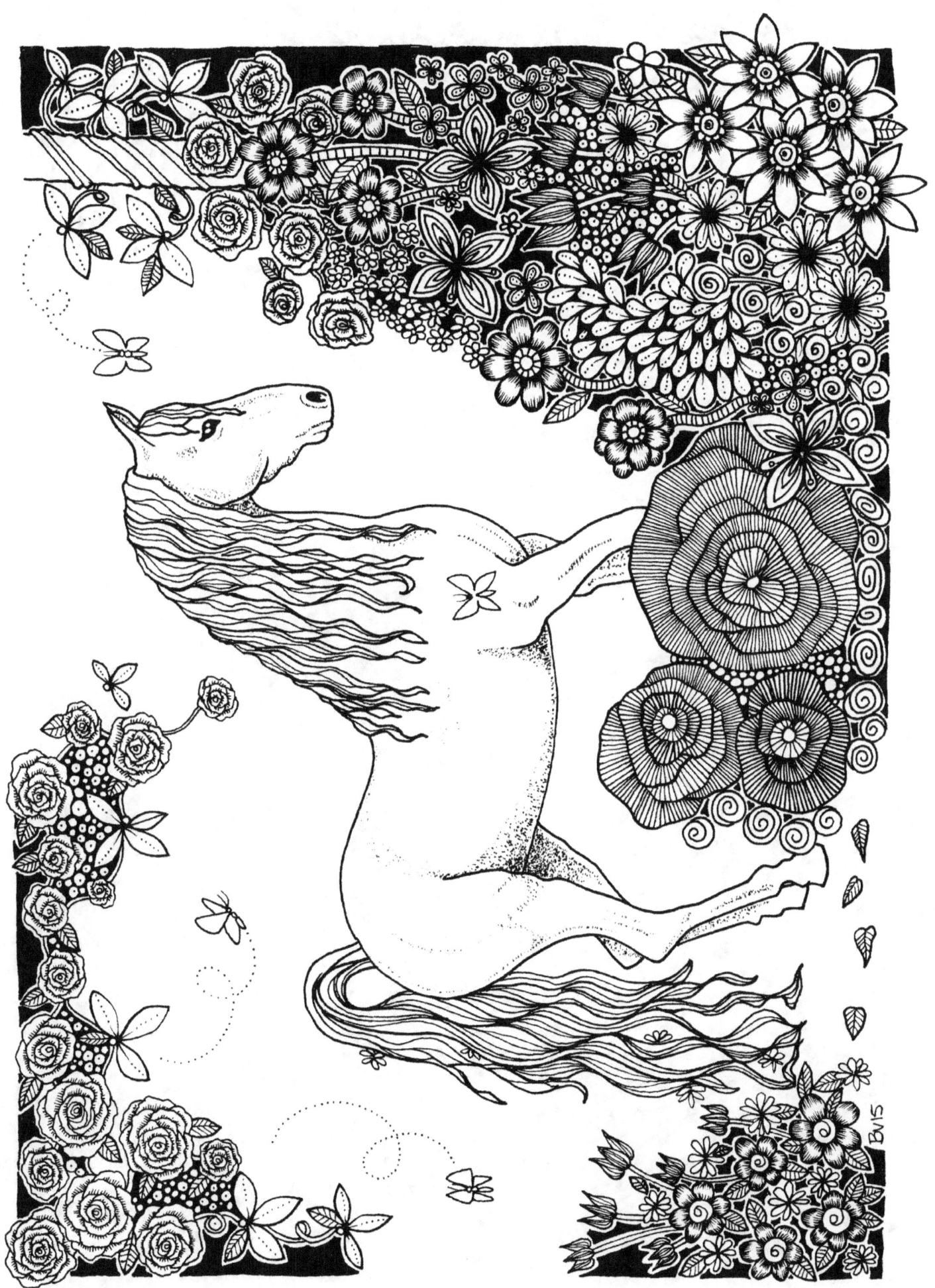

Contributing Artist
Bev Choy
USA

Facebook : bevchoyart
Facebook Group : MixedMediaSupport
Etsy : BevChoyArt

Colors of Whimsy 3

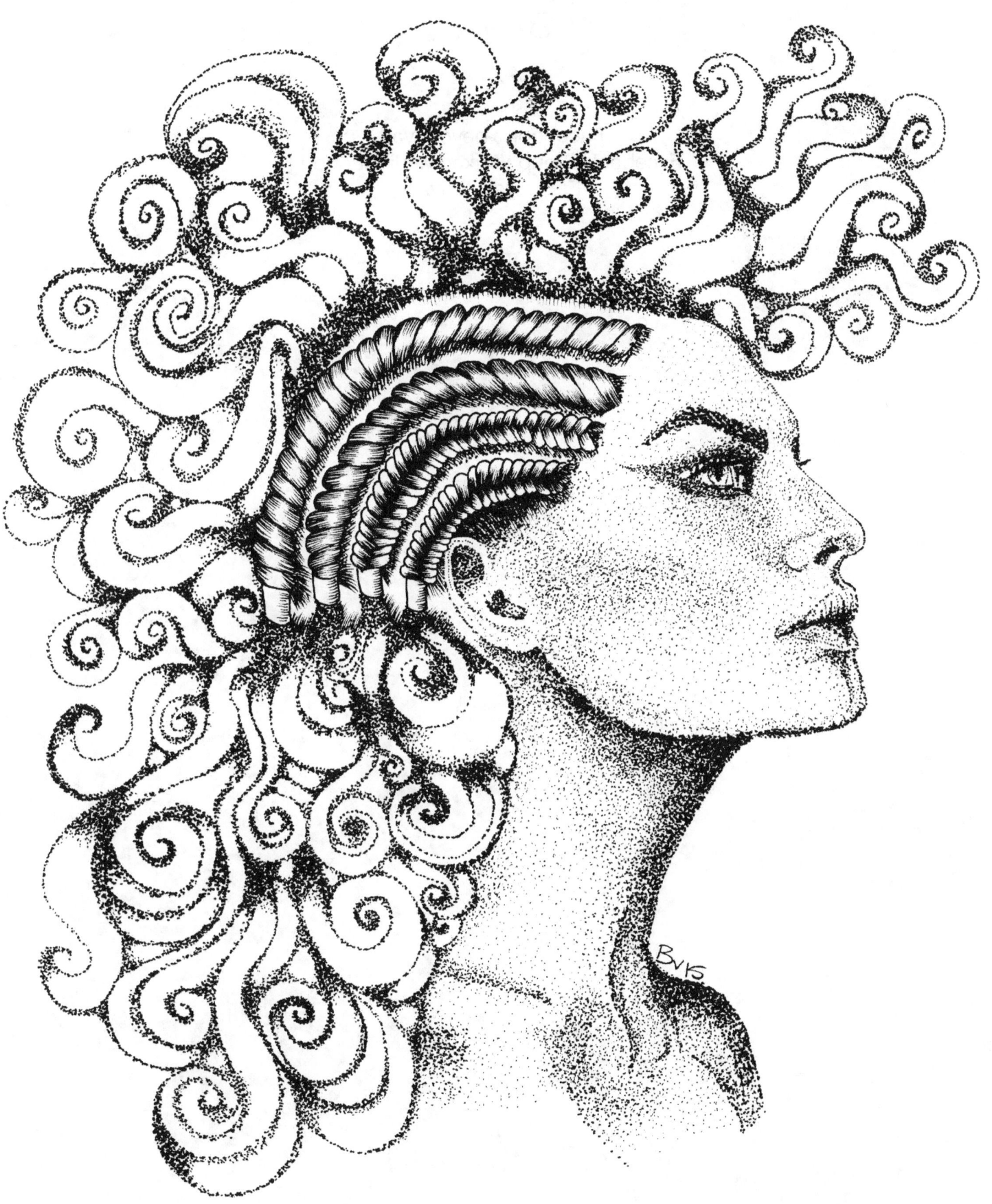

Contributing Artist
Bev Choy
USA

Facebook : bevchoyart
Facebook Group : MixedMediaSupport
Etsy : BevChoyArt

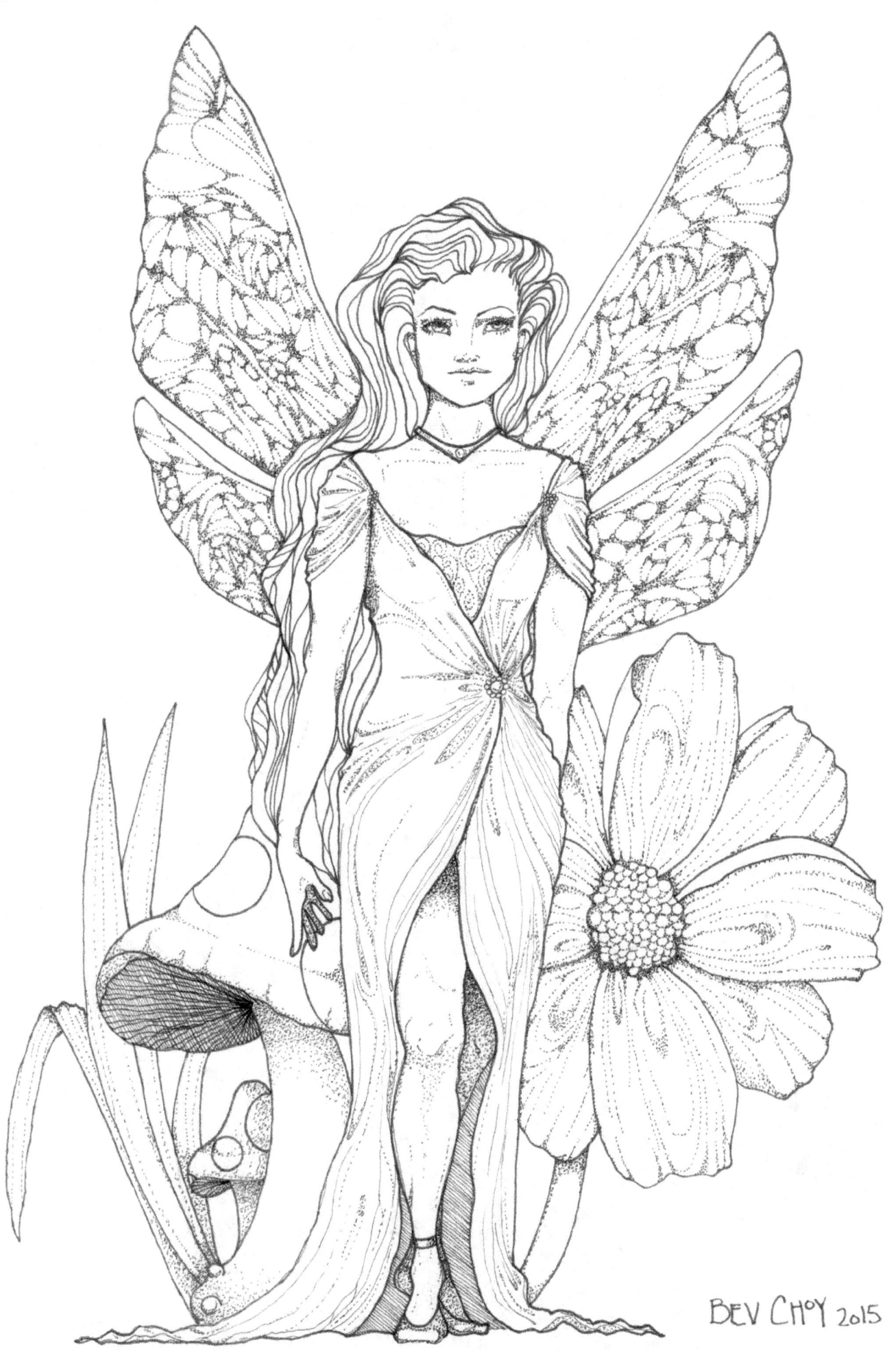

Contributing Artist
Bev Choy
USA

Facebook : bevchoyart
Facebook Group : MixedMediaSupport
Etsy : BevChoyArt

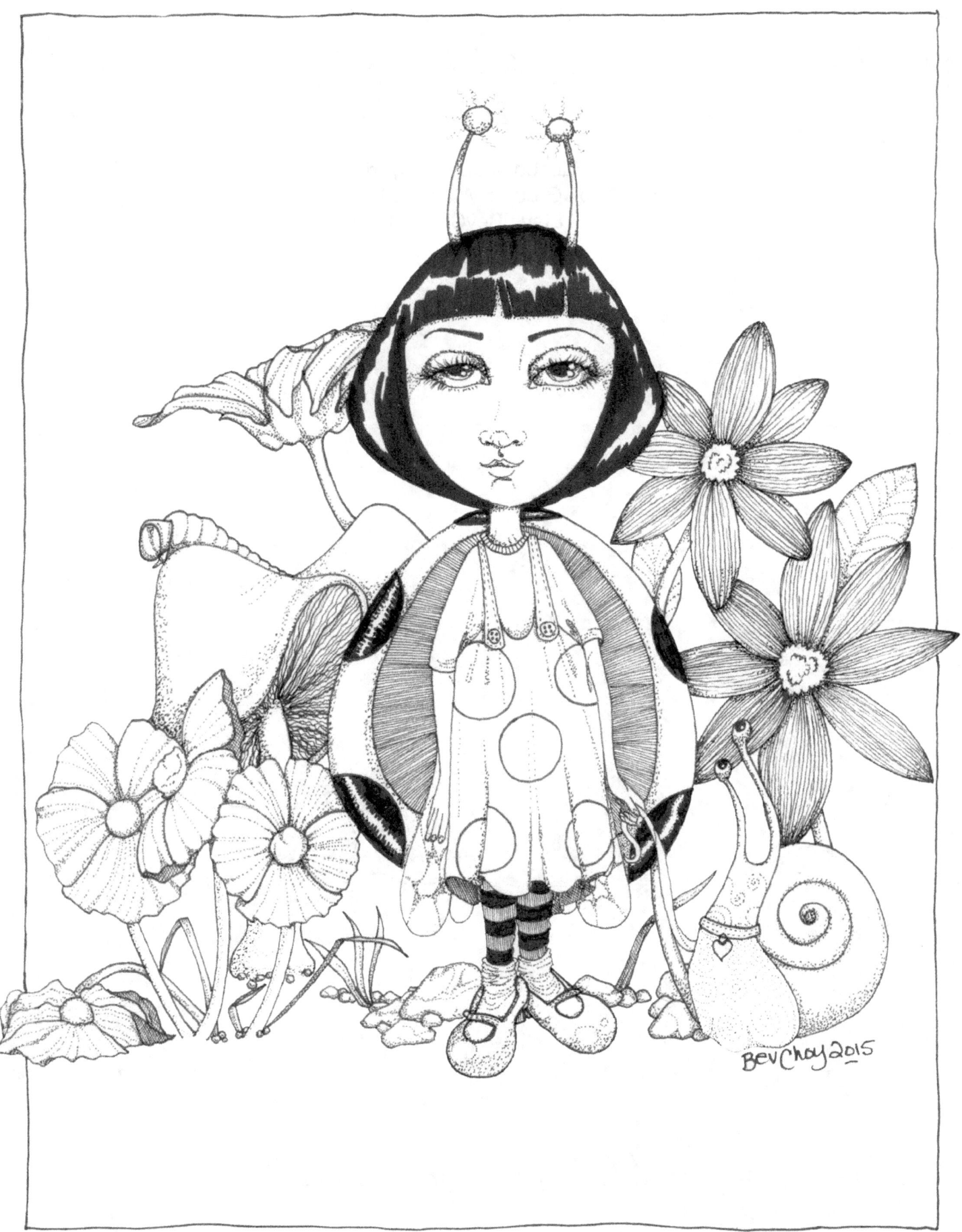

Contributing Artist
Bev Choy
USA

Facebook : bevchoyart
Facebook Group : MixedMediaSupport
Etsy : BevChoyArt

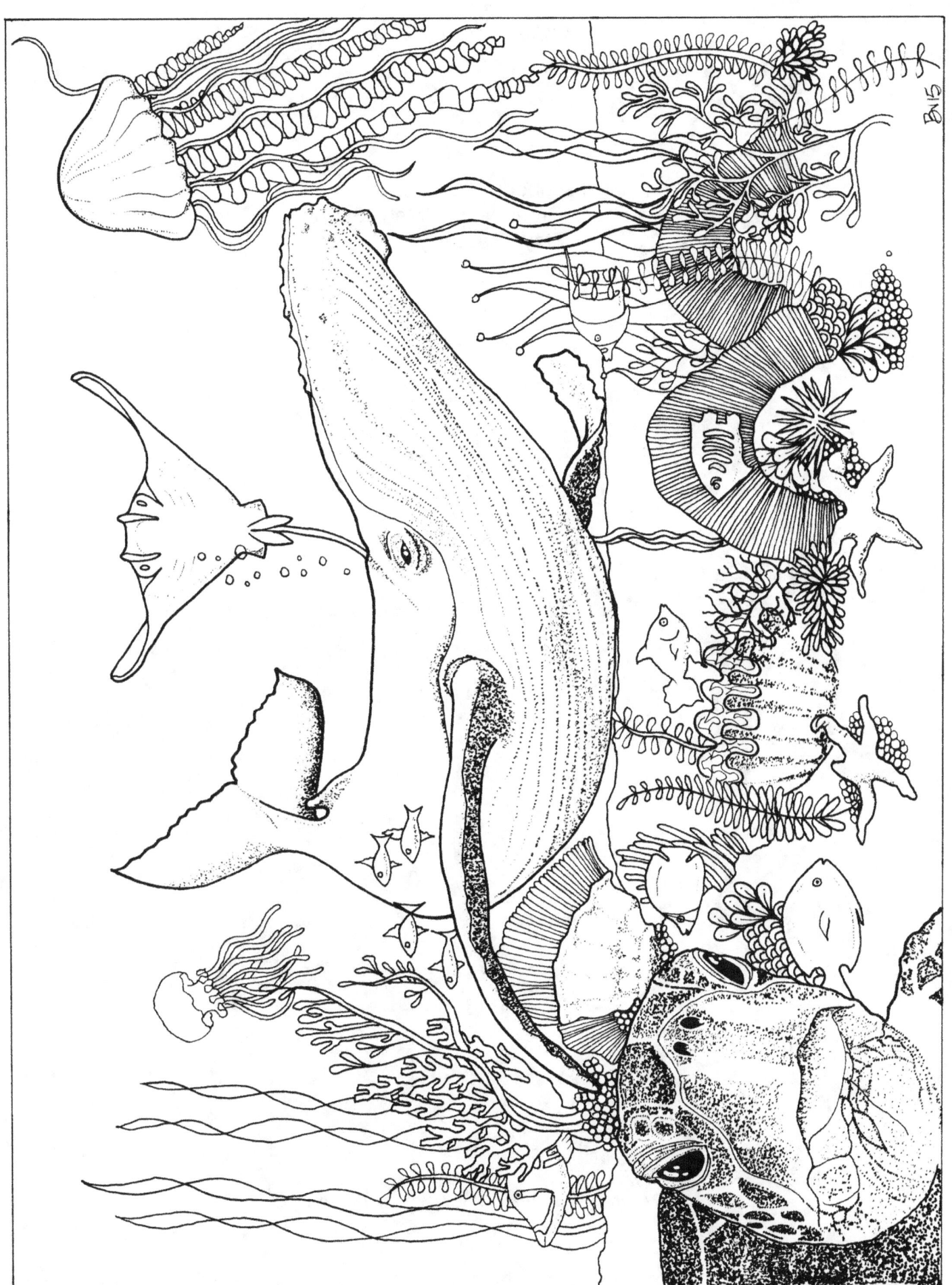

Contributing Artist
Bev Choy
USA

Facebook : bevchoyart
Facebook Group : MixedMediaSupport
Etsy : BevChoyArt

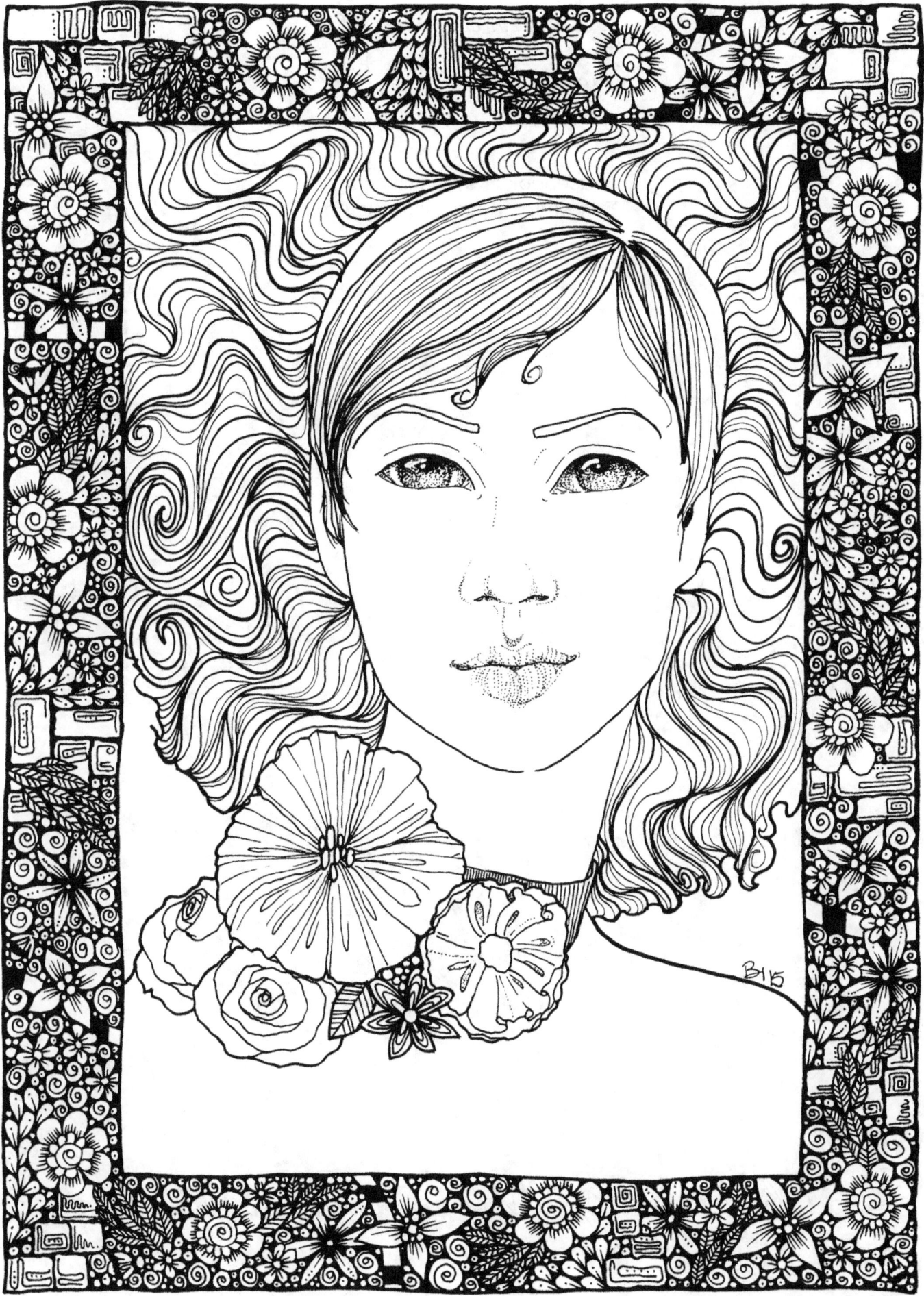

Contributing Artist
Casey "Keyesay" Gilmore
USA

Facebook : keyesaysfineart
Etsy shop : KeyesaysVisualArt

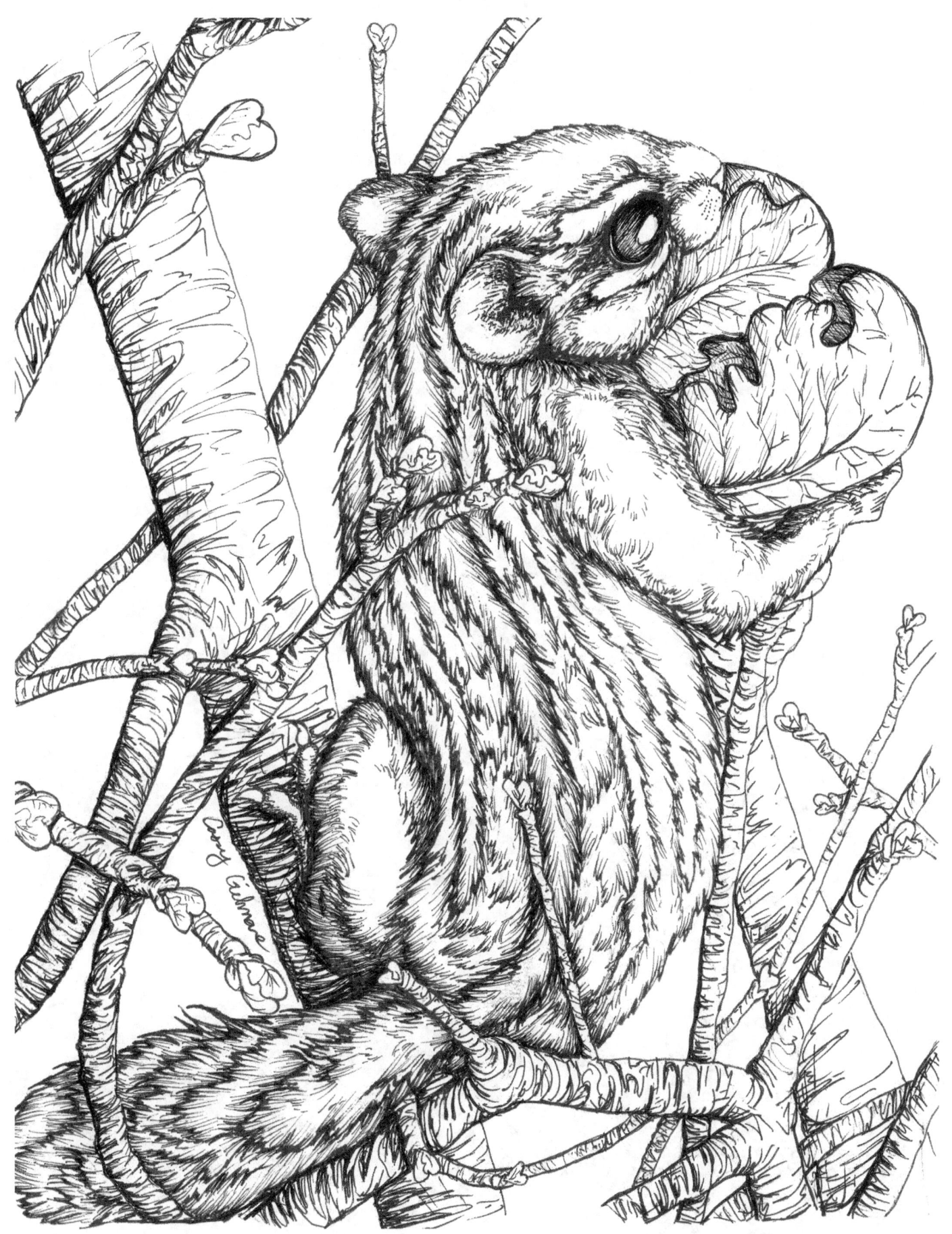

Contributing Artist
Casey "Keyesay" Gilmore
USA

Facebook : keyesaysfineart
Etsy shop : KeyesaysVisualArt

Global Doodle Gems Valentines Collection Volume 2

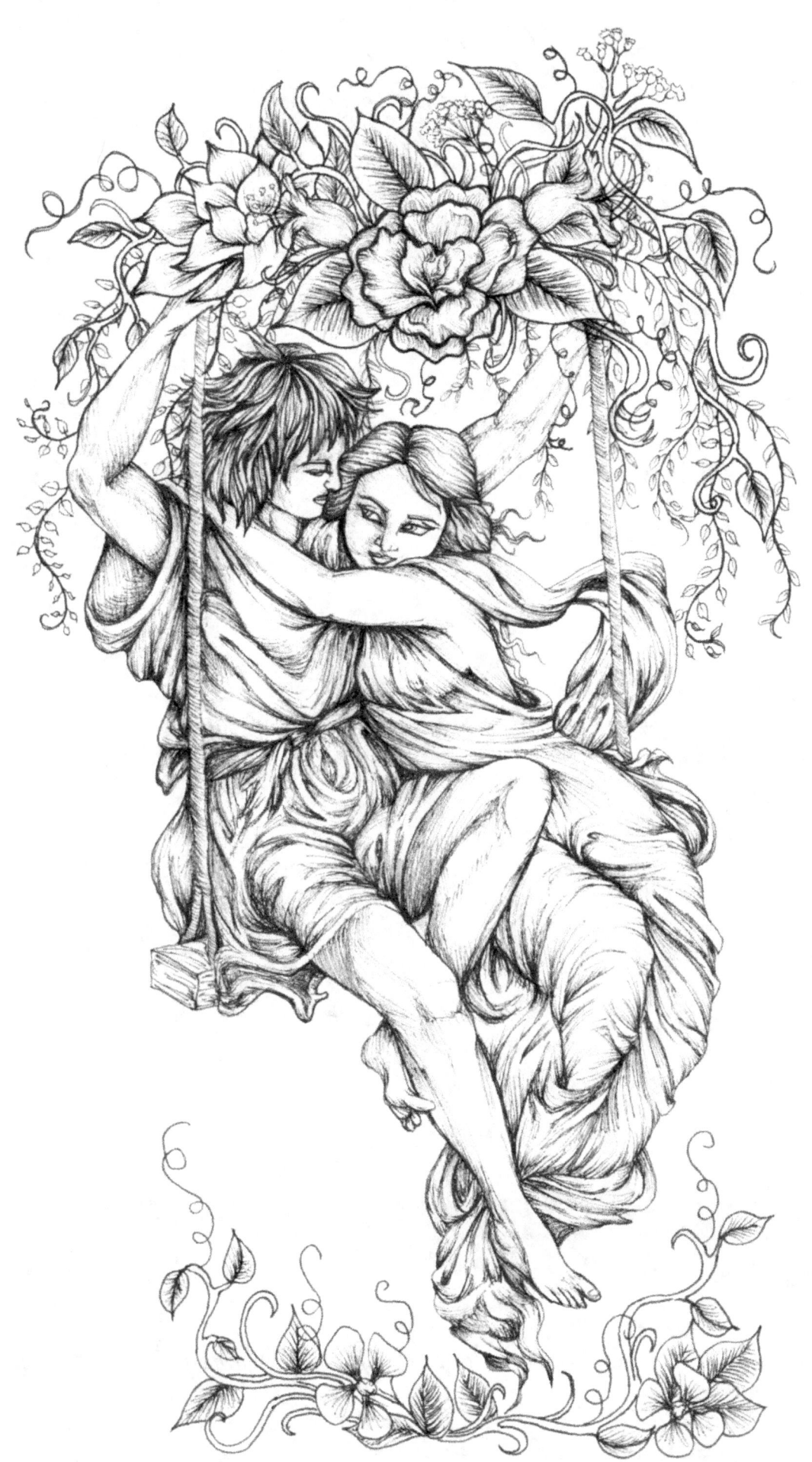

Contributing Artist
Cynthia Kloeter
USA

Facebook : CynthiaKloeter

Global Doodle Gems Volume 5

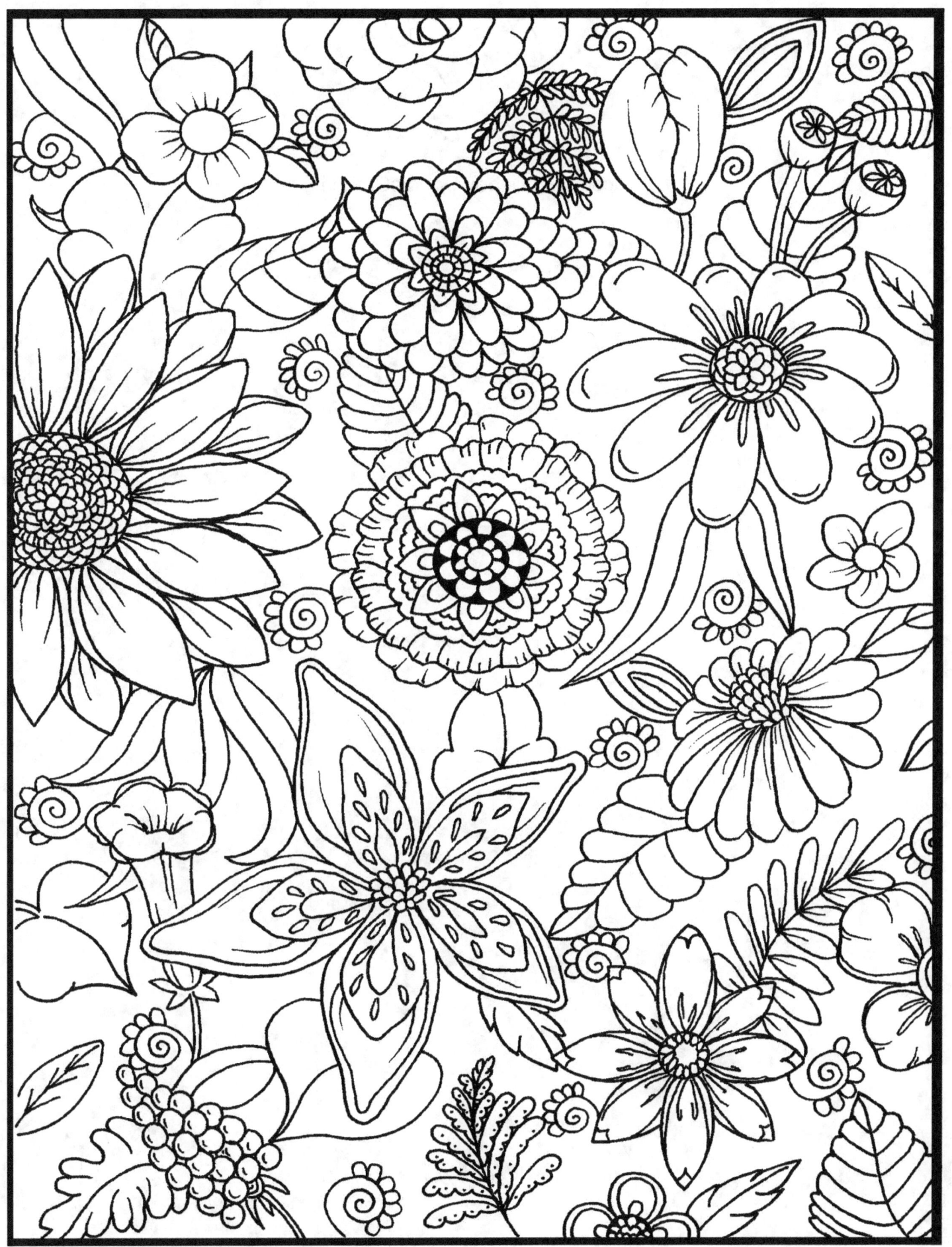

Contributing Artist
Debbie Lai
Taiwan

Facebook : DebbieDoodleGarden

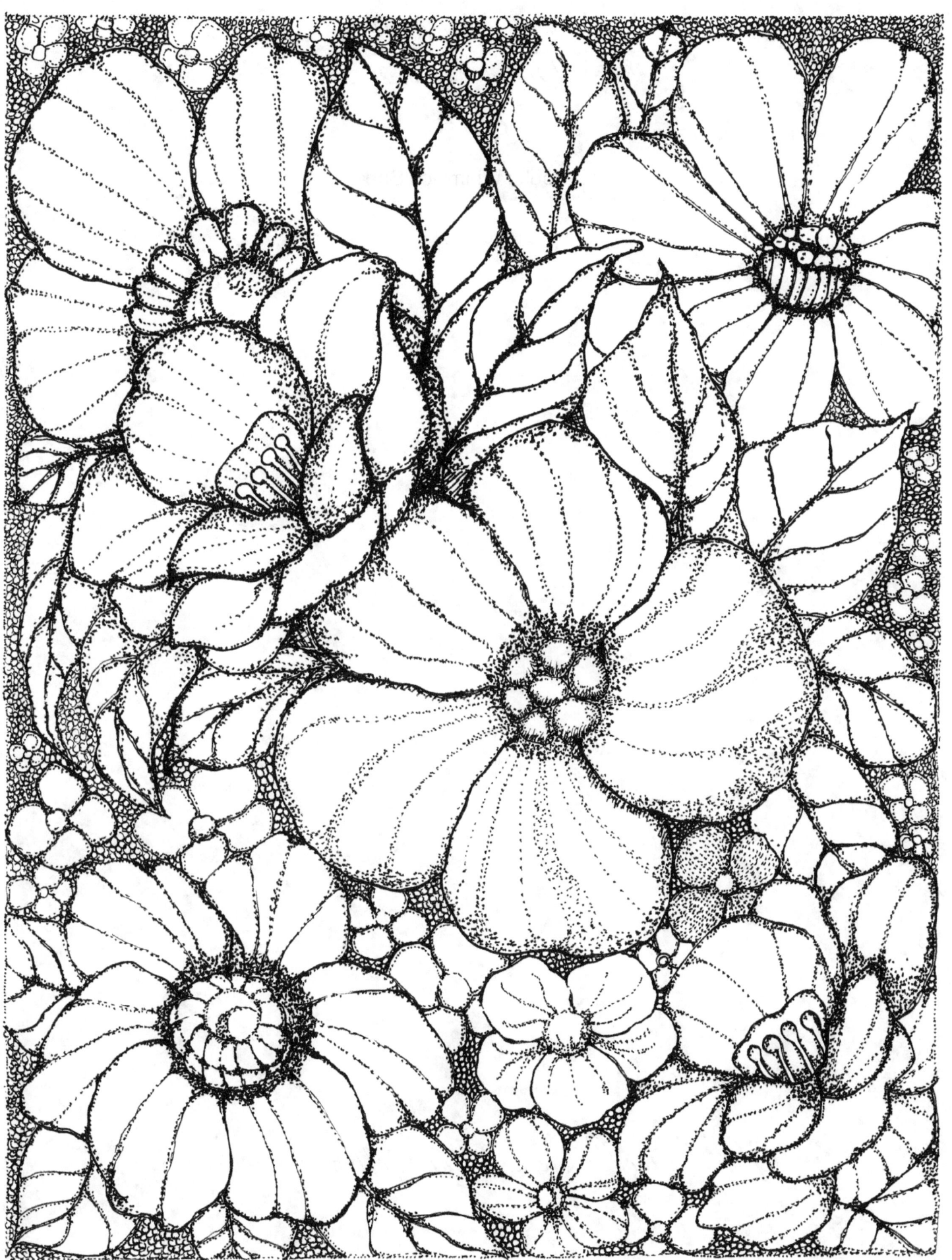

Contributing Artist
Diana Holmes
USA

Facebook : WhimsicalCheers

Global Doodle Gems Mini Collection Volume 3

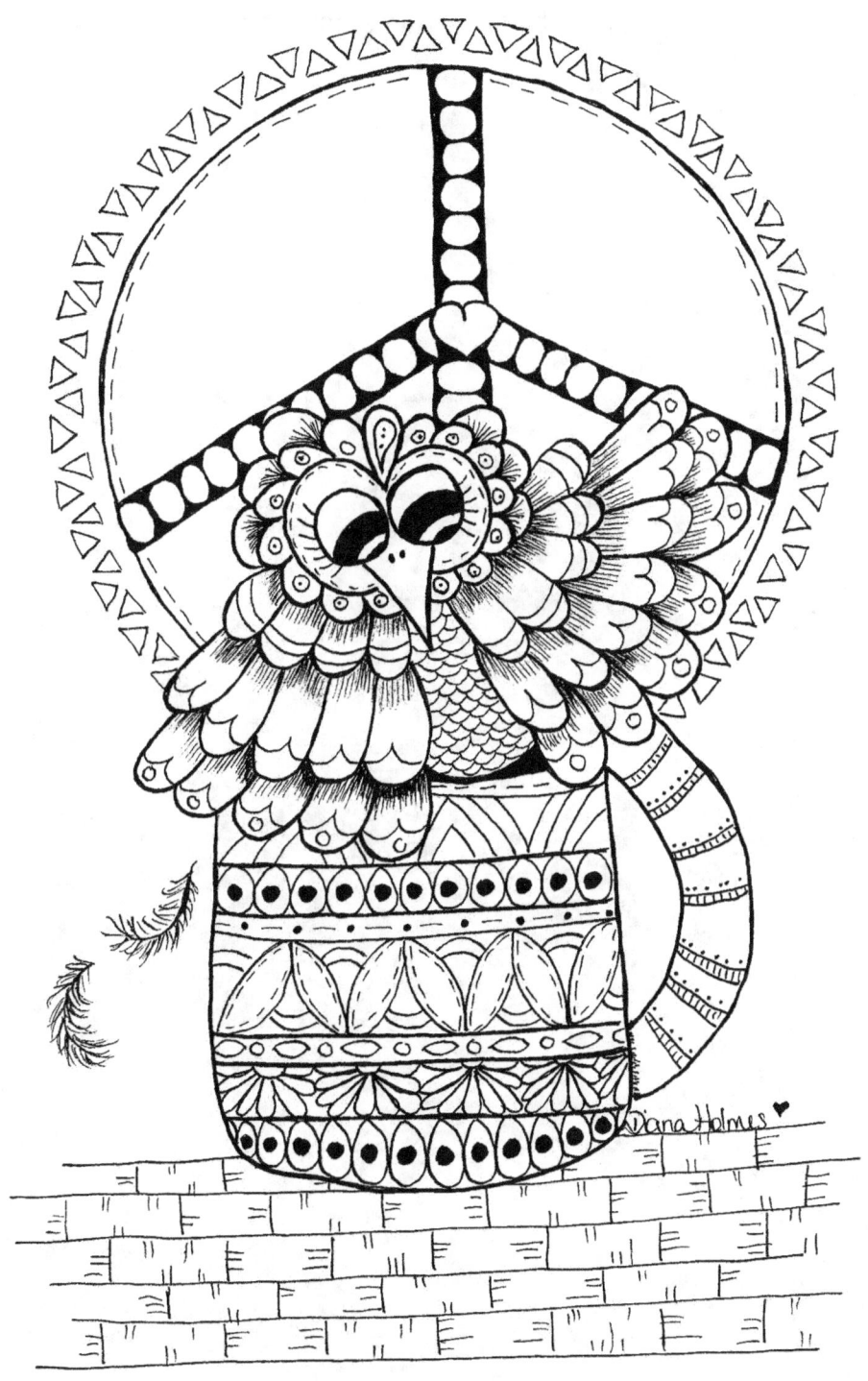

Contributing Artist
Diana Holmes
USA

Facebook : WhimsicalCheers

Global Doodle Gems Volume 10

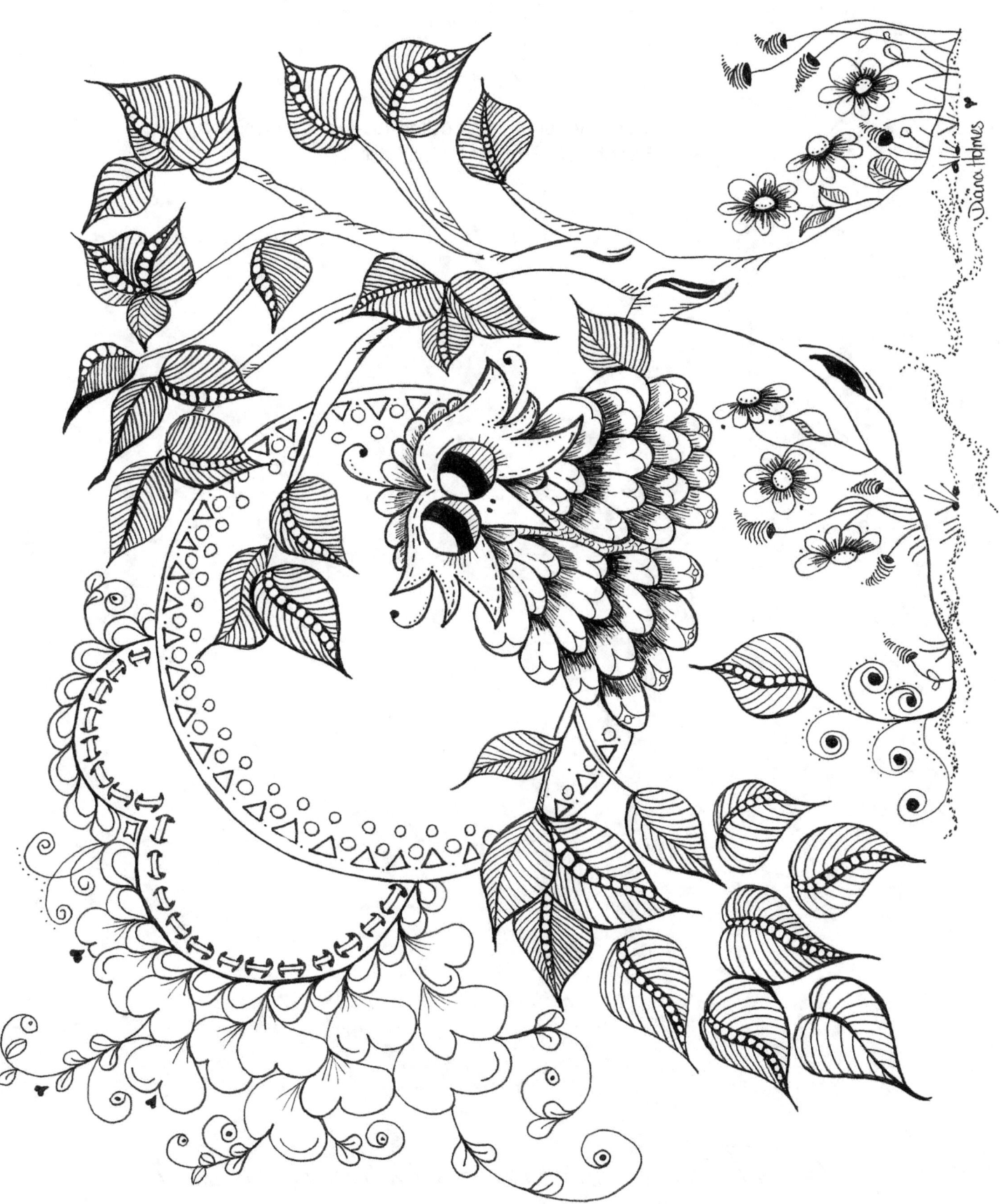

Contributing Artist
DomDomx
France

Facebook : Les-dessins-et-doodles-de-Dom-Domx
Facebook Group : Color.Addict

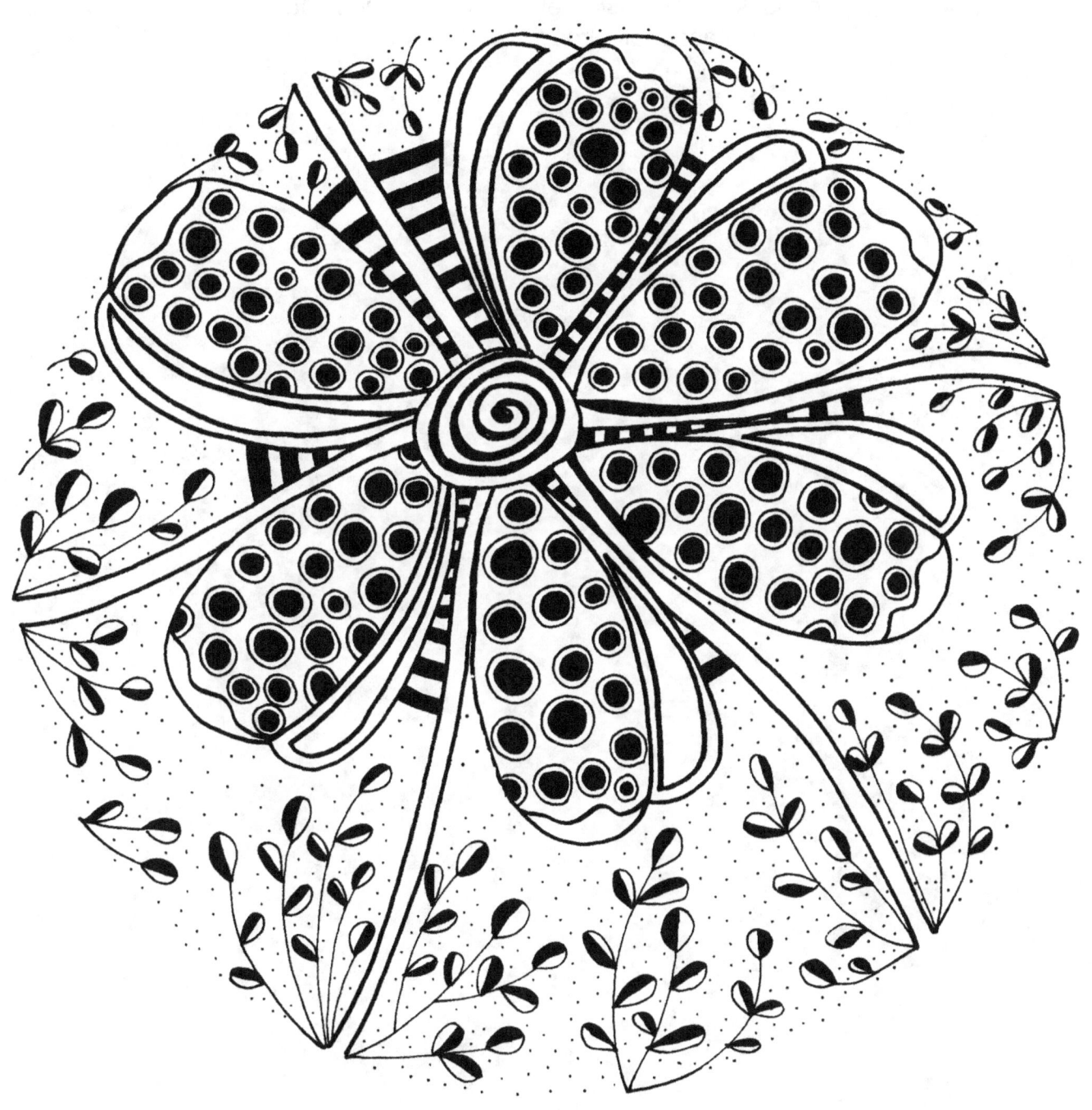

Contributing Artist
DomDomx
France

Facebook : Les-dessins-et-doodles-de-Dom-Domx
Facebook Group : Color.Addict

Global Doodle Gems Volume 1

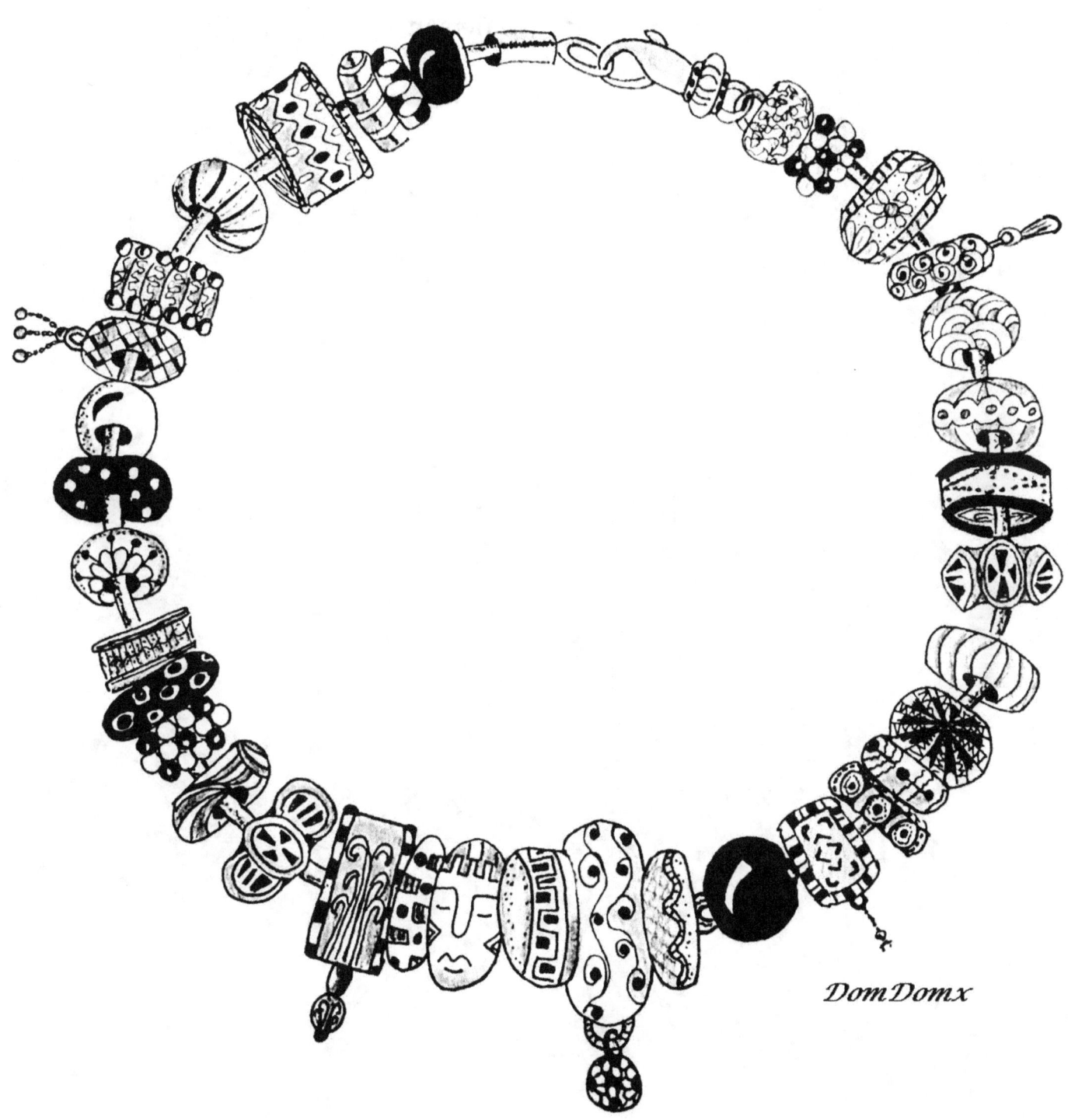

Contributing Artist
Ena Tera Art
Granada, Spain
Facebook : EnaTeraArt

Global Doodle Gems Volume 7

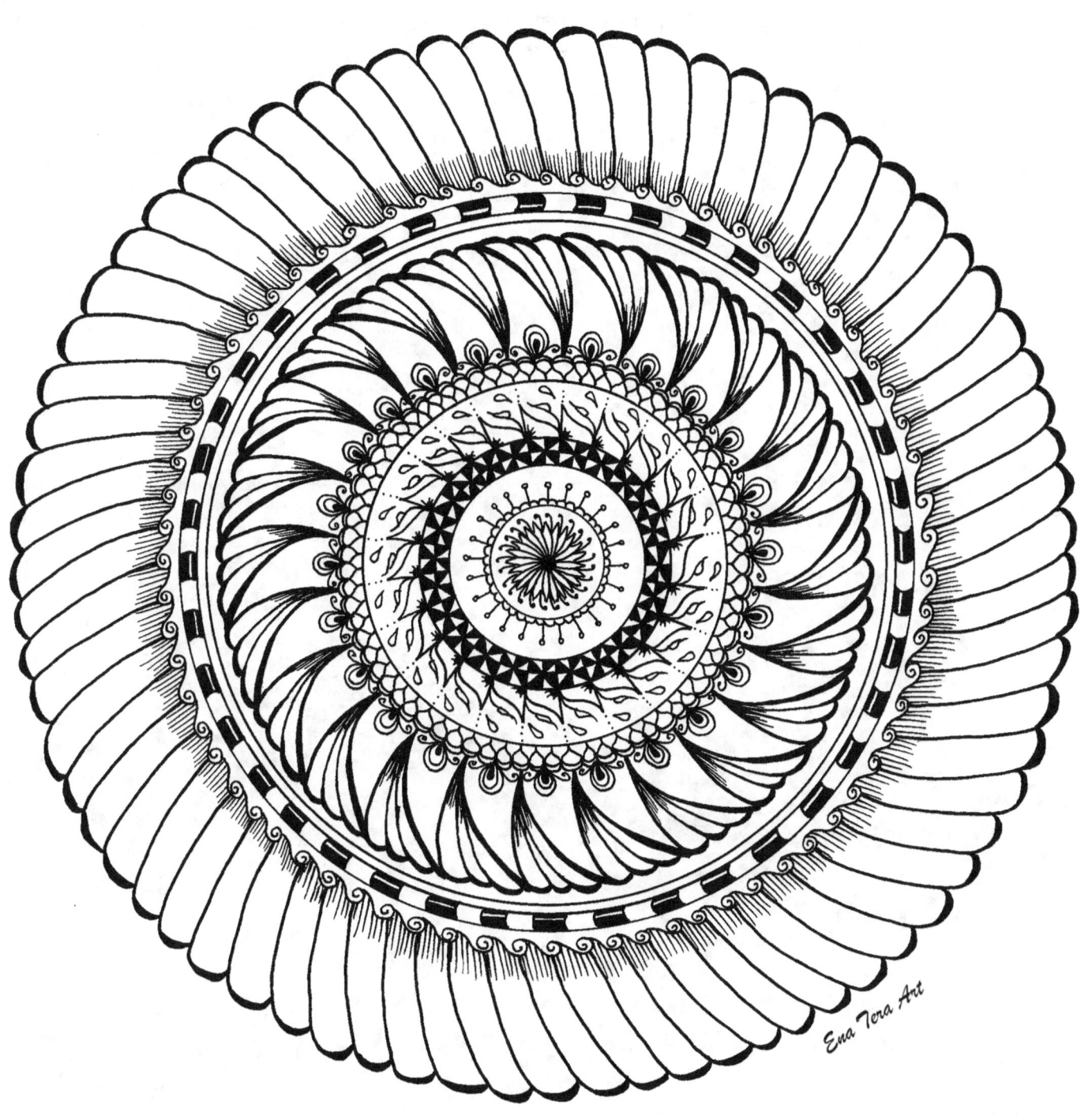

Contributing Artist
Esther Lafiebre
Canarias, Spain

Facebook .esther lafiebre
Instagram estherlafiebre

Global Doodle Gems Volume 2

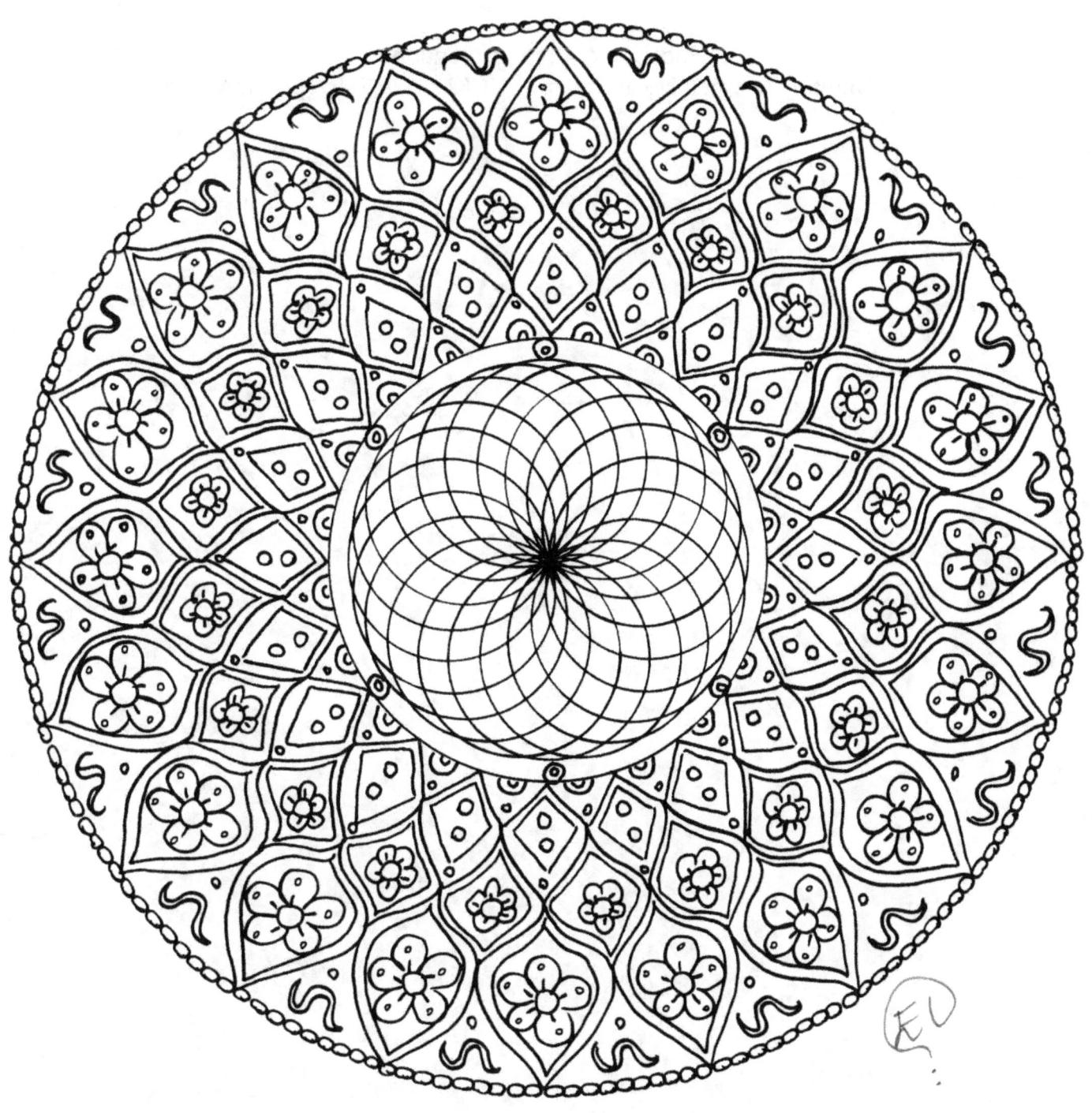

Contributing Artist
Fafahé
France

Facebook : Fafahe-creations
https://www.youtube.com/channel/UCKLs-zt2s5ZsIrFegLjHfoA

Global Doodle Gems Valentines Collection Volume 1

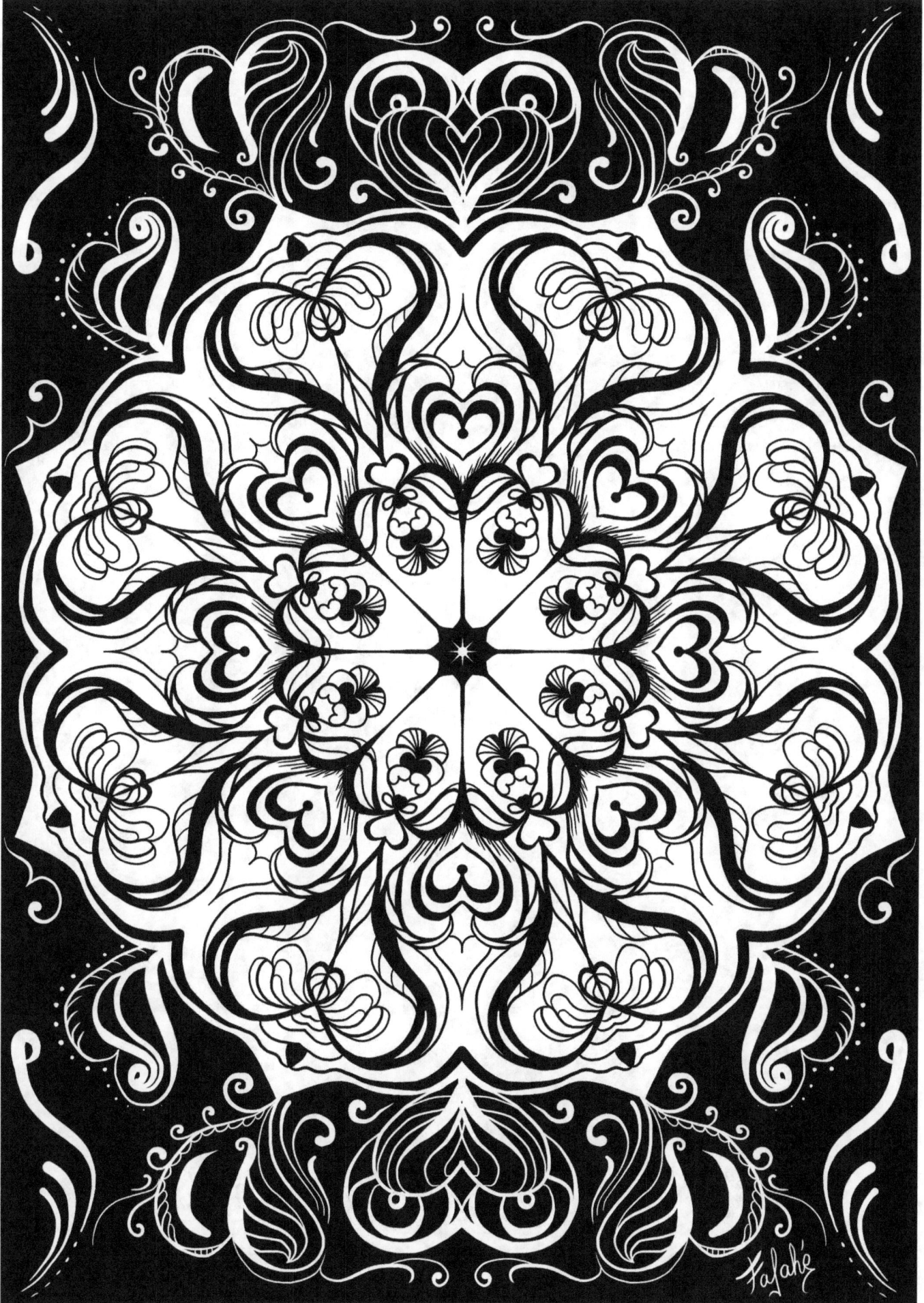

Contributing Artist
Hung Ai-Ling
Taiwan

Facebook : inspiredartLing

Global Doodle Gems Easter Collection Volume 1

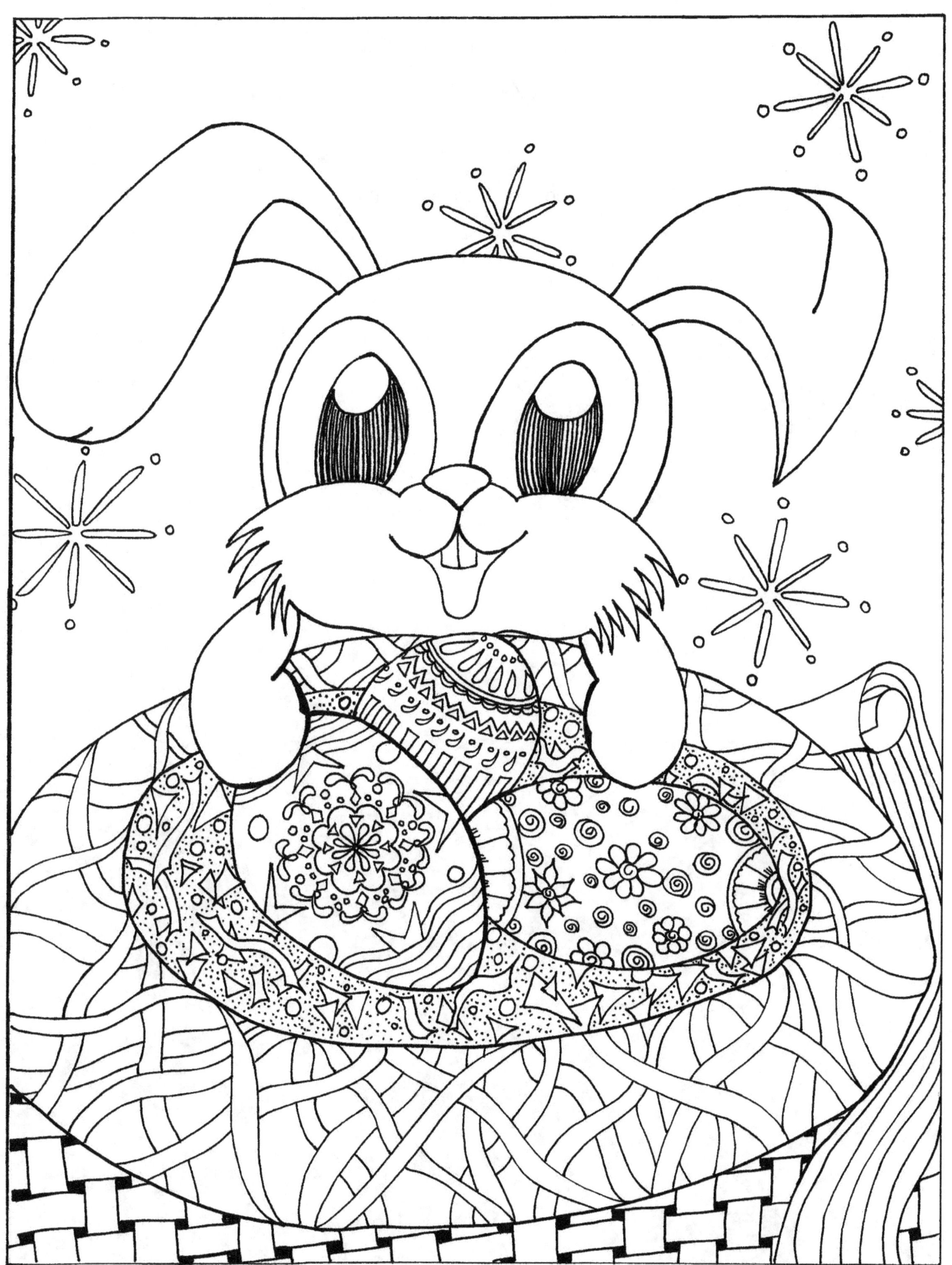

Contributing Artist
Jane Levi
France

Facebook : Cheeky-Cats

Infinity Coloring

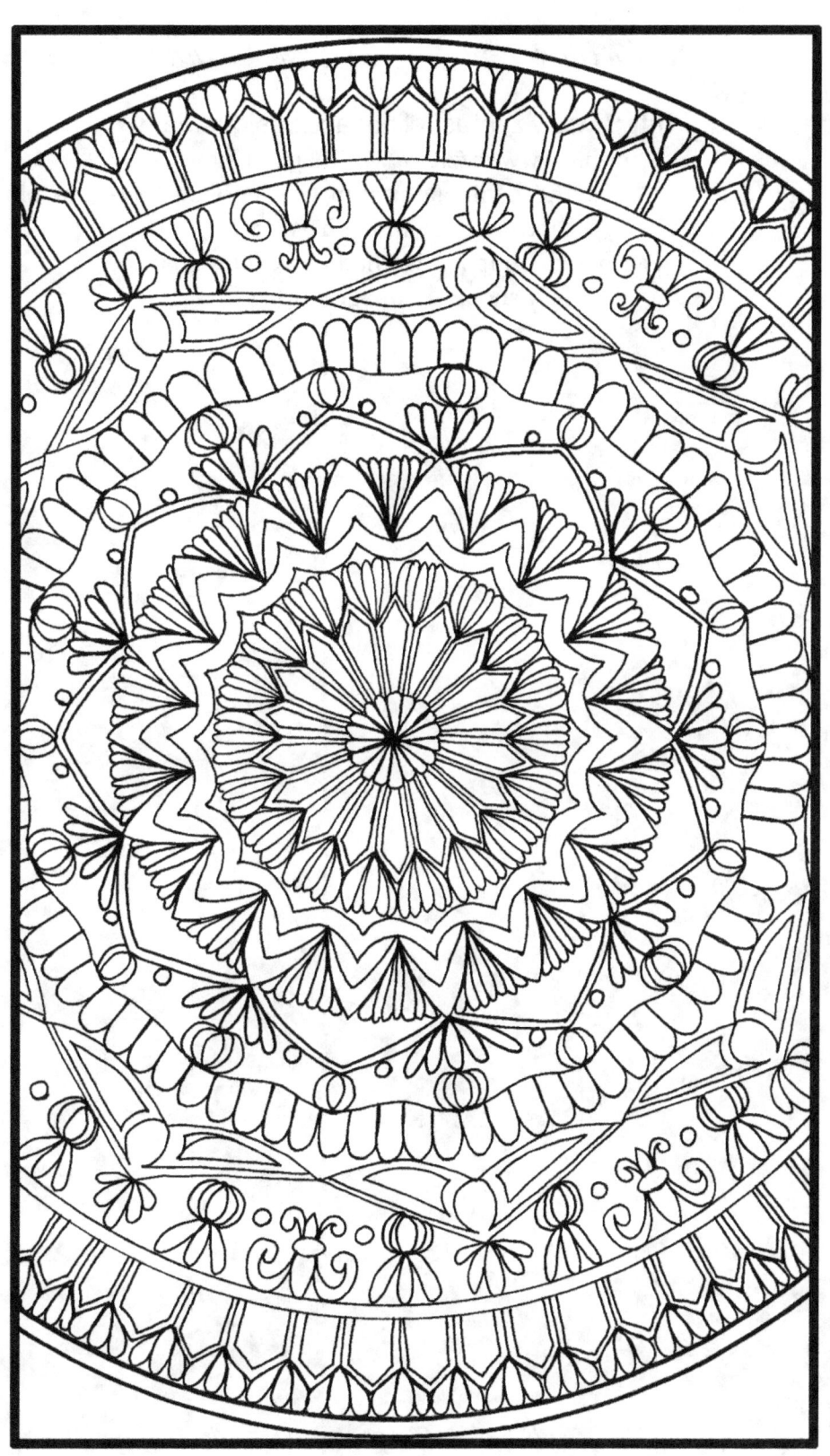

Contributing Artist
Jeanne Burbage
Saskatoon, Saskatchewan Canada

http://www.zentasticlinesanddesigns.ca/
http://www.zazzle.ca/zenimaginarium
http://driverworks.ca/The-Zenimaginarium-Garden-Coloring-Book.php
Facebook : Zenimaginarium
Facebook Group : thisnthatlinesanddesigns
Etsy shop : zenimaginarium

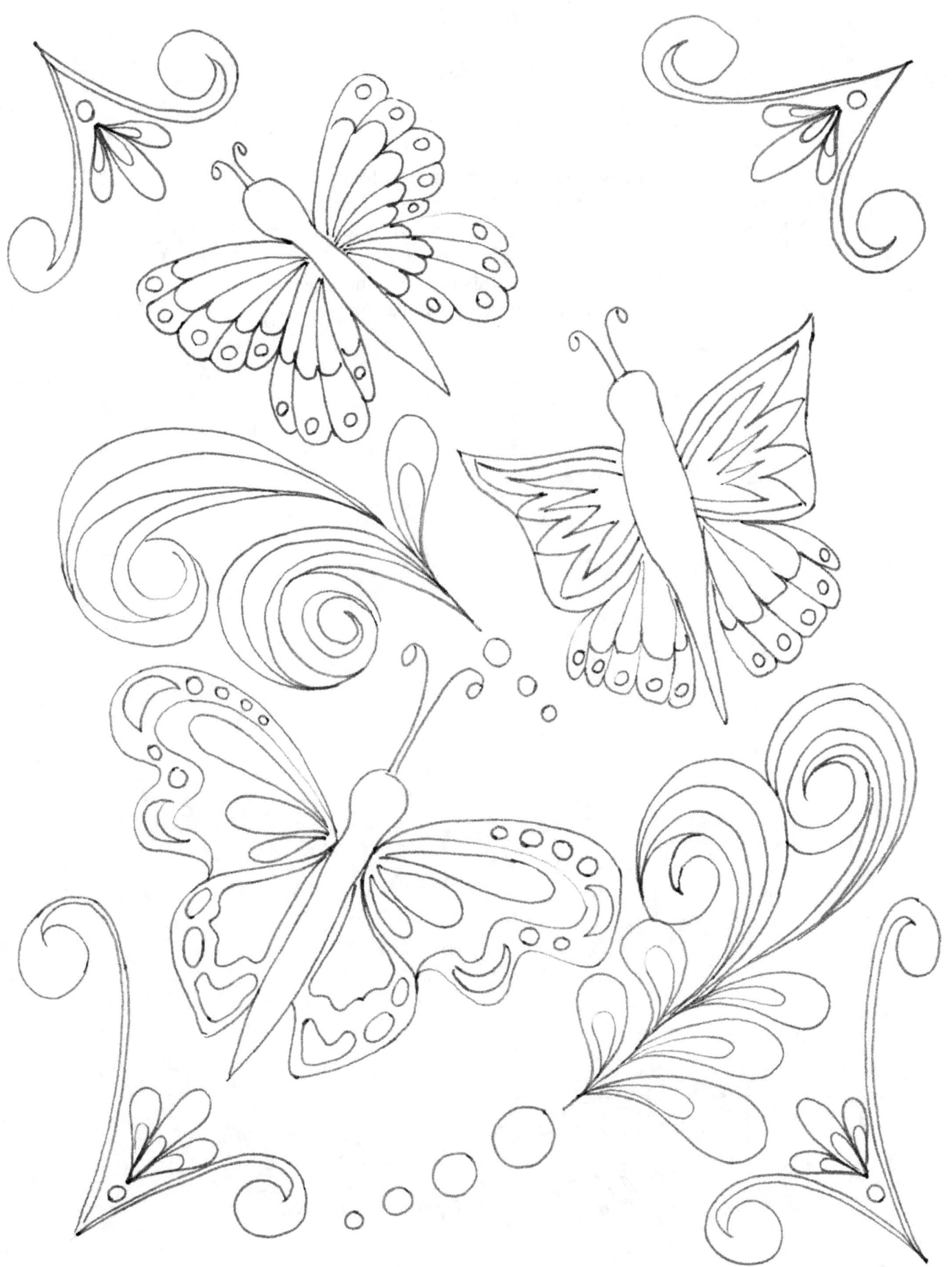

Contributing Artist
Jeanne Burbage
Saskatoon, Saskatchewan Canada

http://www.zentasticlinesanddesigns.ca/
http://www.zazzle.ca/zenimaginarium
http://driverworks.ca/The-Zenimaginarium-Garden-Coloring-Book.php
Facebook : Zenimaginarium
Facebook Group : thisnthatlinesanddesigns
Etsy shop : zenimaginarium

Global Doodle Gems Volume 7

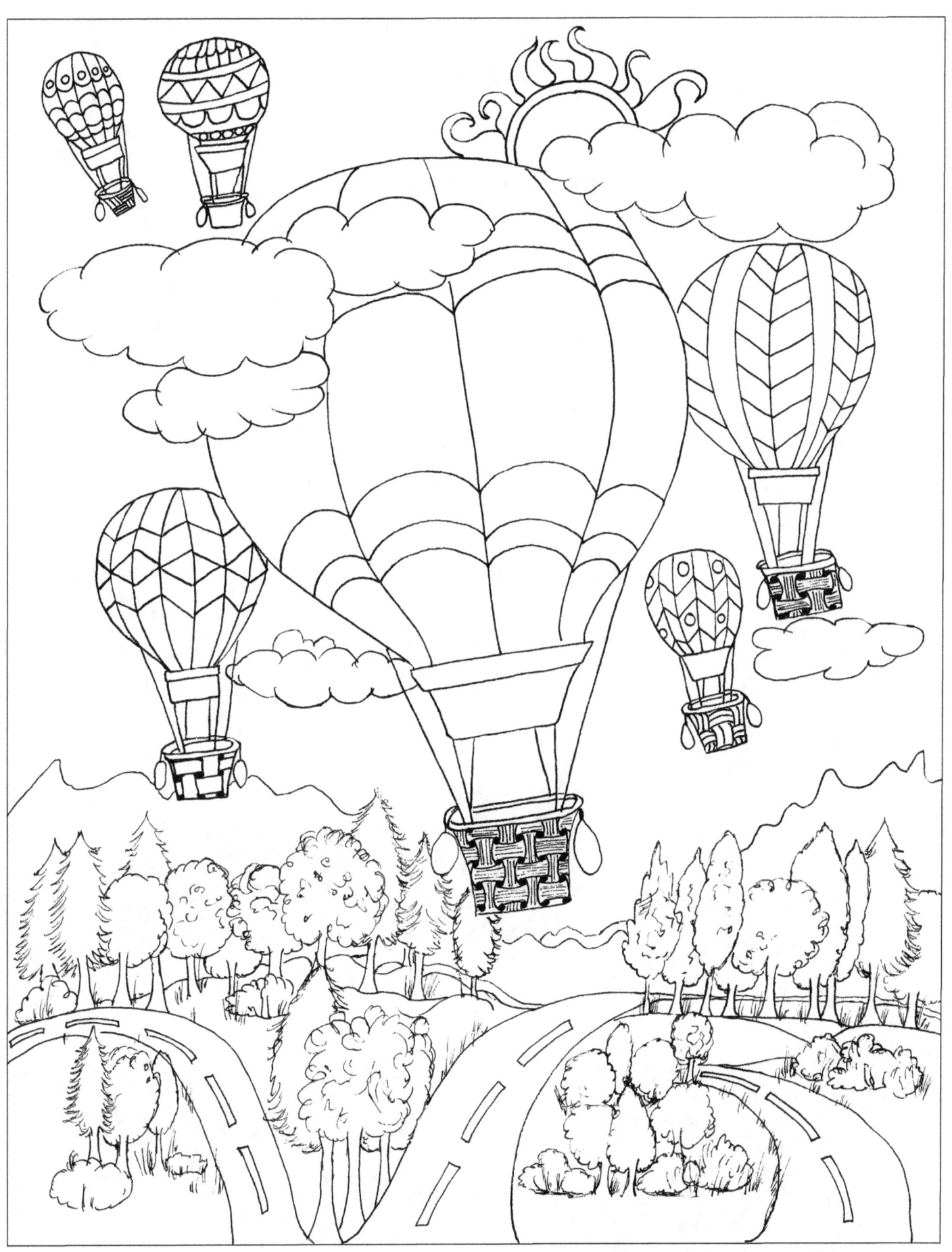

Contributing Artist
Jenny Wei
Taiwan

Facebook : zentanglefun

Global Doodle Gems Valentines Collection Volume 1

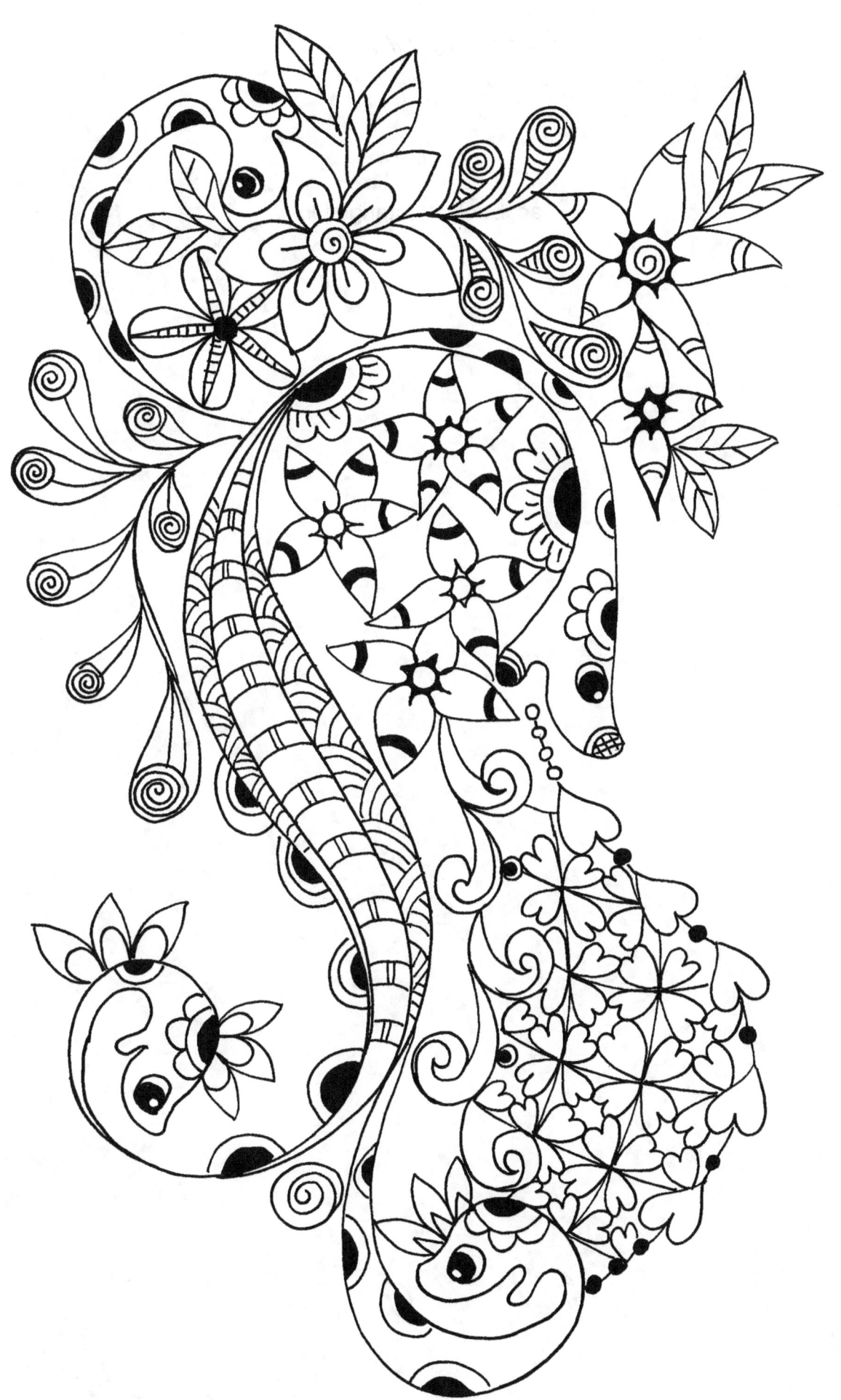

Contributing Artist
Jenny Wei
Taiwan

Facebook : zentanglefun

Global Doodle Gems Volume 5

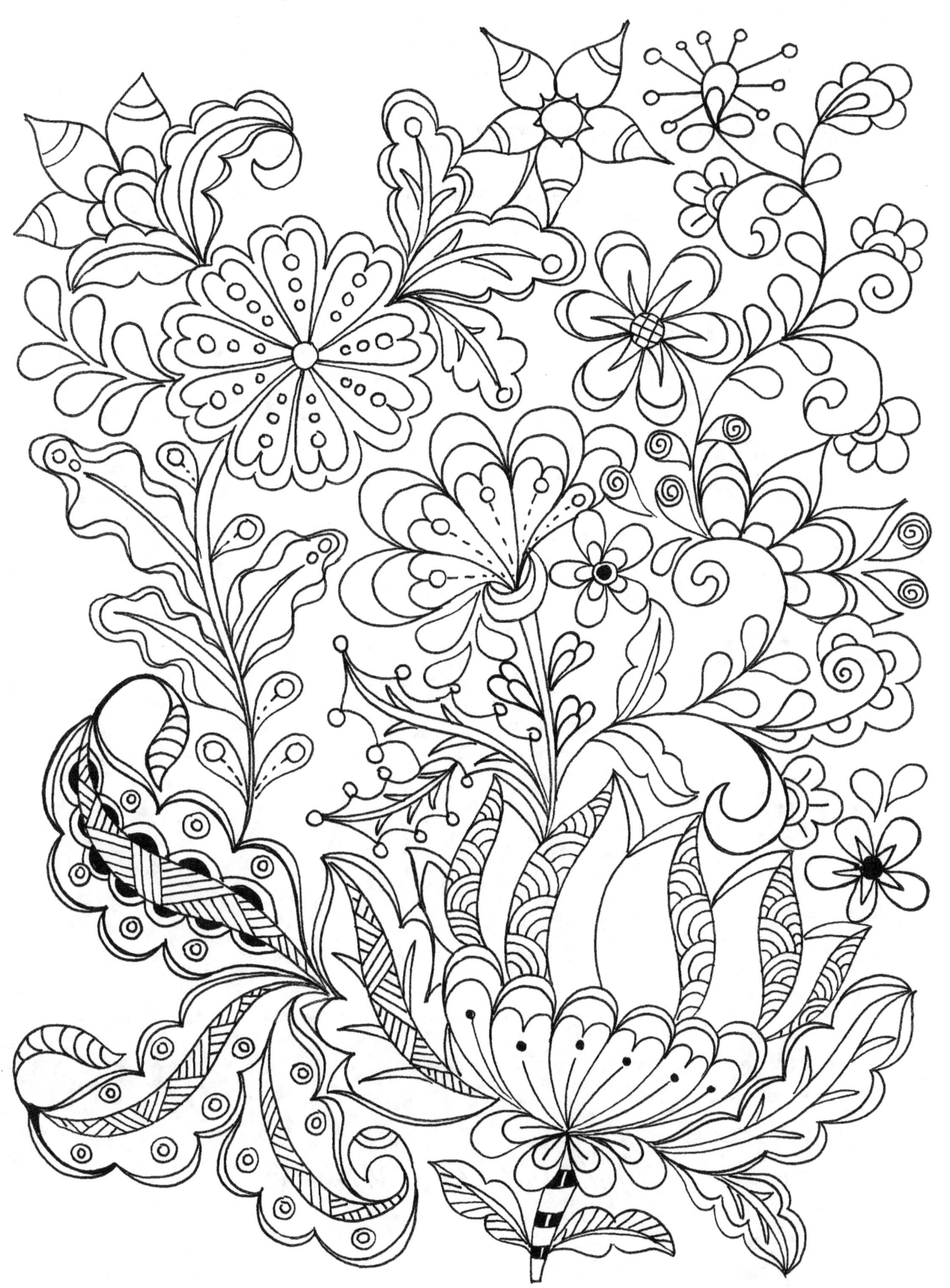

Contributing Artist
Jenny Wei
Taiwan

Facebook : zentanglefun

Global Doodle Gems Volume 5

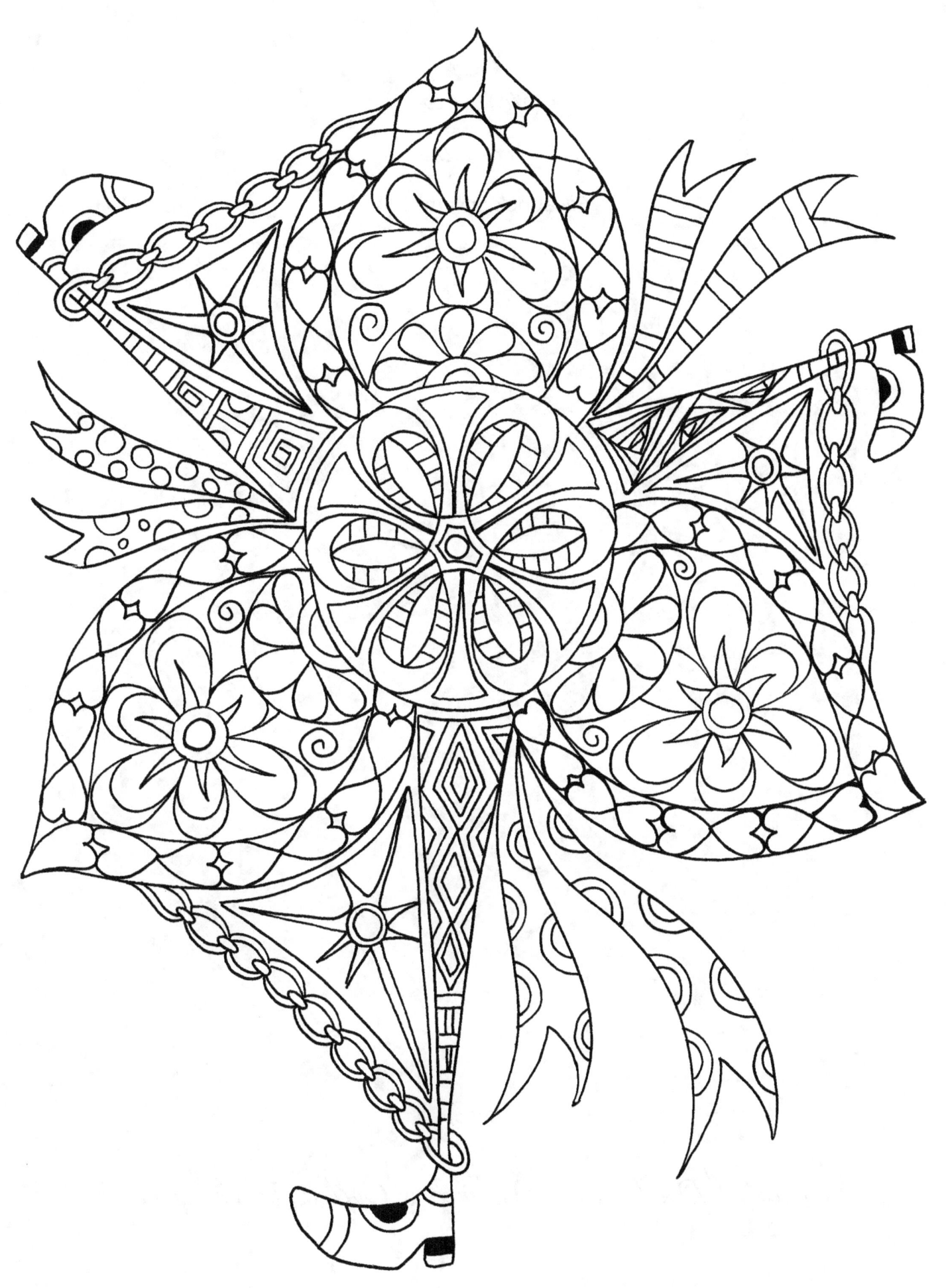

Contributing Artist
Jodi Ho
Taiwan

Facebook : riverho1688

Global Doodle Gems Valentines Collection Volume 1

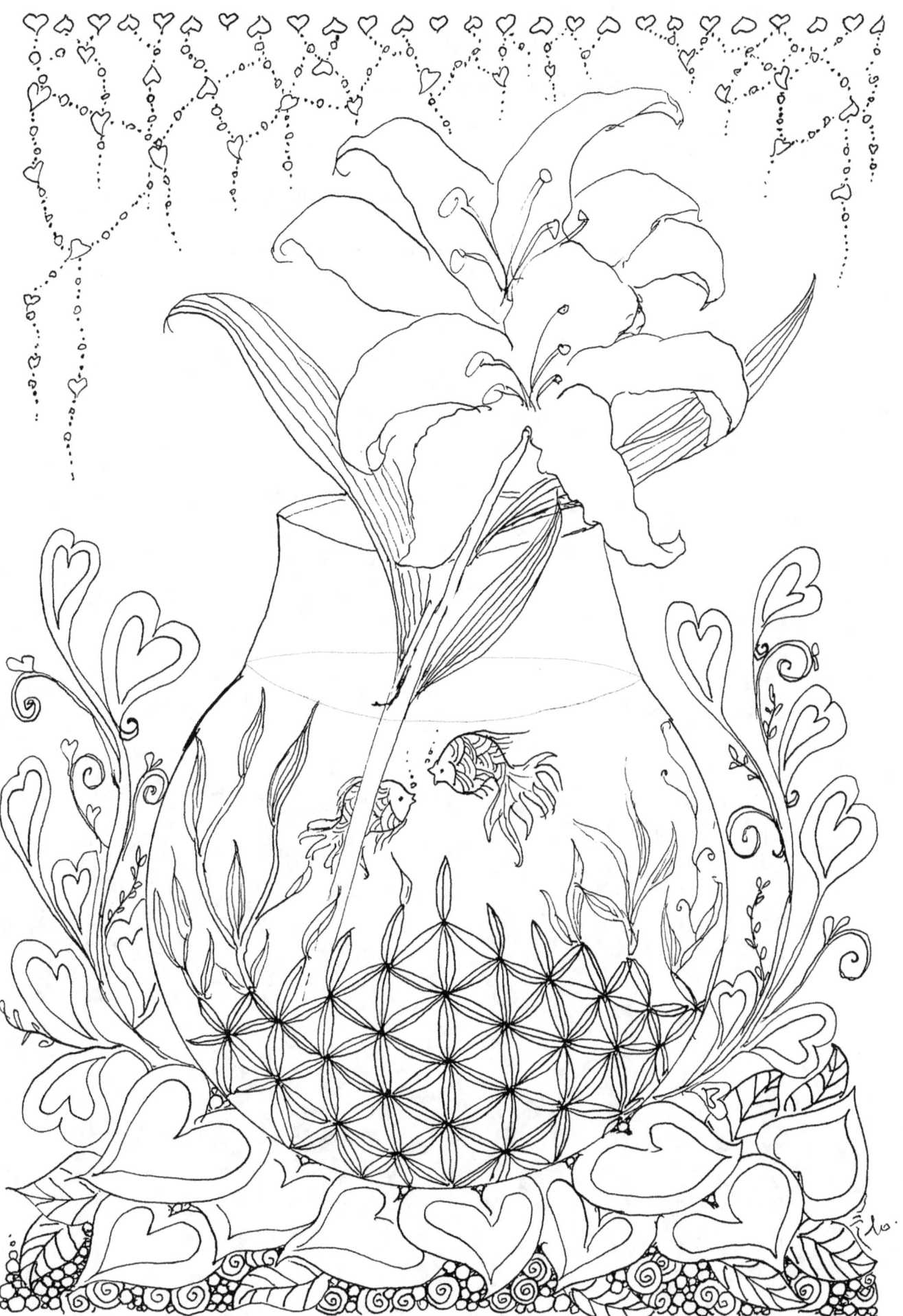

Contributing Artist
MWMS-Johanna Ans
The Netherlands

Blog : mywaymystylejohannaans.wordpress.com

Facebook : Johanna-Ans-My-creative-site

Cat Gems

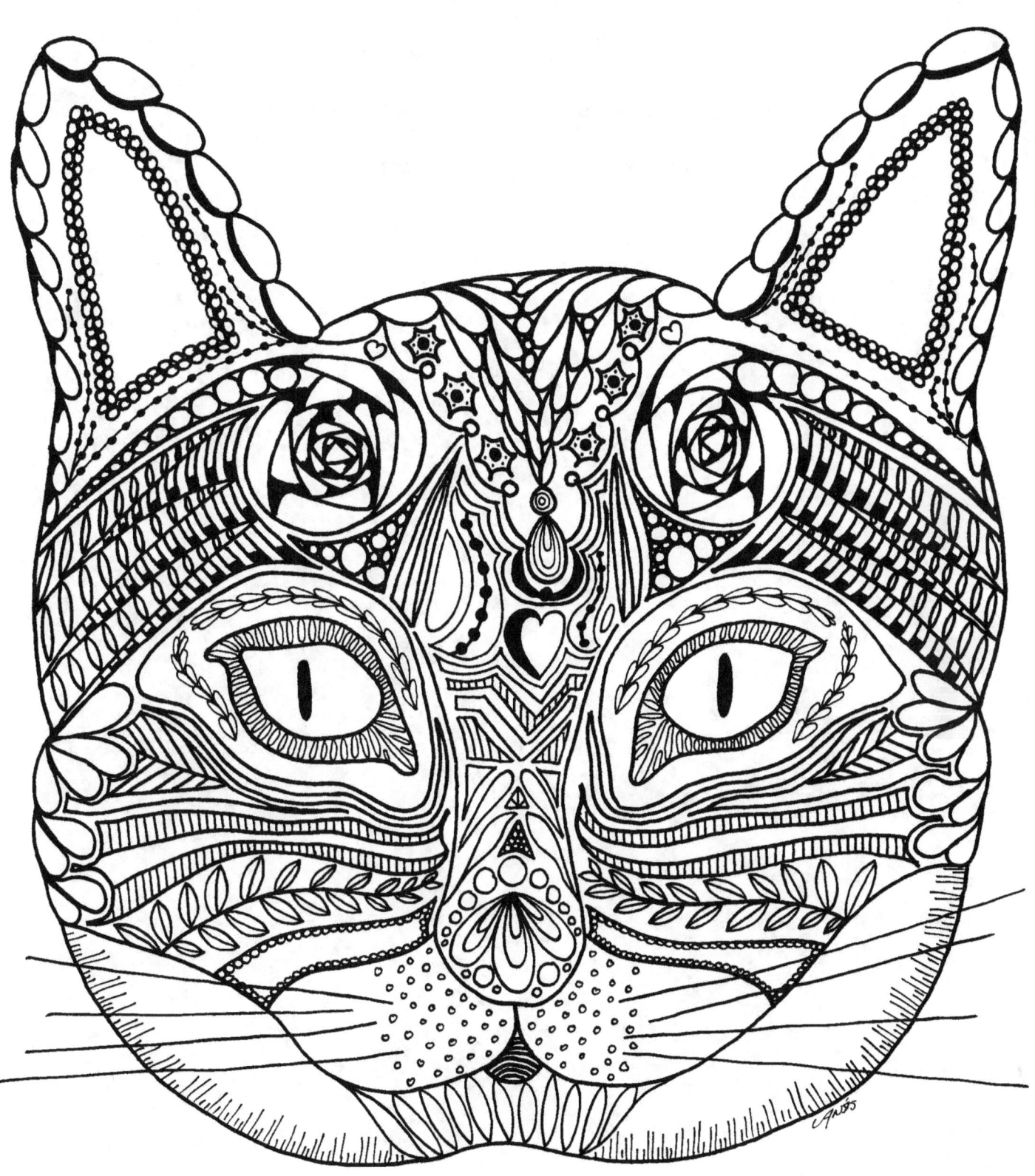

Contributing Artist
MWMS-Johanna Ans
The Netherlands

Blog : mywaymystylejohannaans.wordpress.com

Facebook : Johanna-Ans-My-creative-site

Cat Gems

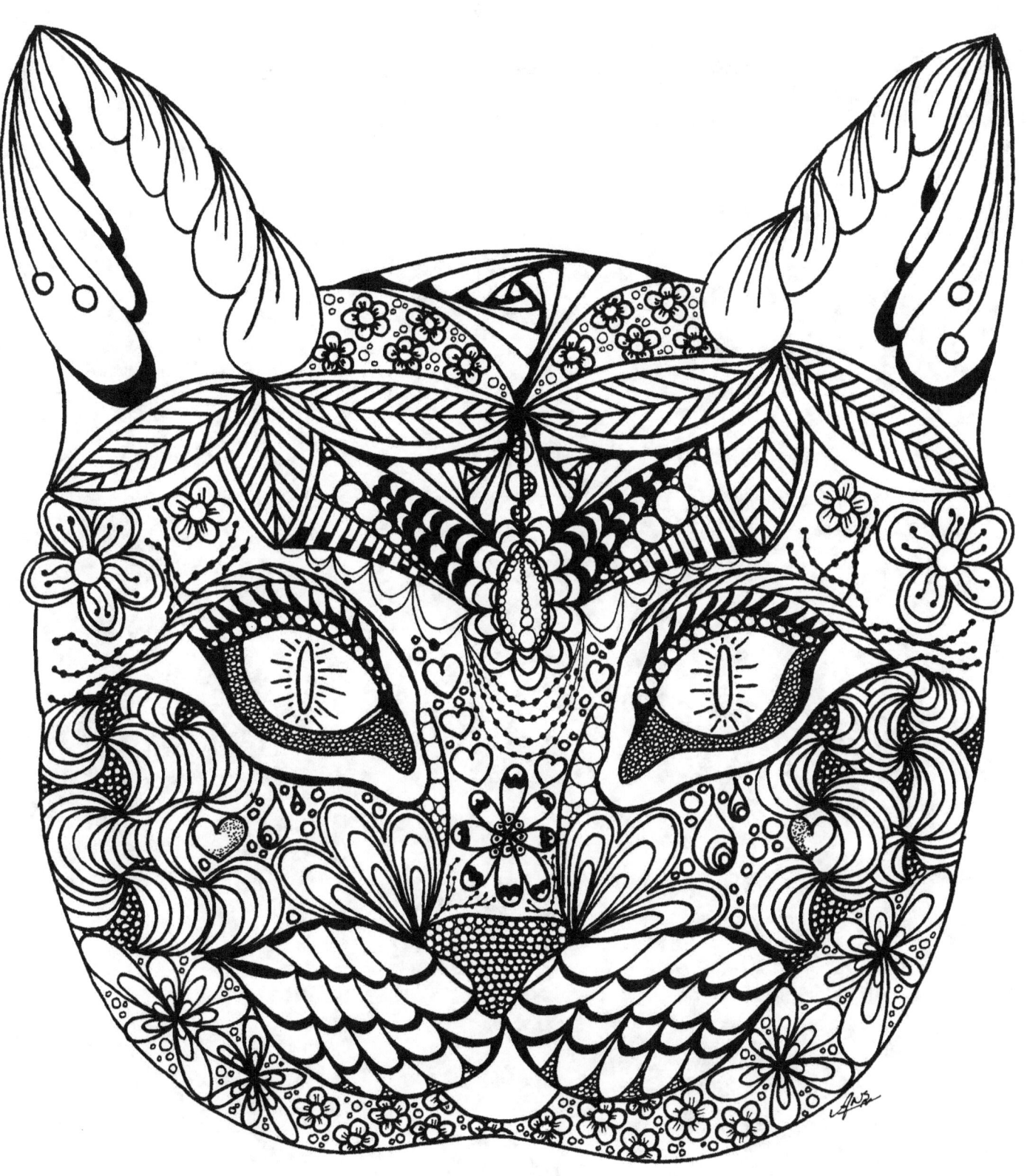

Contributing Artist
MWMS-Johanna Ans
The Netherlands

Blog : mywaymystylejohannaans.wordpress.com

Facebook : Johanna-Ans-My-creative-site

Cat Gems

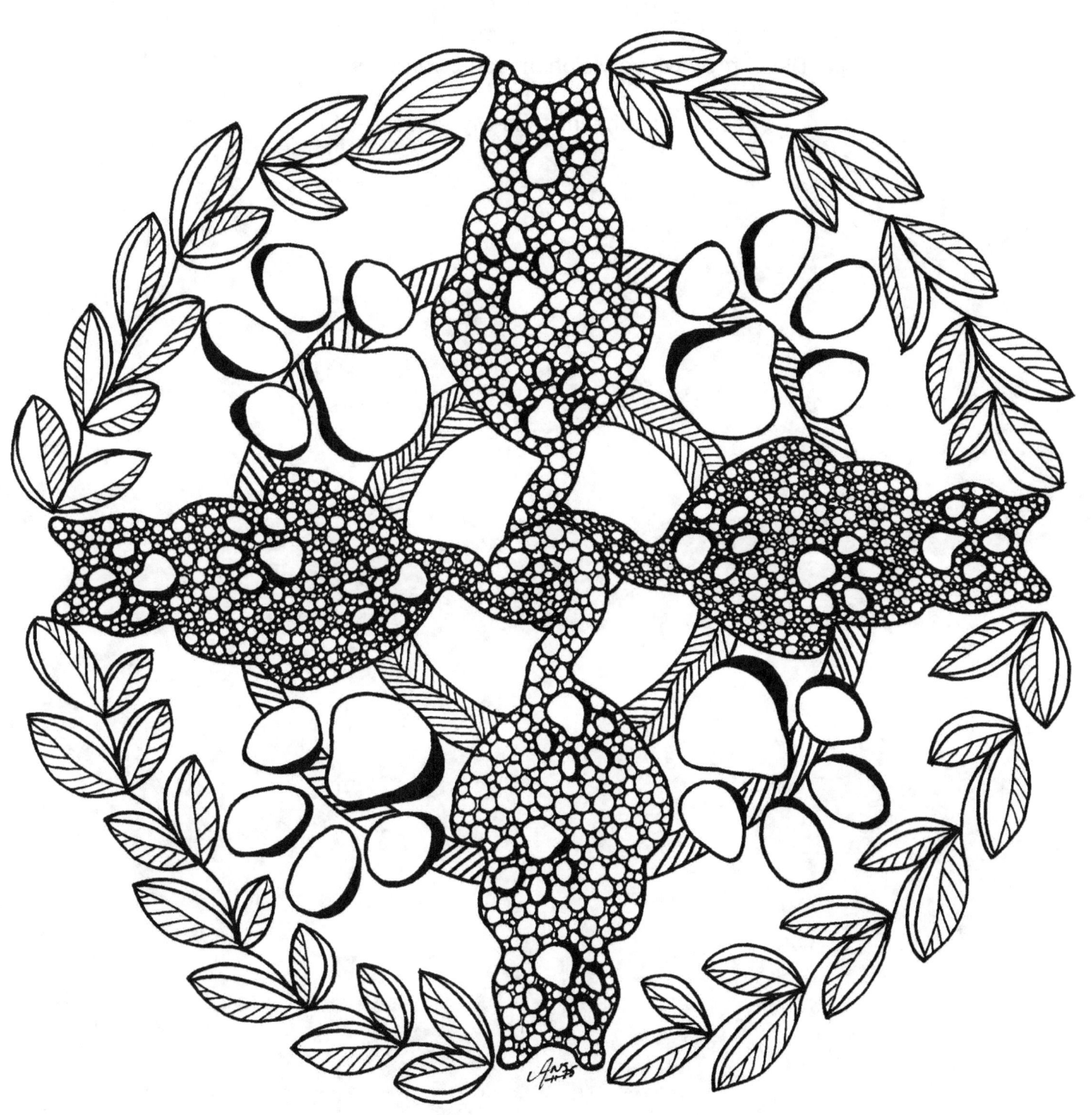

Contributing Artist
MWMS-Johanna Ans
The Netherlands

Blog : mywaymystylejohannaans.wordpress.com

Facebook : Johanna-Ans-My-creative-site

Cat Gems

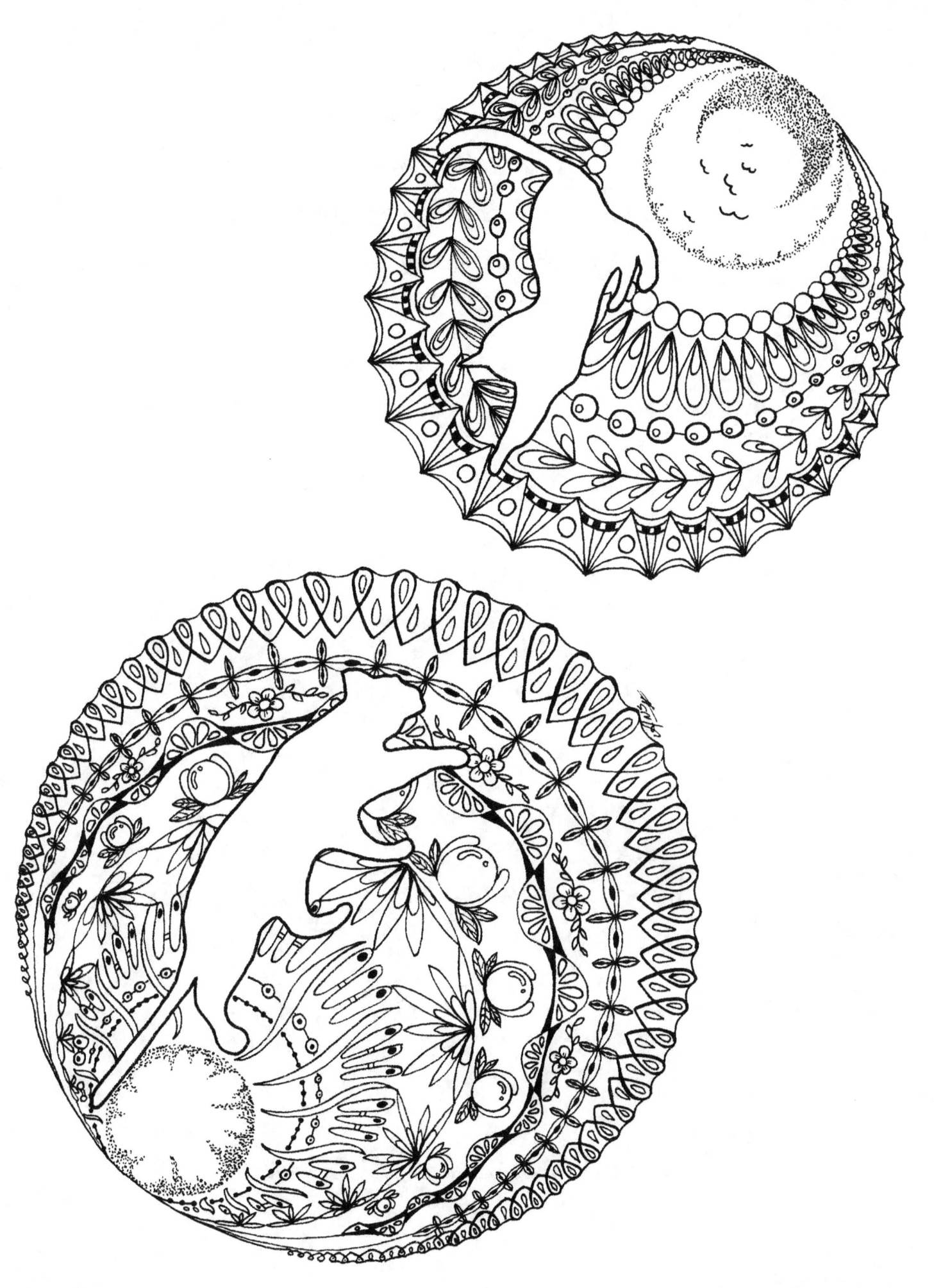

Contributing Artist
MWMS-Johanna Ans
The Netherlands

Blog : mywaymystylejohannaans.wordpress.com

Facebook : Johanna-Ans-My-creative-site

Twister-Gems-Doodle-Do-Book

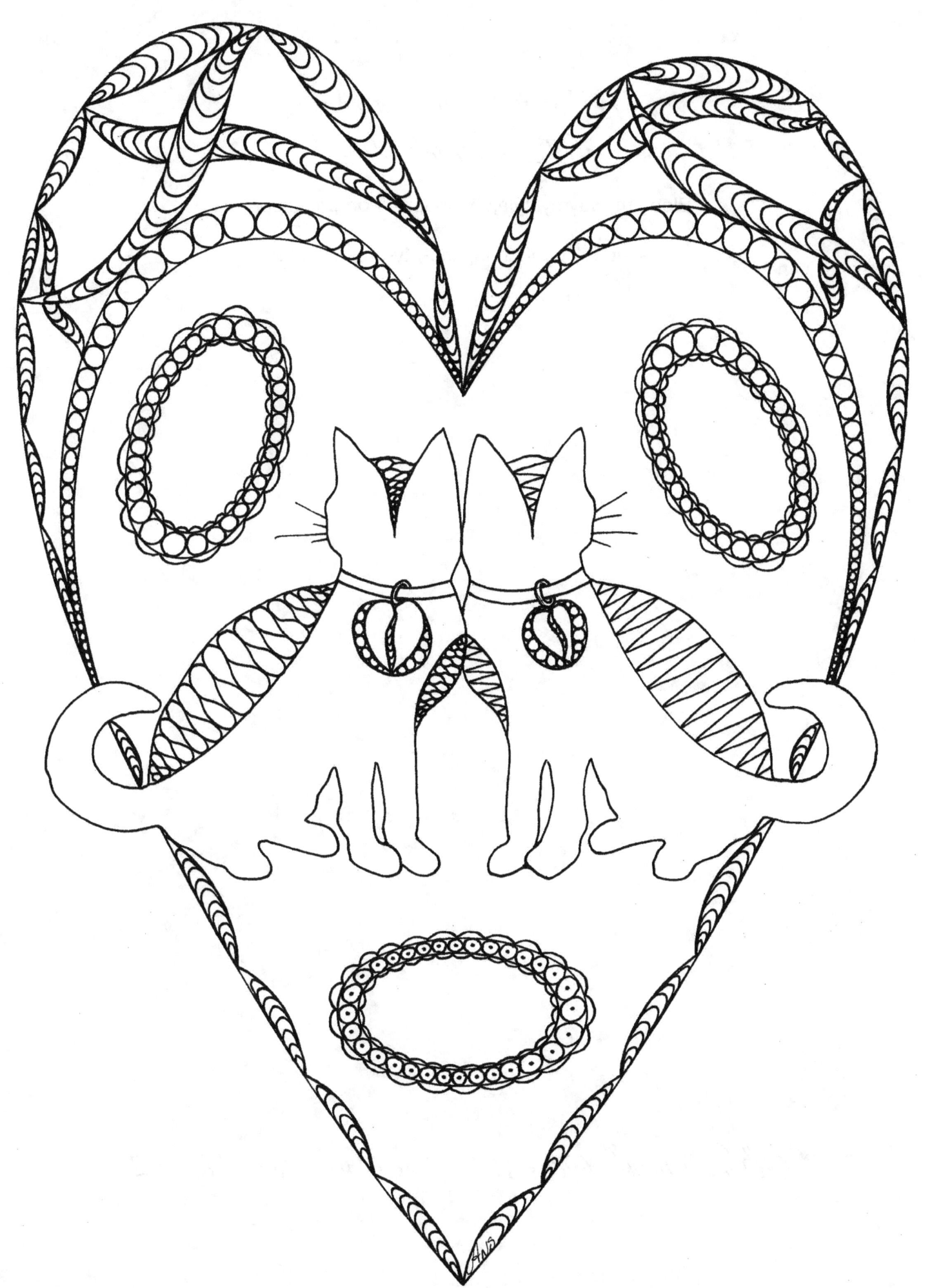

Contributing Artist
MWMS-Johanna Ans
The Netherlands

Blog : mywaymystylejohannaans.wordpress.com

Facebook : Johanna-Ans-My-creative-site

Contributing Artist
Joseph Shivery
USA

Facebook : The-Broken-Mind-of-Joes-Ink
Payhip shop : joesinkearthlinknet

The Broken Mind of Joe's Ink 1

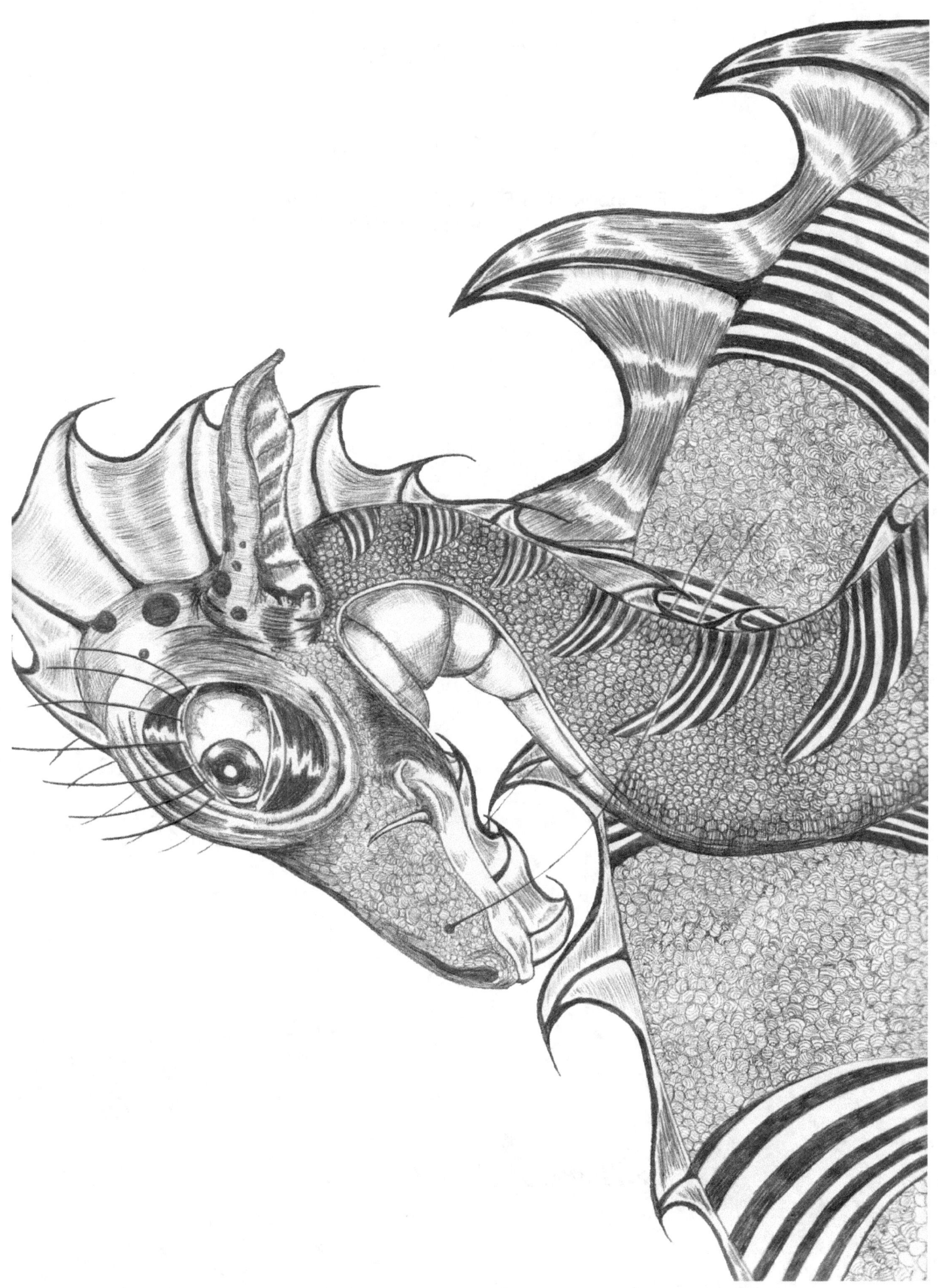

Contributing Artist
Joseph Shivery
USA

Facebook : The-Broken-Mind-of-Joes-Ink
Payhip shop : joesinkearthlinknet

The Broken Mind of Joe's Ink 2

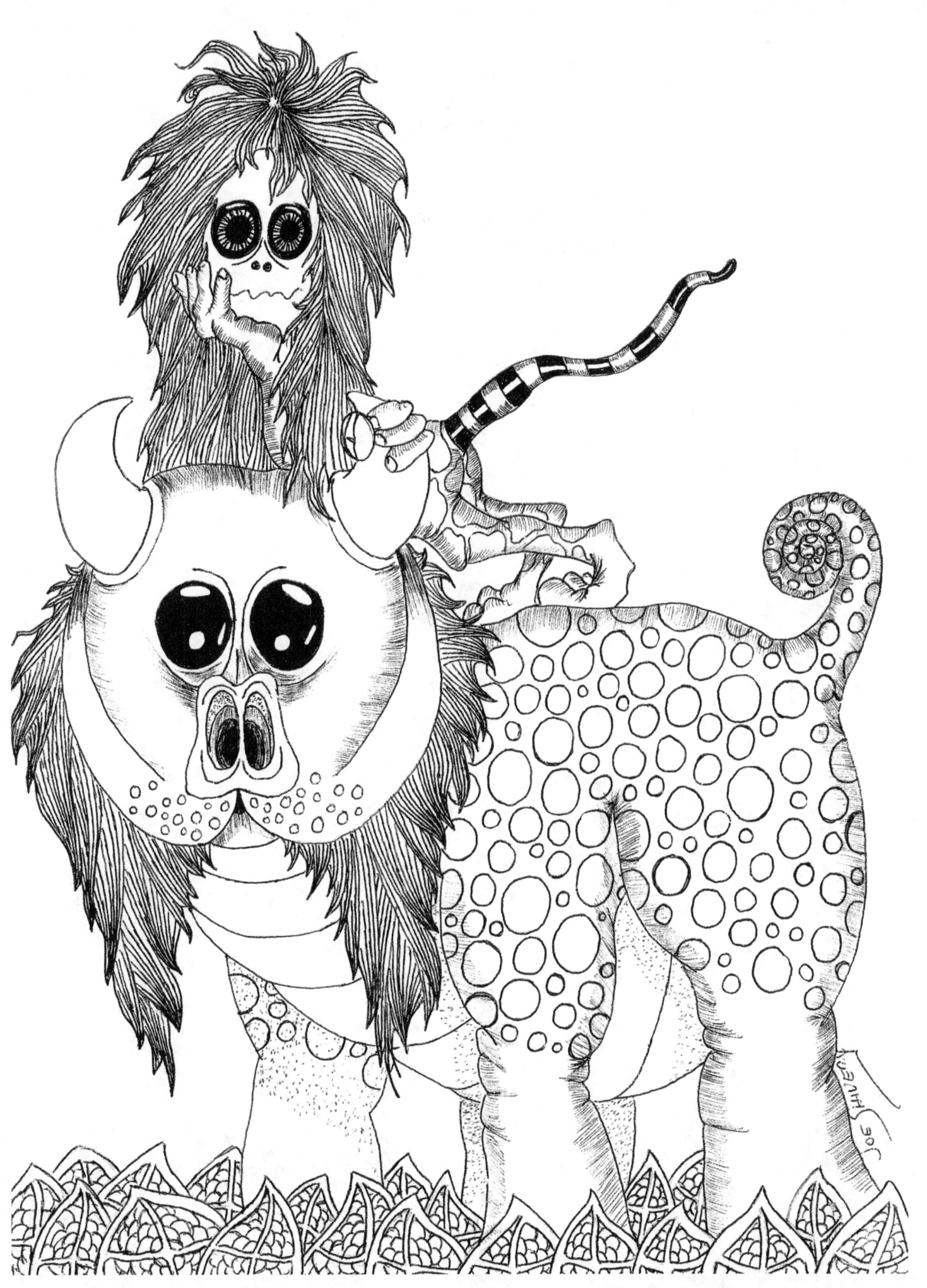

Contributing Artist
Joseph Shivery
USA

Facebook : The-Broken-Mind-of-Joes-Ink
Payhip shop : joesinkearthlinknet

The Broken Mind of Joe's Ink 2

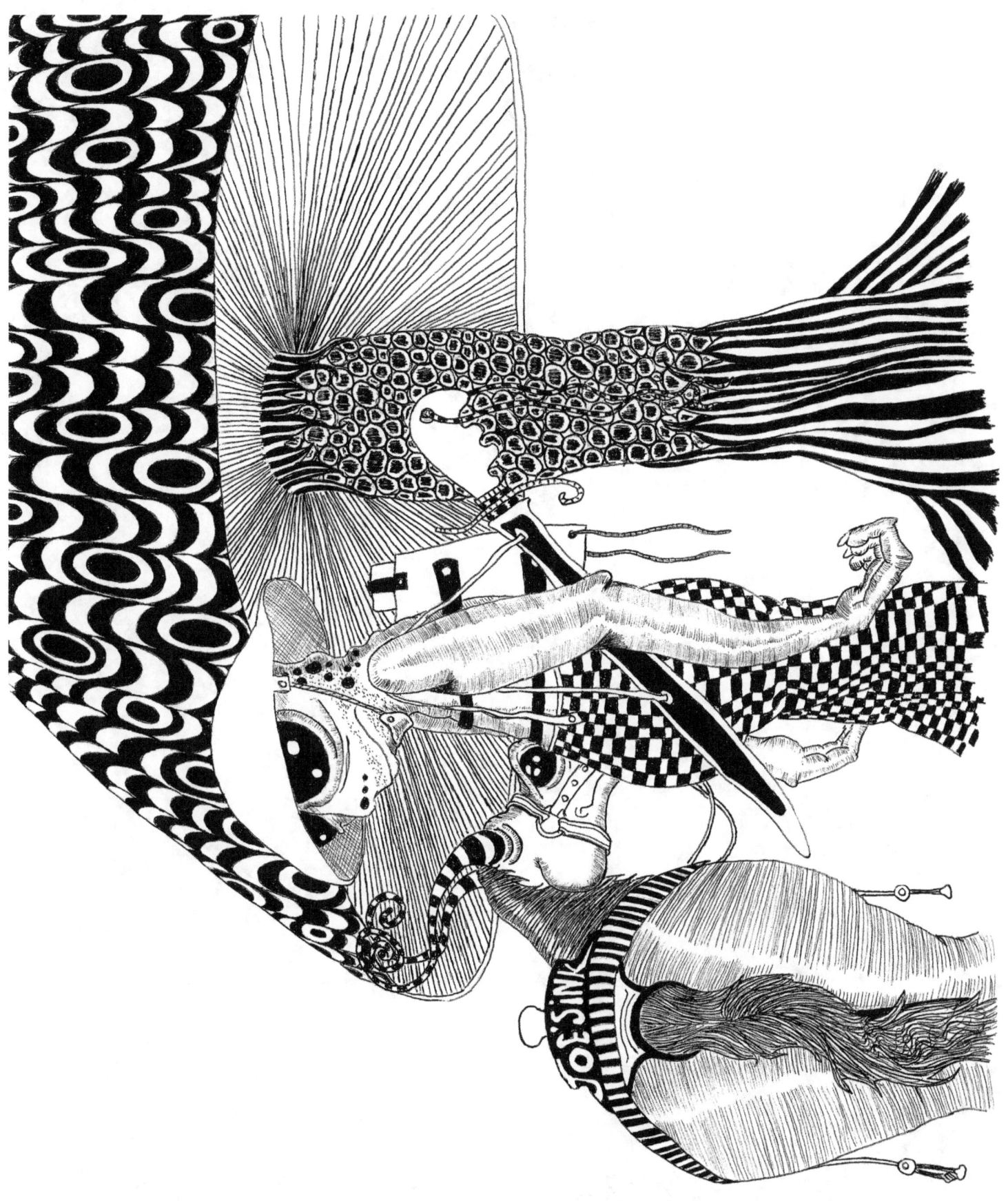

Contributing Artist
Joseph Shivery
USA

Facebook : The-Broken-Mind-of-Joes-Ink
Payhip shop : joesinkearthlinknet

Global Doodle Gems Volume 4

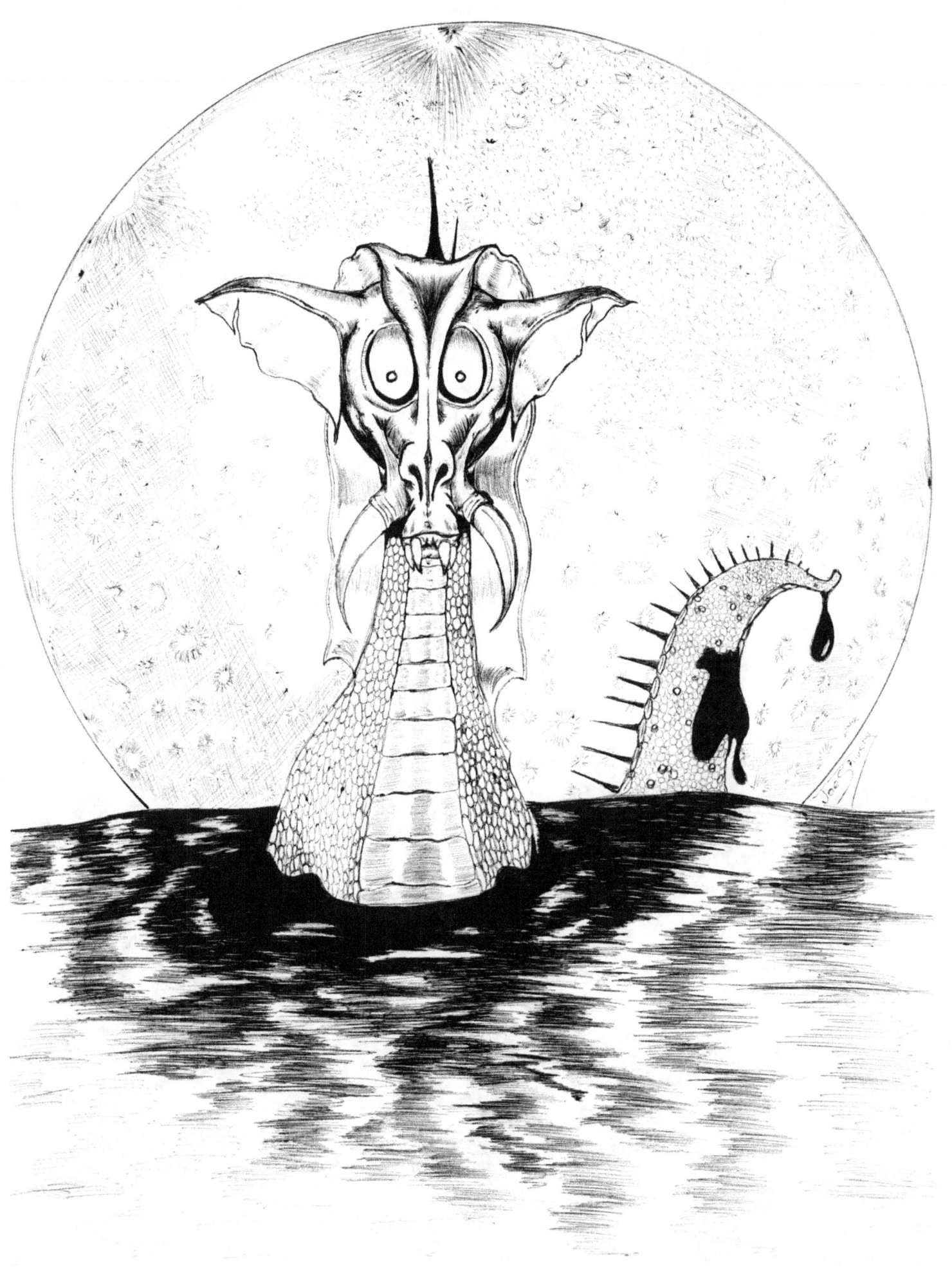

Contributing Artist
Karim Benyagoub
Algeria

Facebook : karimdesignscoloring
Facebook Group : karimcoloringbooks
Twitter : karim_designs
More books by Karim : http://amazon.com/author/karimbenyagoub/

Global Doodle Gems Volume 1

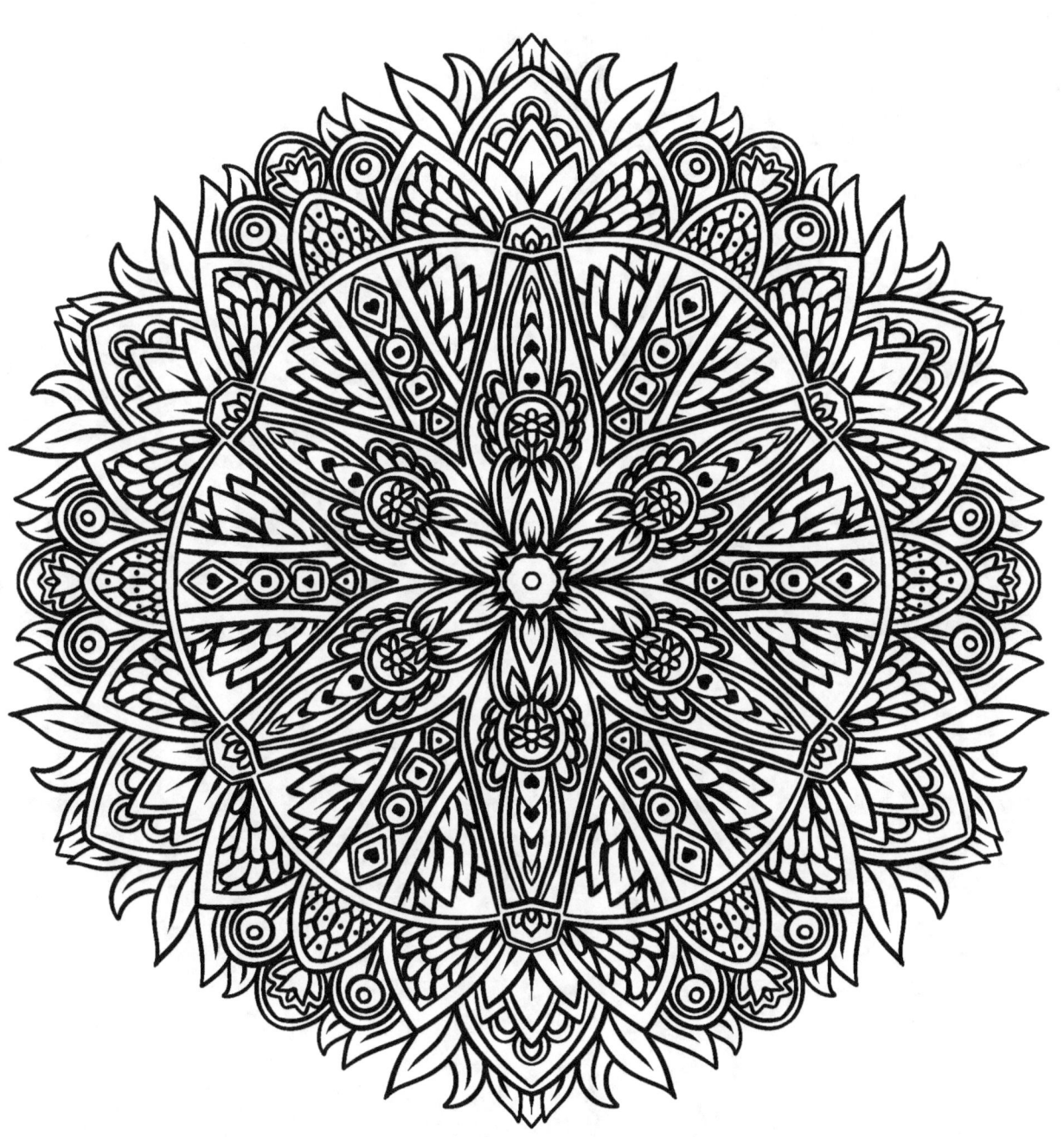

Contributing Artist
Laurie Beauchamp
USA

Dazzling Dragons

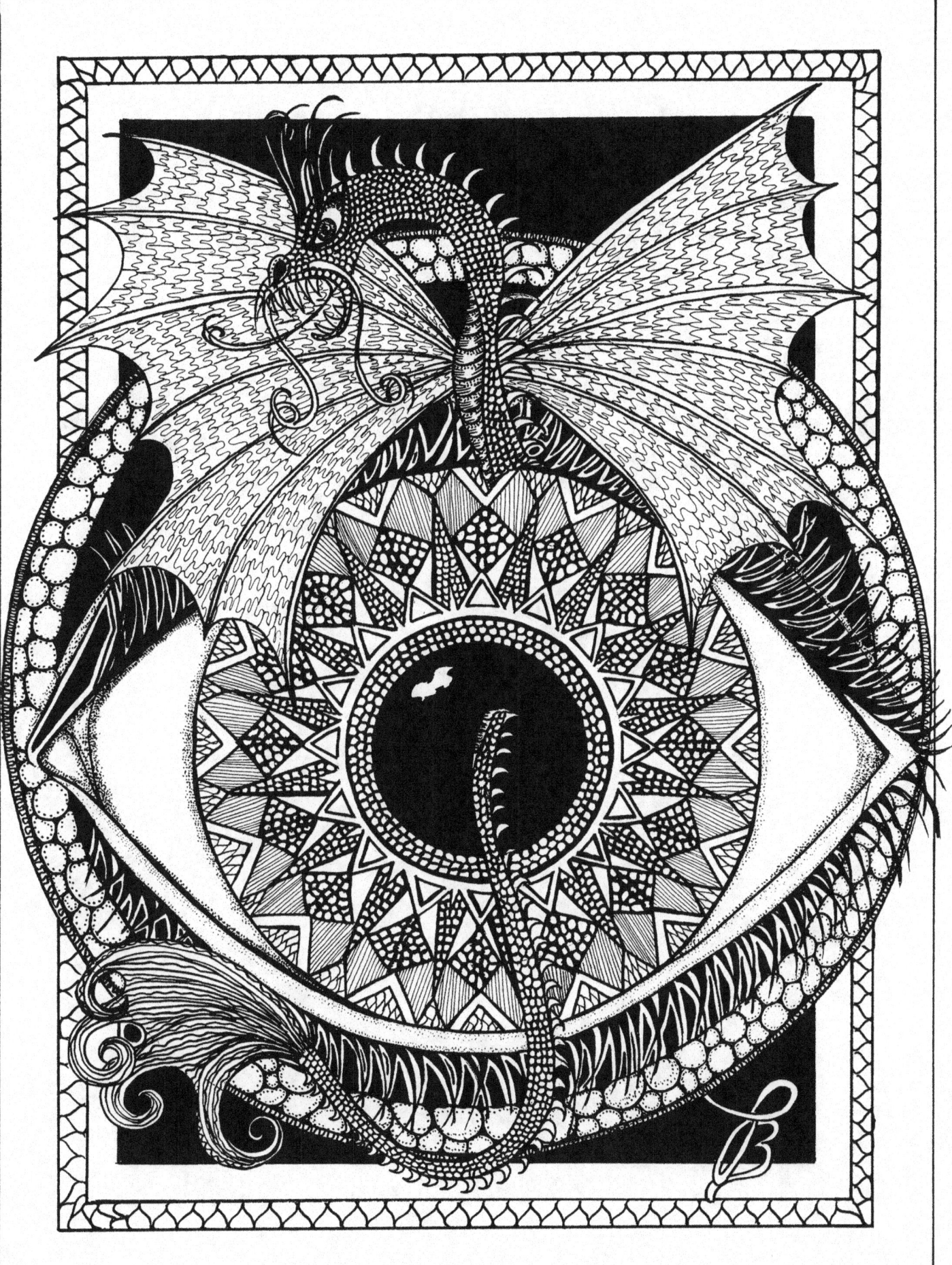

Contributing Artist
Laurie Beauchamp
USA

Dazzling Dragons

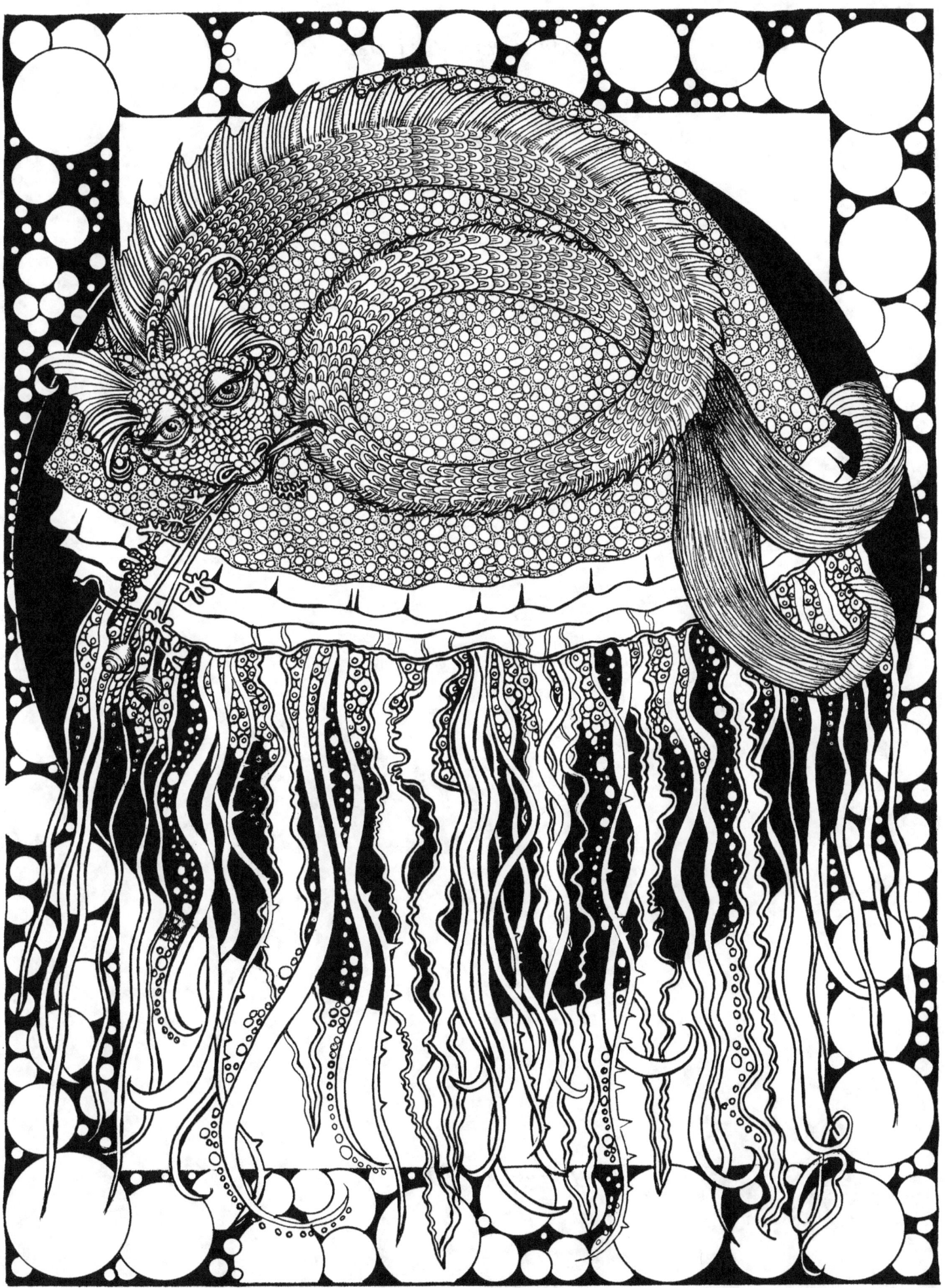

Contributing Artist
Laurie Beauchamp
USA

Dazzling Dragons

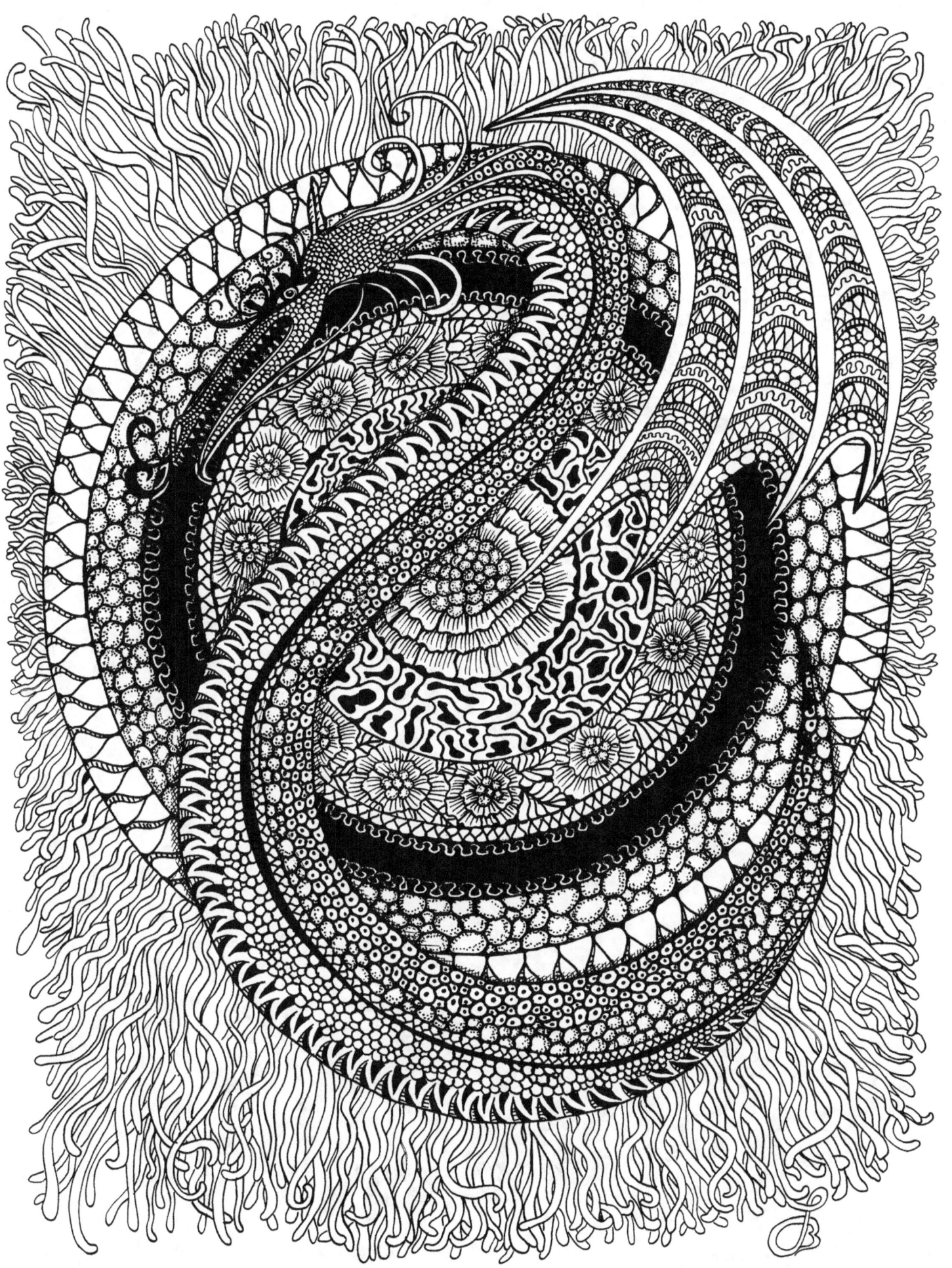

Contributing Artist
Laurie Beauchamp
USA

Dazzling Dragons

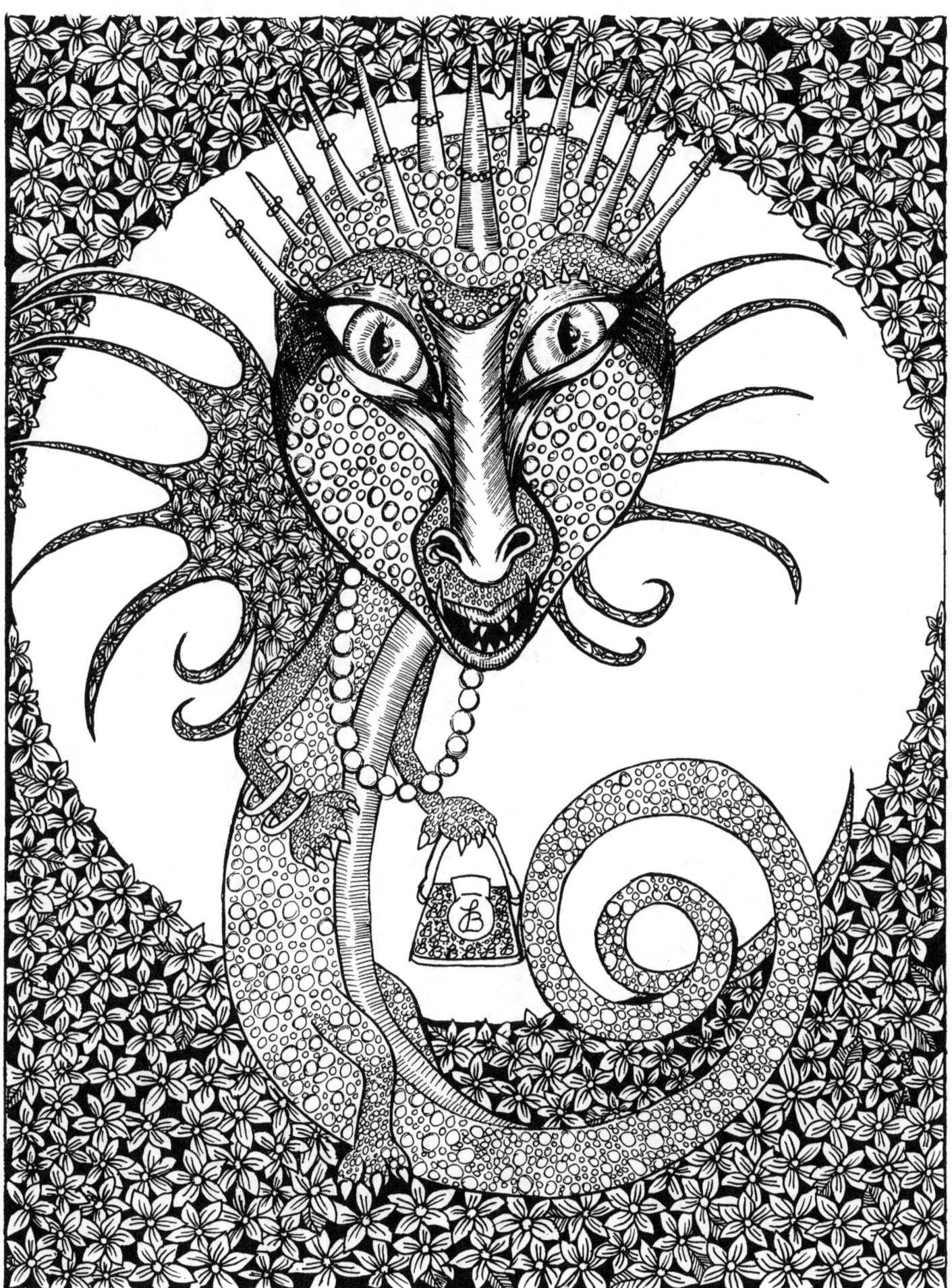

Contributing Artist
Laurie Beauchamp
USA

Dazzling Dragons

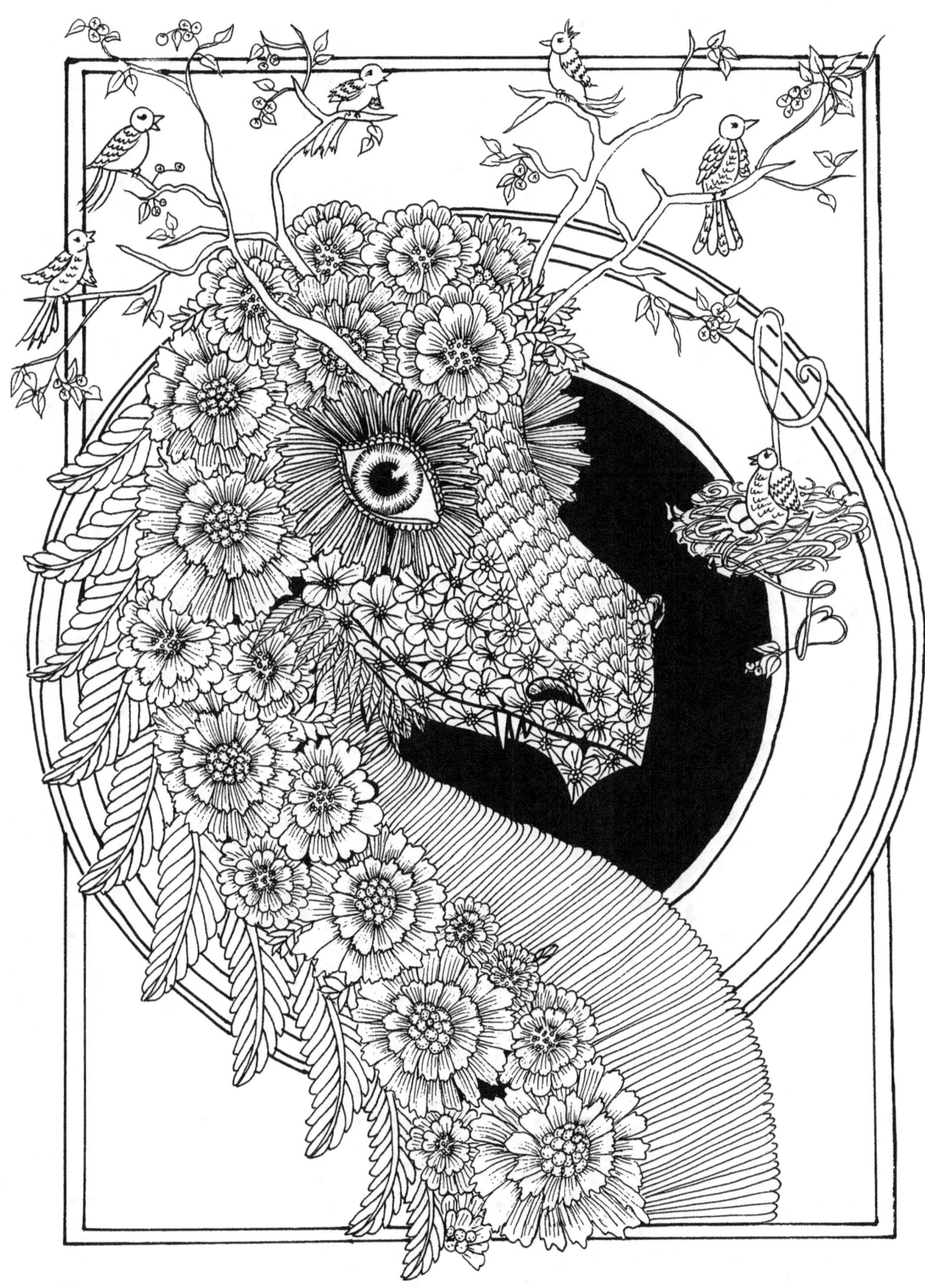

Contributing Artist
Laurie Beauchamp
USA

Dazzling Dragons

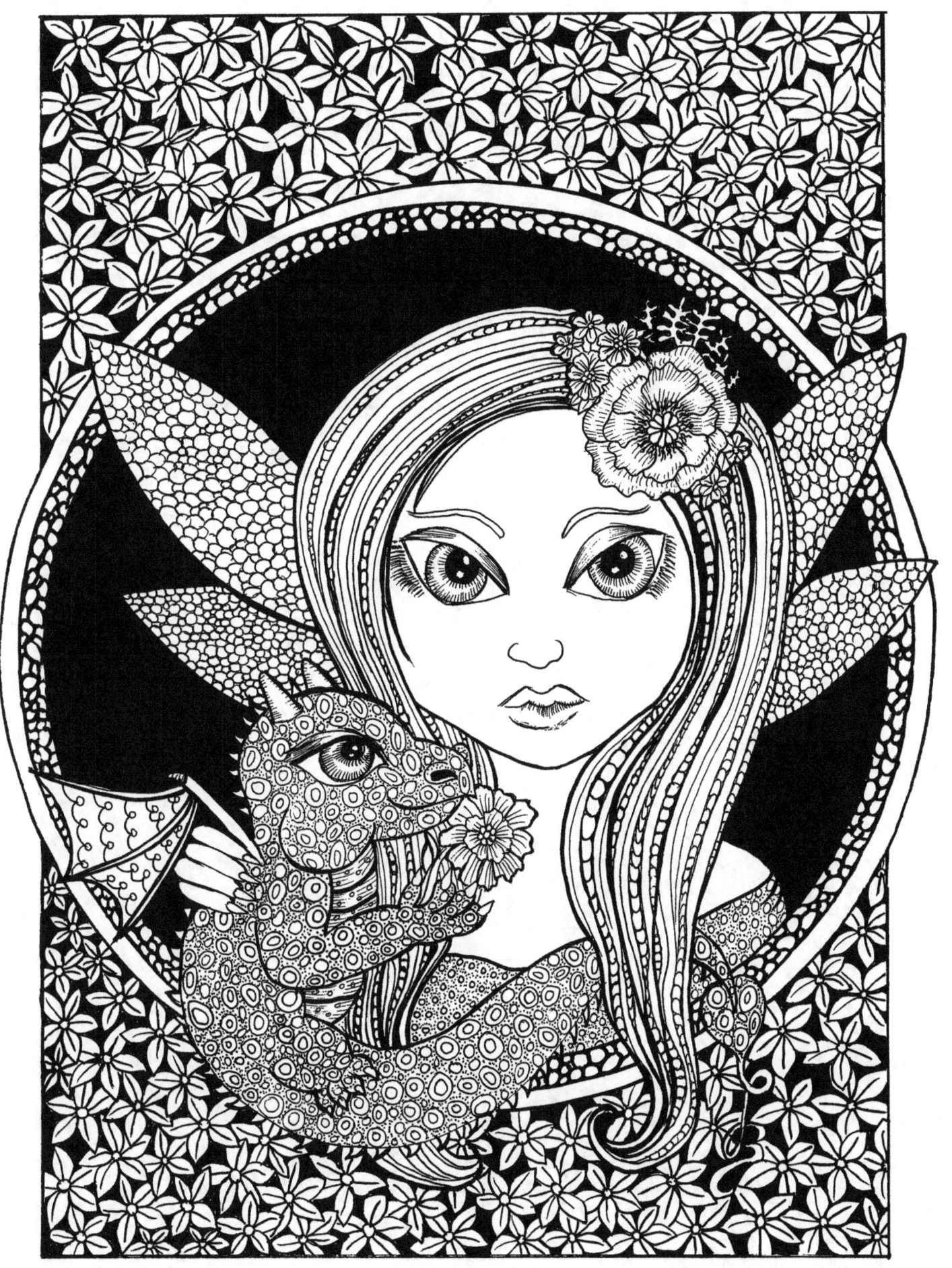

Contributing Artist
Laurie Beauchamp
USA

Global Doodle Gems Easter Collection Volume 1

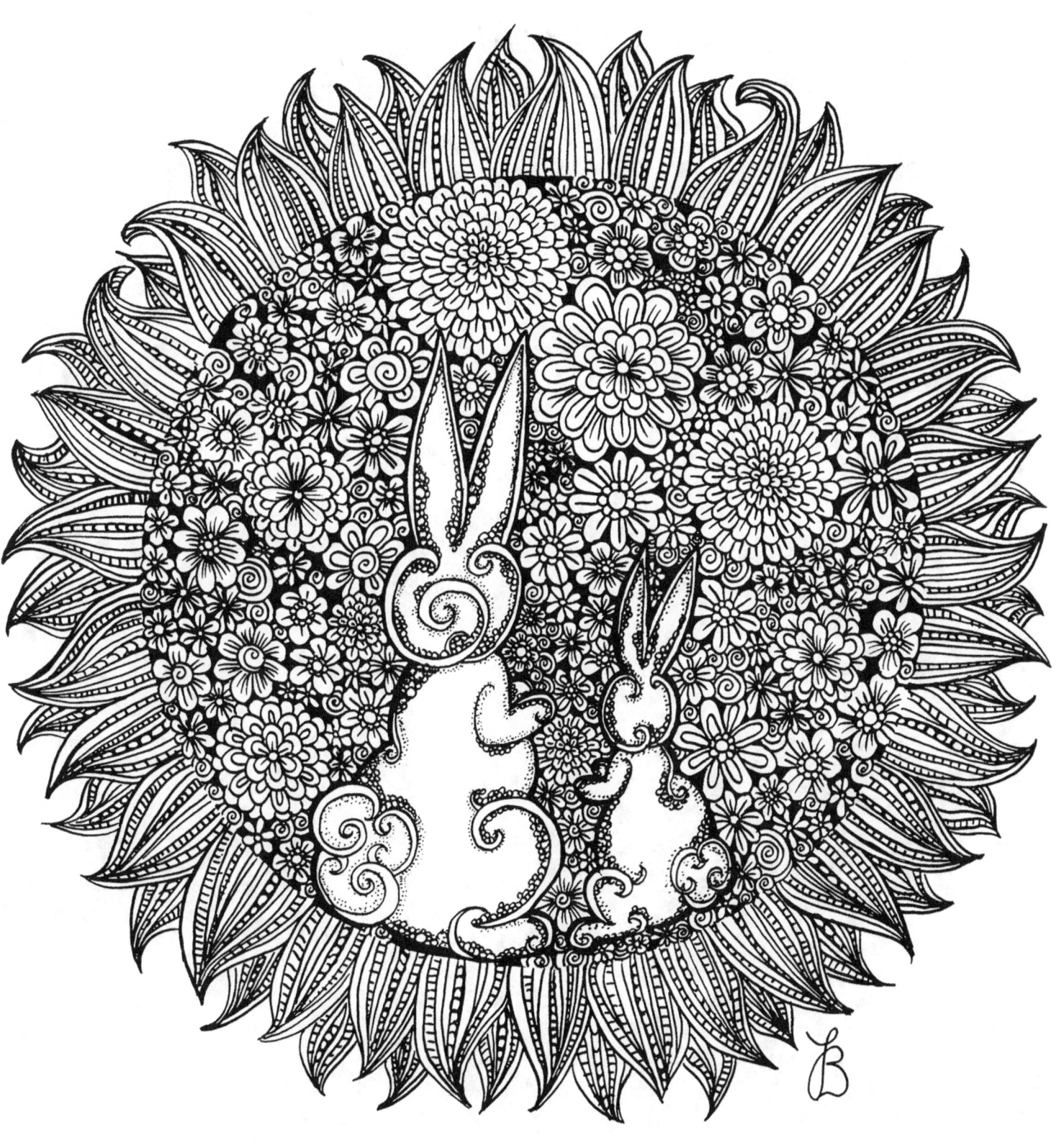

*Contributing Artist
Laurie Beauchamp
USA*

Global Doodle Gems Easter Collection Volume 1

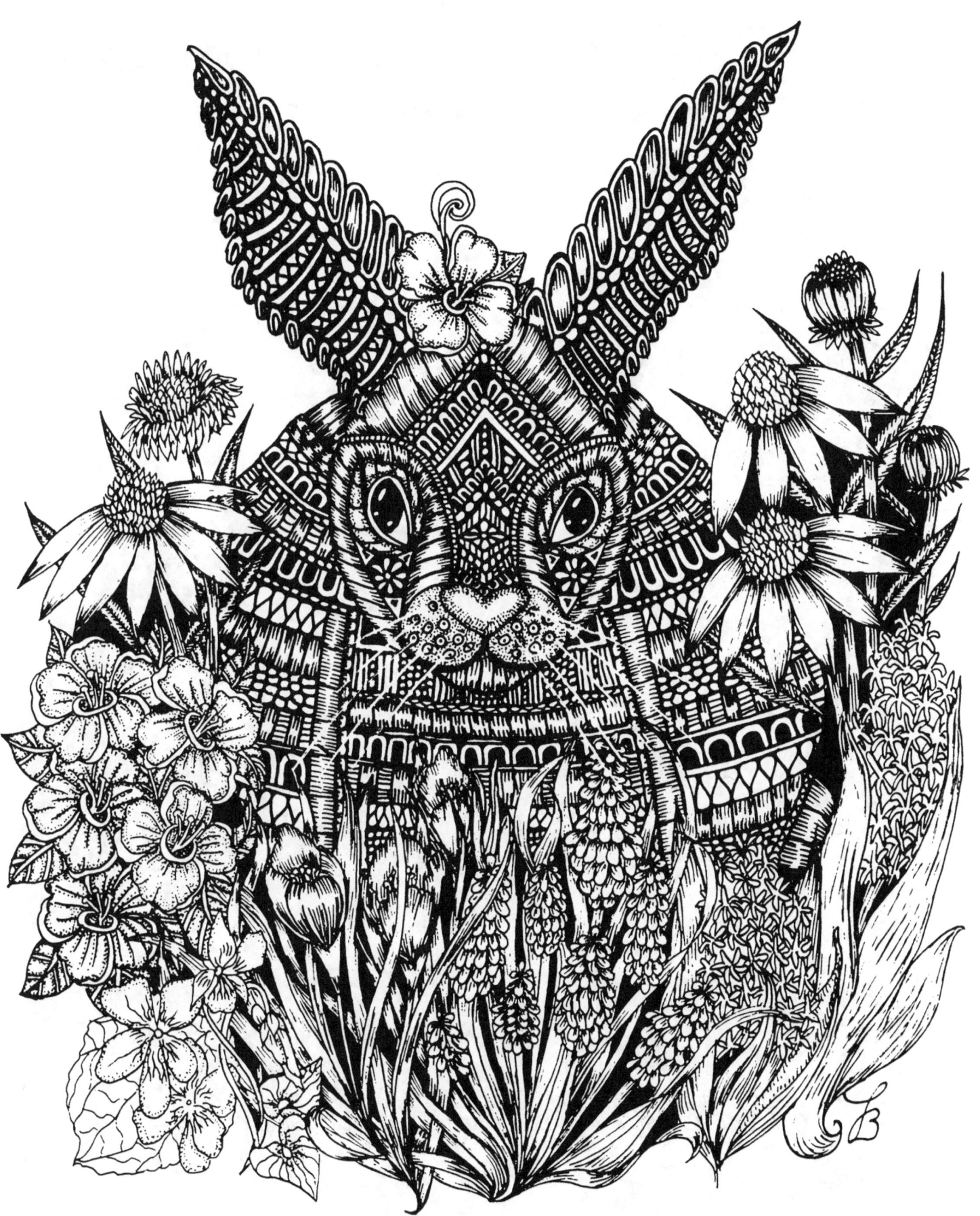

Contributing Artist
Leaf Yeh
Taiwan

Facebook : leaf.Painting

Global Doodle Gems Flowers Collection Volume 2

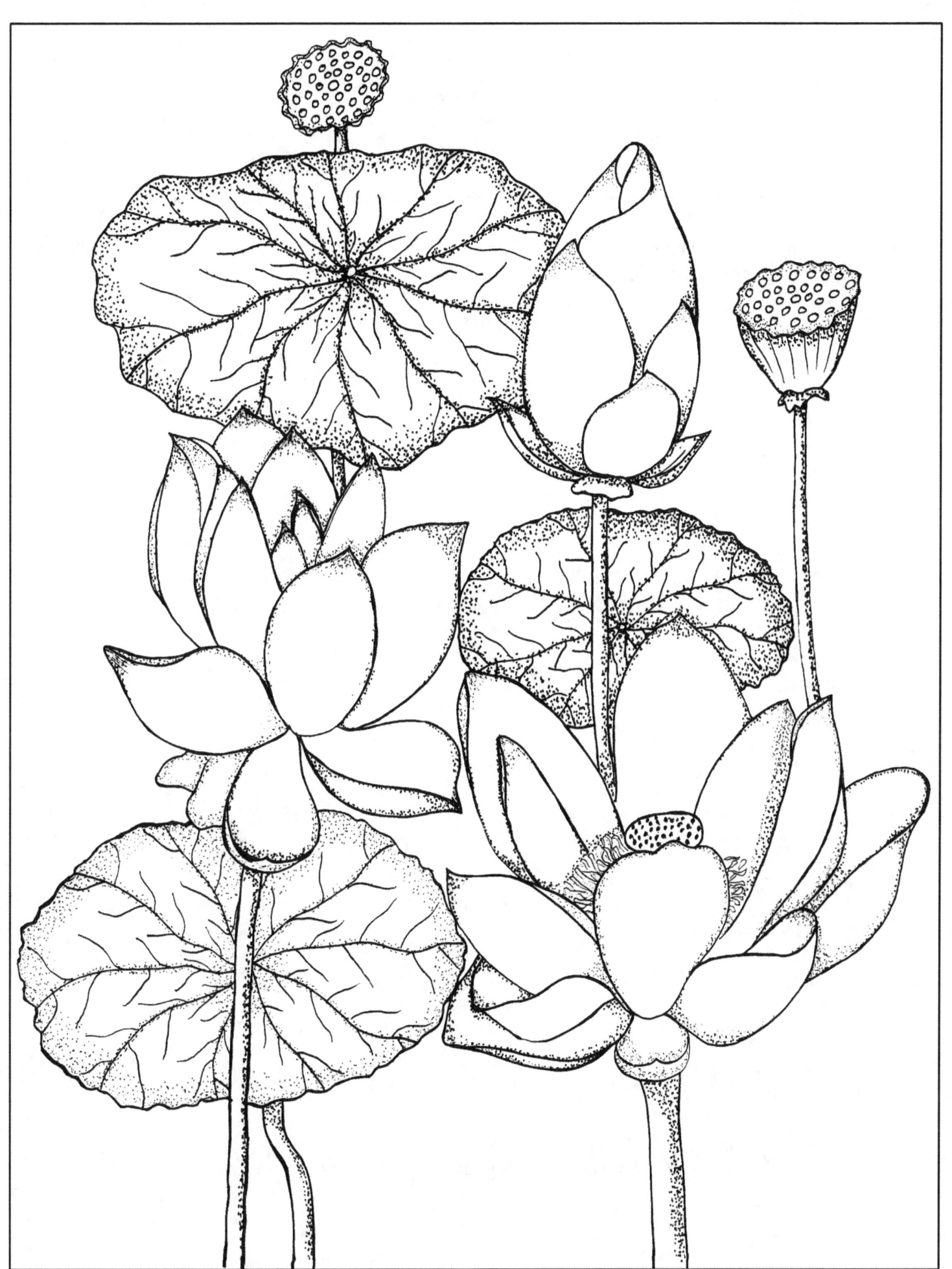

Contributing Artist
Leen Margot
France

Facebook Group : https://www.facebook.com/groups/666909036736080/

More Books : http://www.alittlemarket.com/dessins/fr_offre_speciale_saint_valentin_une_boite_de_feutres_maped_colorpep_s_brush_offerte_avec_ma_pause_a_moi_et_mille_-12935453.html

Twitter : leenmargot

Global Doodle Gems Gems Collection Volume 1

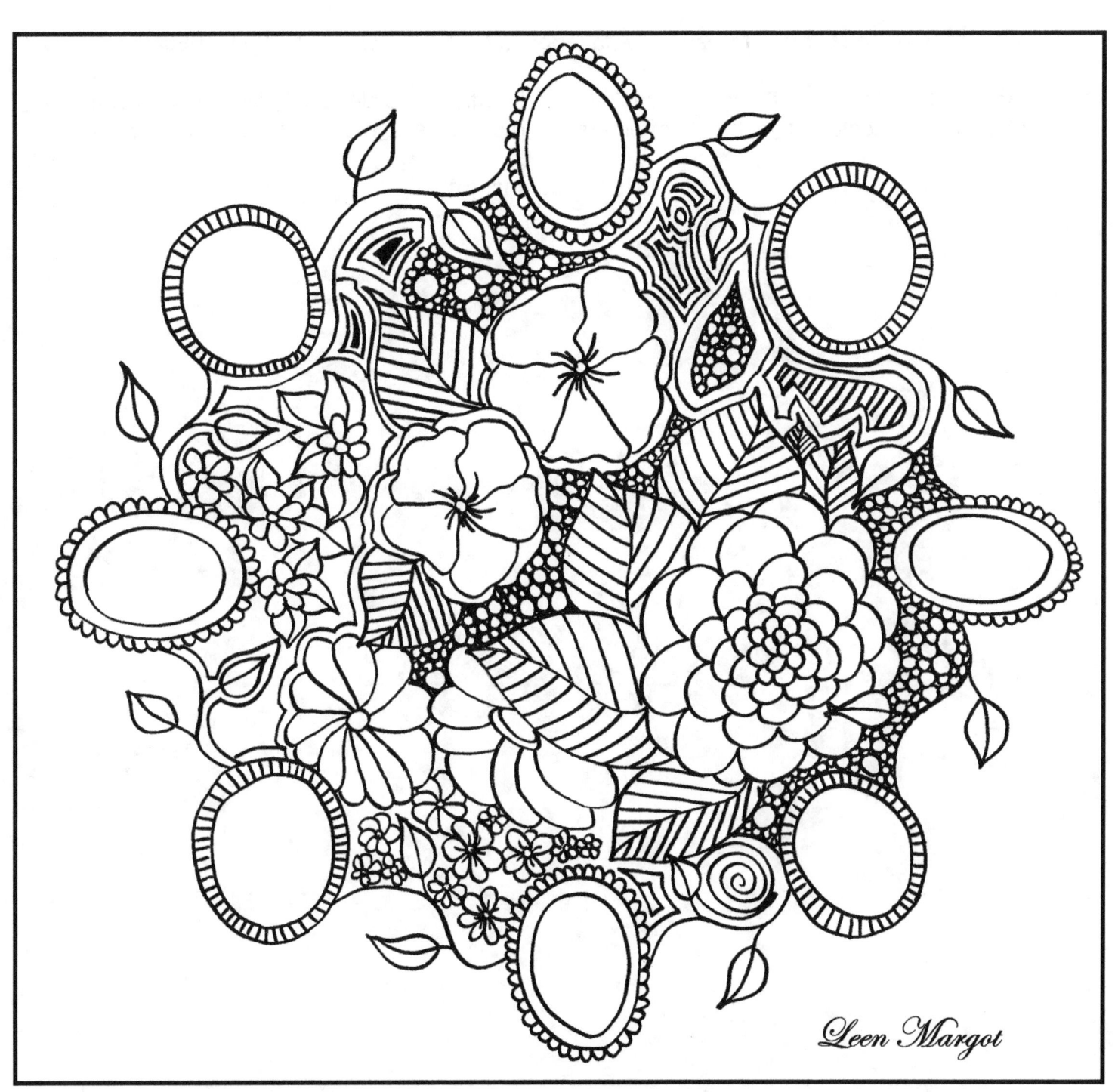

Contributing Artist
Leen Margot
France

Facebook Group : https://www.facebook.com/groups/666909036736080/

More Books : http://www.alittlemarket.com/dessins/fr_offre_speciale_saint_valentin_une_boite_de_feutres_maped_colorpep_s_brush_offerte_avec_ma_pause_a_moi_et_mille_-12935453.html

Twitter : leenmargot

Harmony

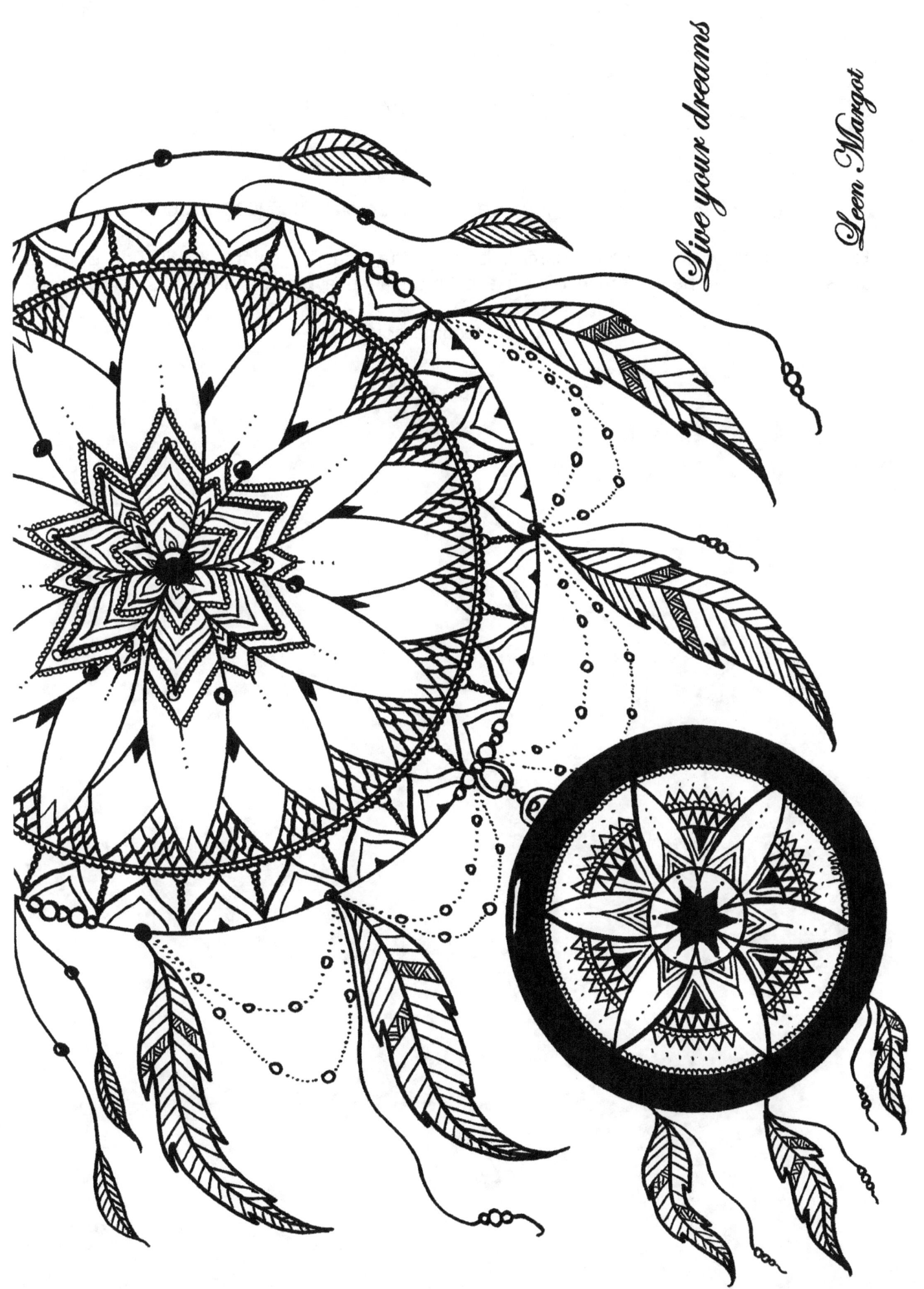

Contributing Artist
Leen Margot
France

Facebook Group : https://www.facebook.com/groups/666909036736080/

More Books : http://www.alittlemarket.com/dessins/fr_offre_speciale_saint_valentin_une_boite_de_feutres_maped_colorpep_s_brush_offerte_avec_ma_pause_a_moi_et_mille_-12935453.html

Twitter : leenmargot

Harmony

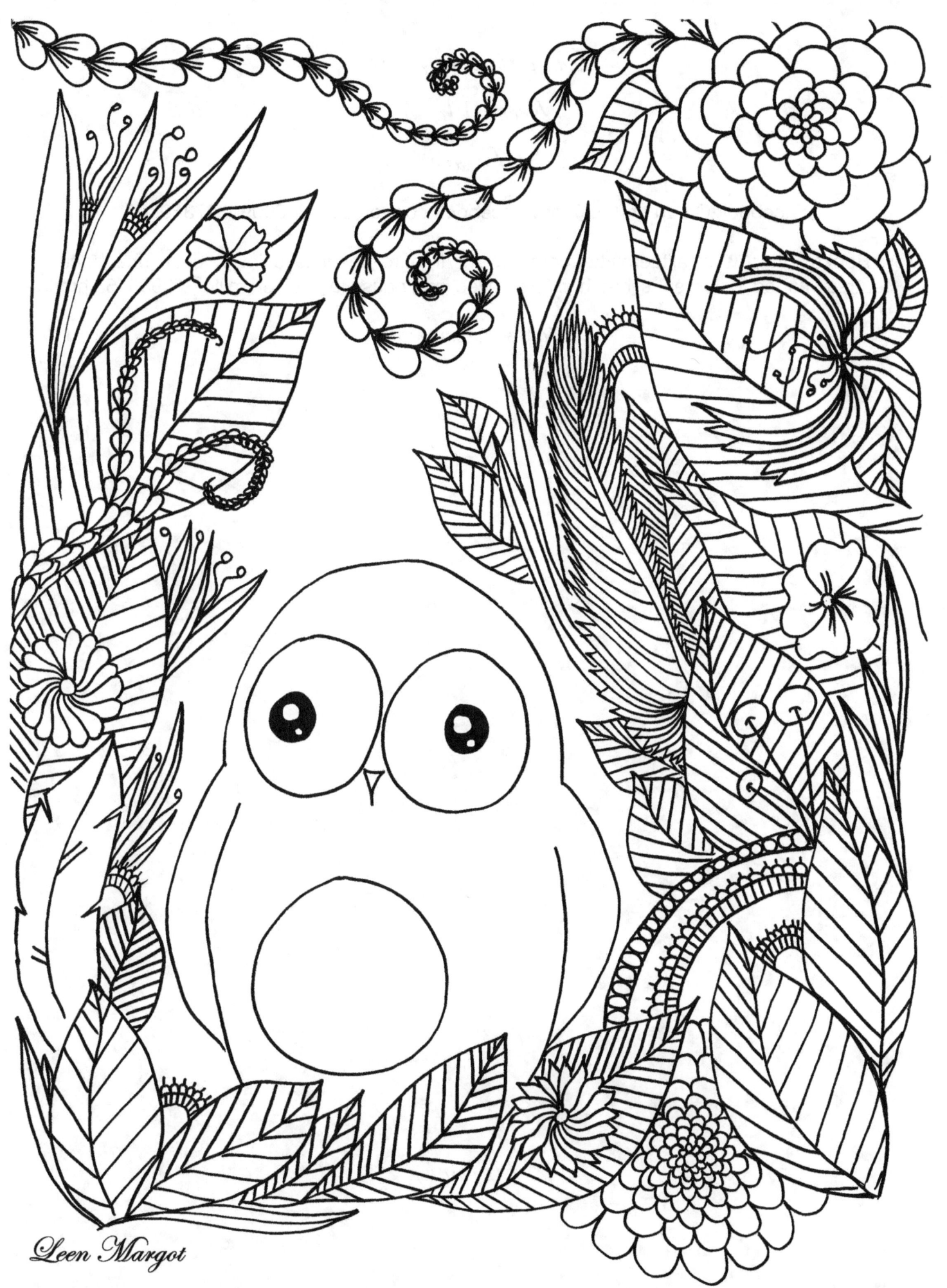

Contributing Artist
Leen Margot
France

Facebook Group : https://www.facebook.com/groups/666909036736080/

More Books : http://www.alittlemarket.com/dessins/fr_offre_speciale_saint_valentin_une_boite_de_feutres_maped_colorpep_s_brush_offerte_avec_ma_pause_a_moi_et_mille_-12935453.html

Twitter : leenmargot

Harmony

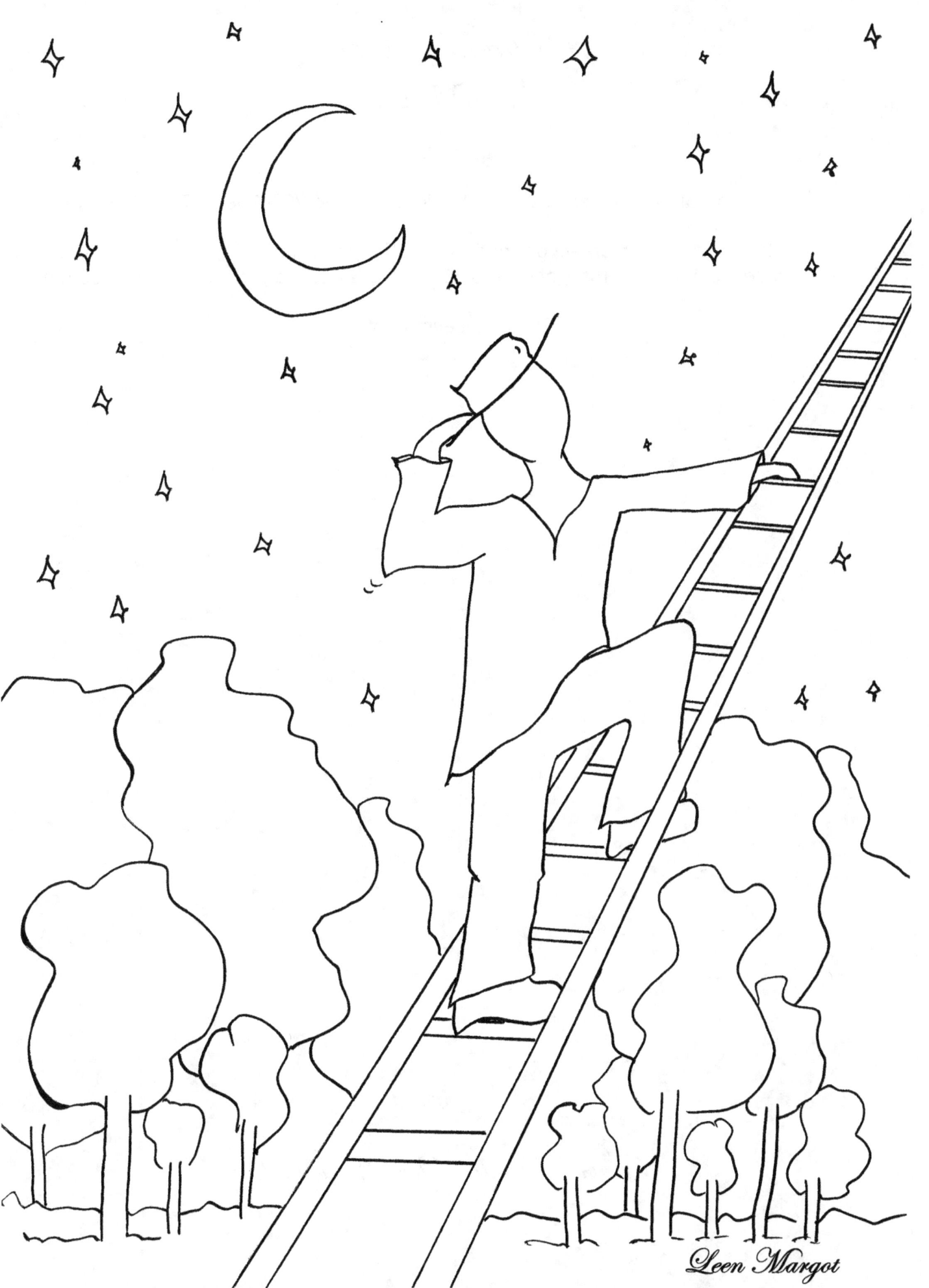

Contributing Artist
Leen Margot
France

Facebook Group : https://www.facebook.com/groups/666909036736080/

More Books : http://www.alittlemarket.com/dessins/fr_offre_speciale_saint_valentin_une_boite_de_feutres_maped_colorpep_s_brush_offerte_avec_ma_pause_a_moi_et_mille_-12935453.html

Twitter : leenmargot

Global Doodle Gems Volume 1

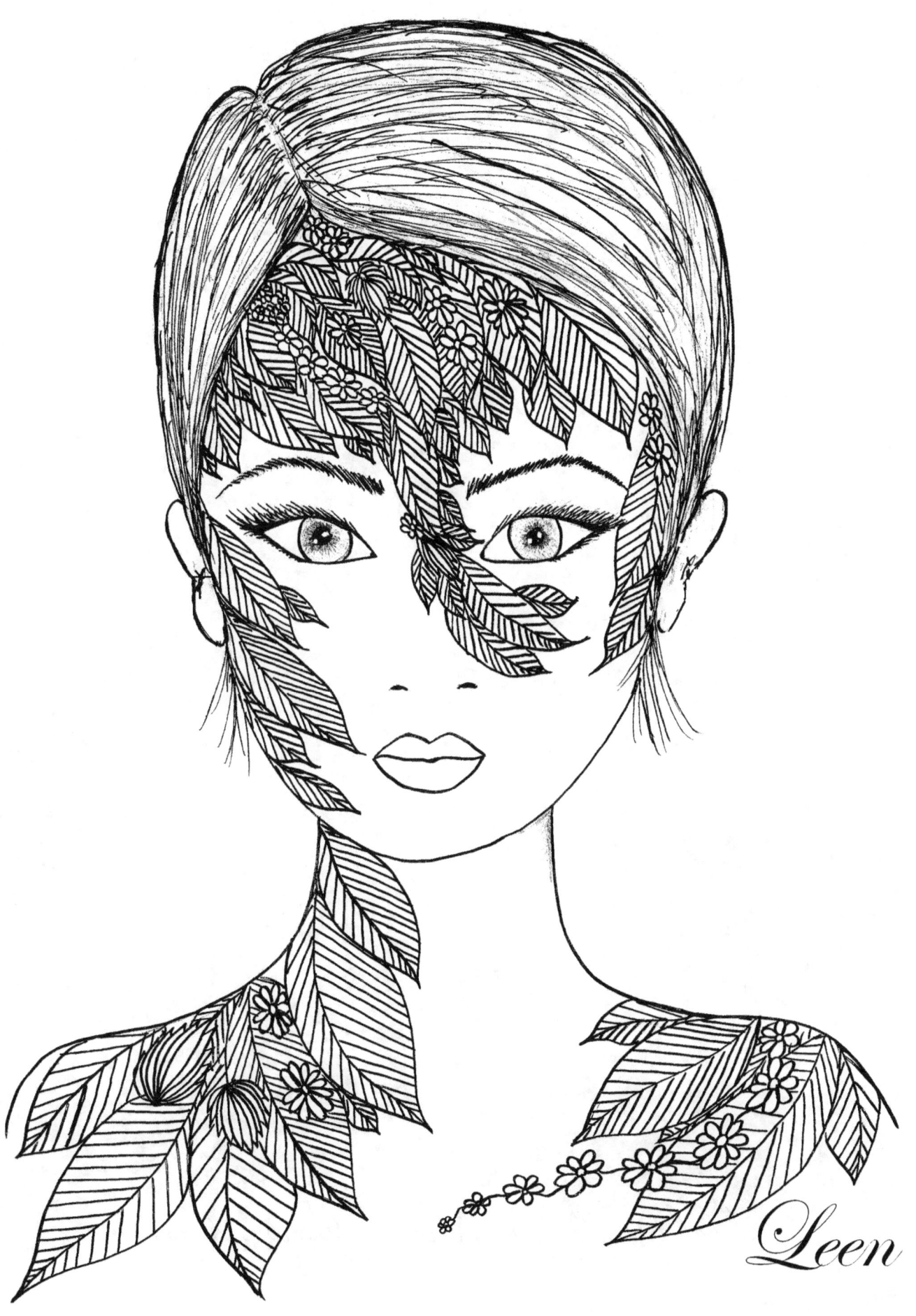

Contributing Artist
Lilan Chen
Taiwan

Facebook : lilanchen.art

Global Doodle Gems Mini Collection Volume 4

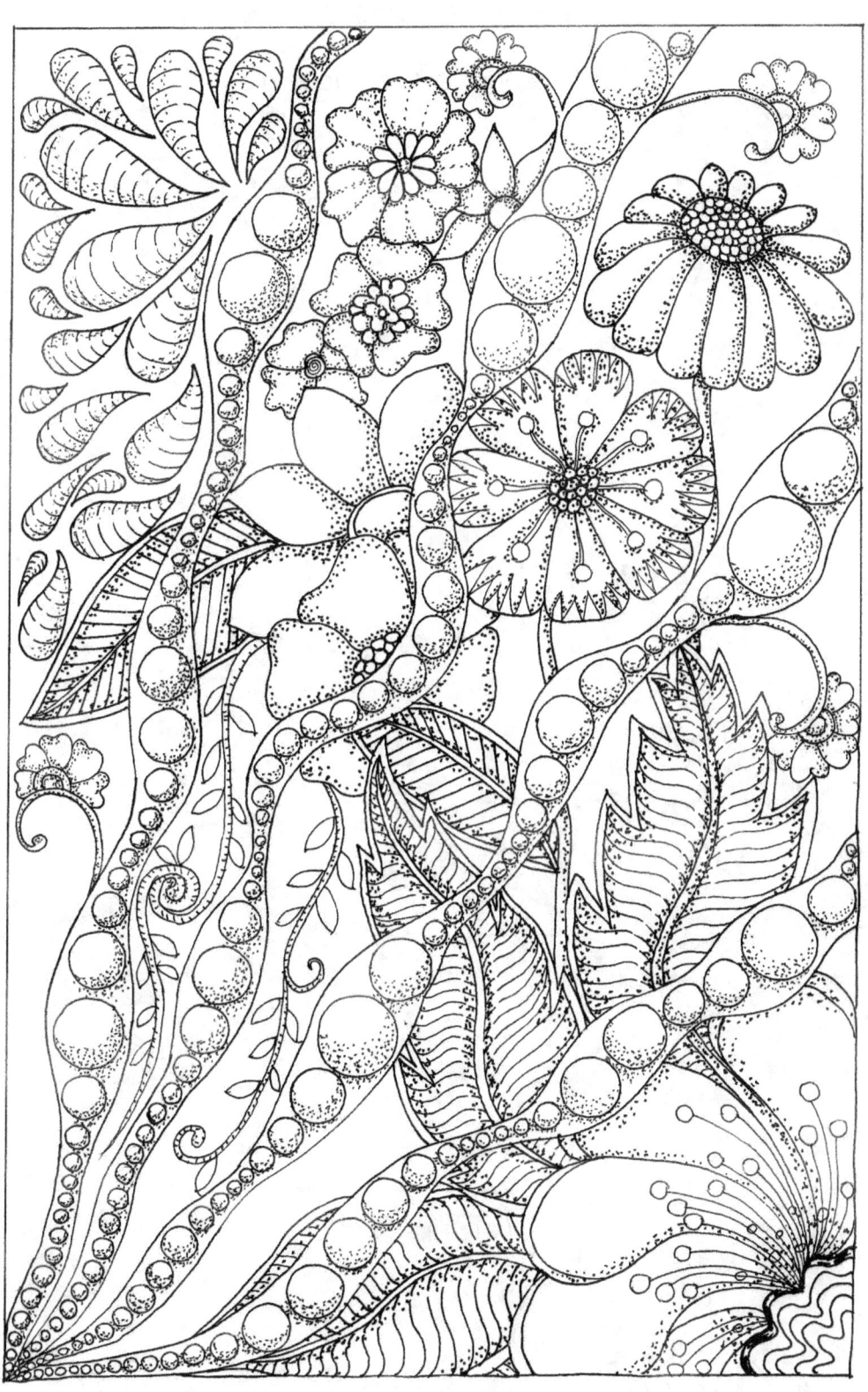

Contributing Artist
Lynne McGee
Brisbane, Australia

Facebook : Colorandtangle

Global Doodle Gems Mini Collection Volume 1

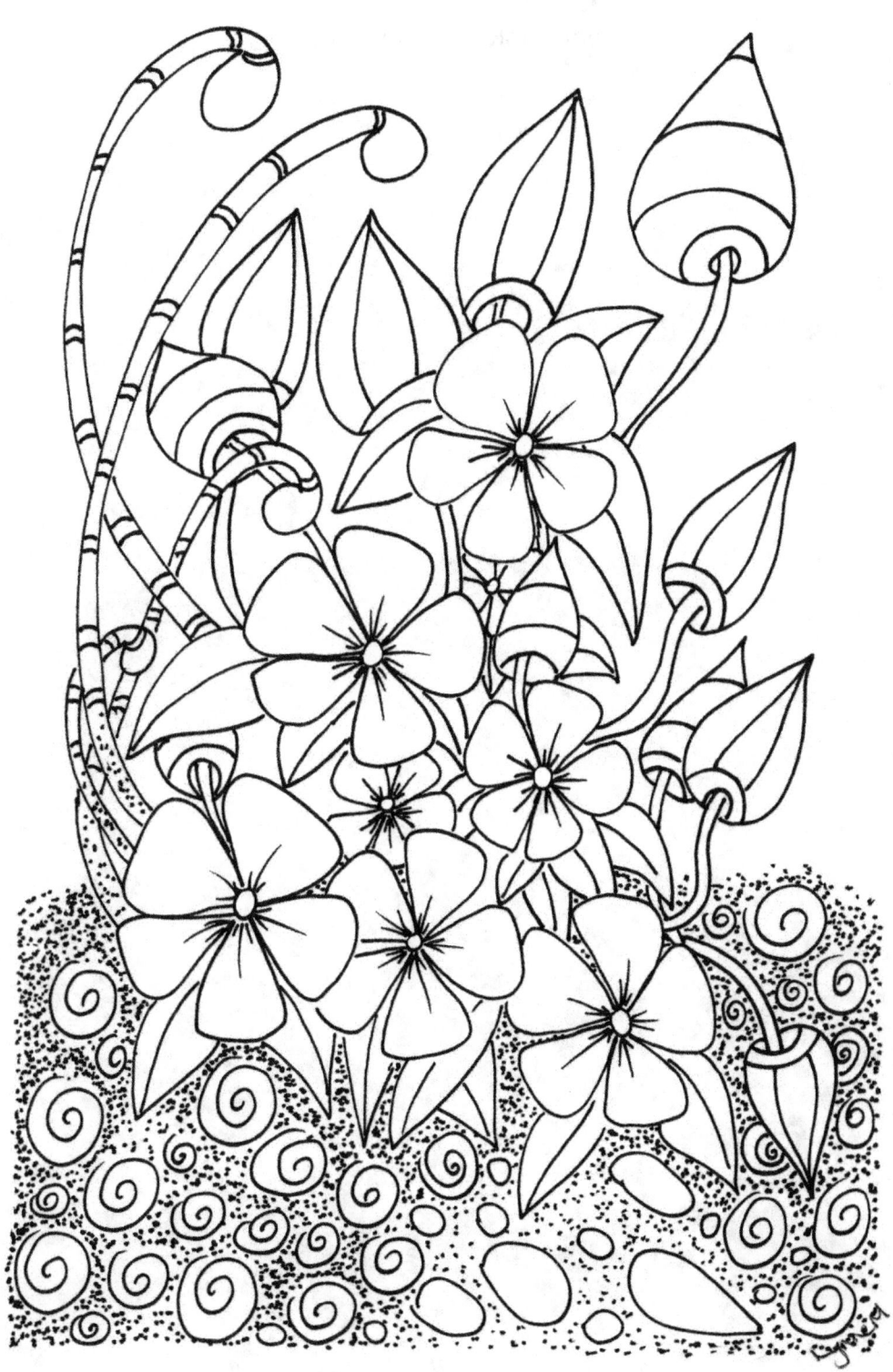

Contributing Artist
Lynni Ex
UK

Facebook : Lynniex Doodles

Global Doodle Gems Volume 5

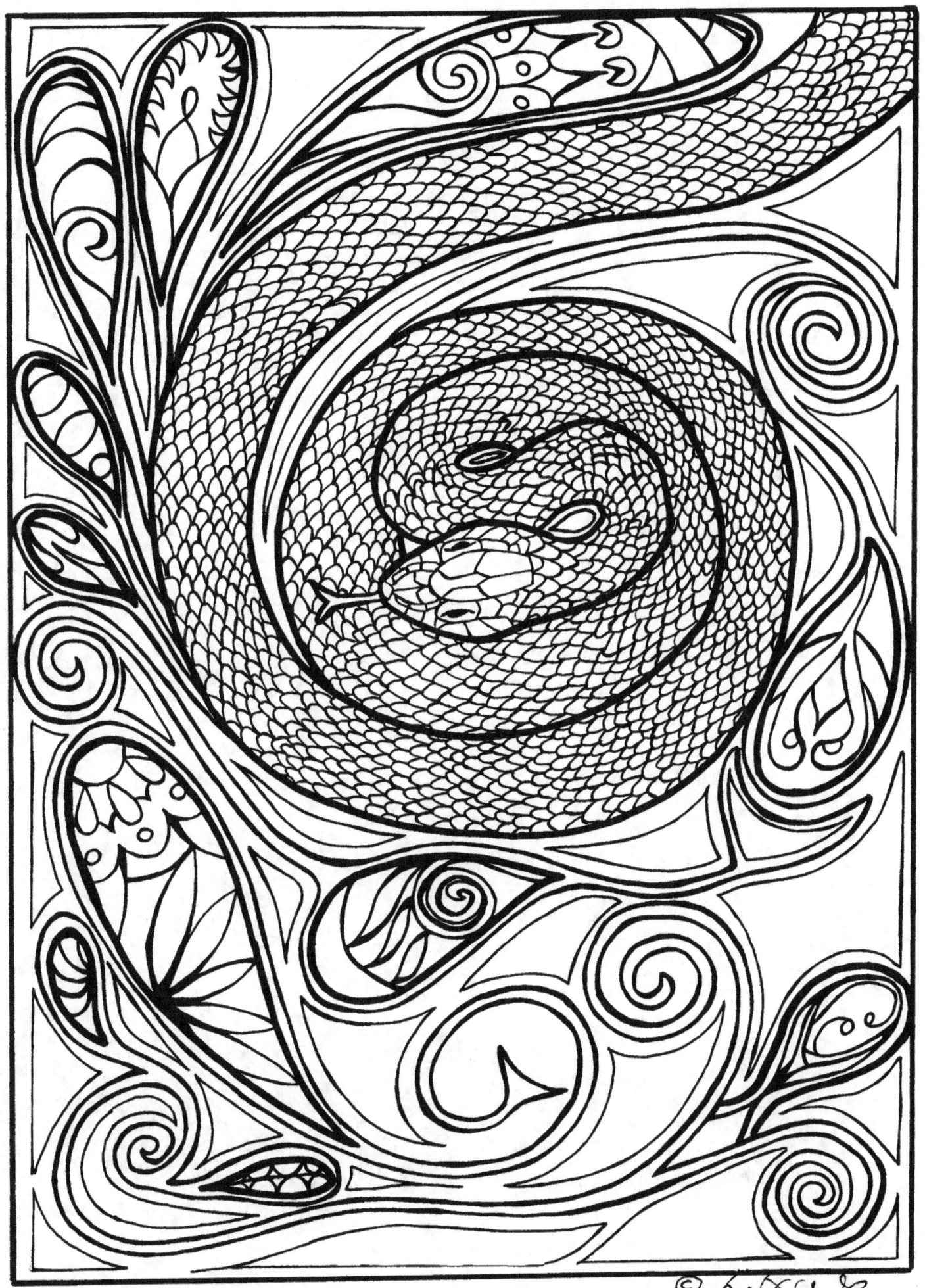

Contributing Artist
Maggie Lin
Taiwan

Facebook : maggiezentangle

Global Doodle Gems Christmas Collection Volume 2

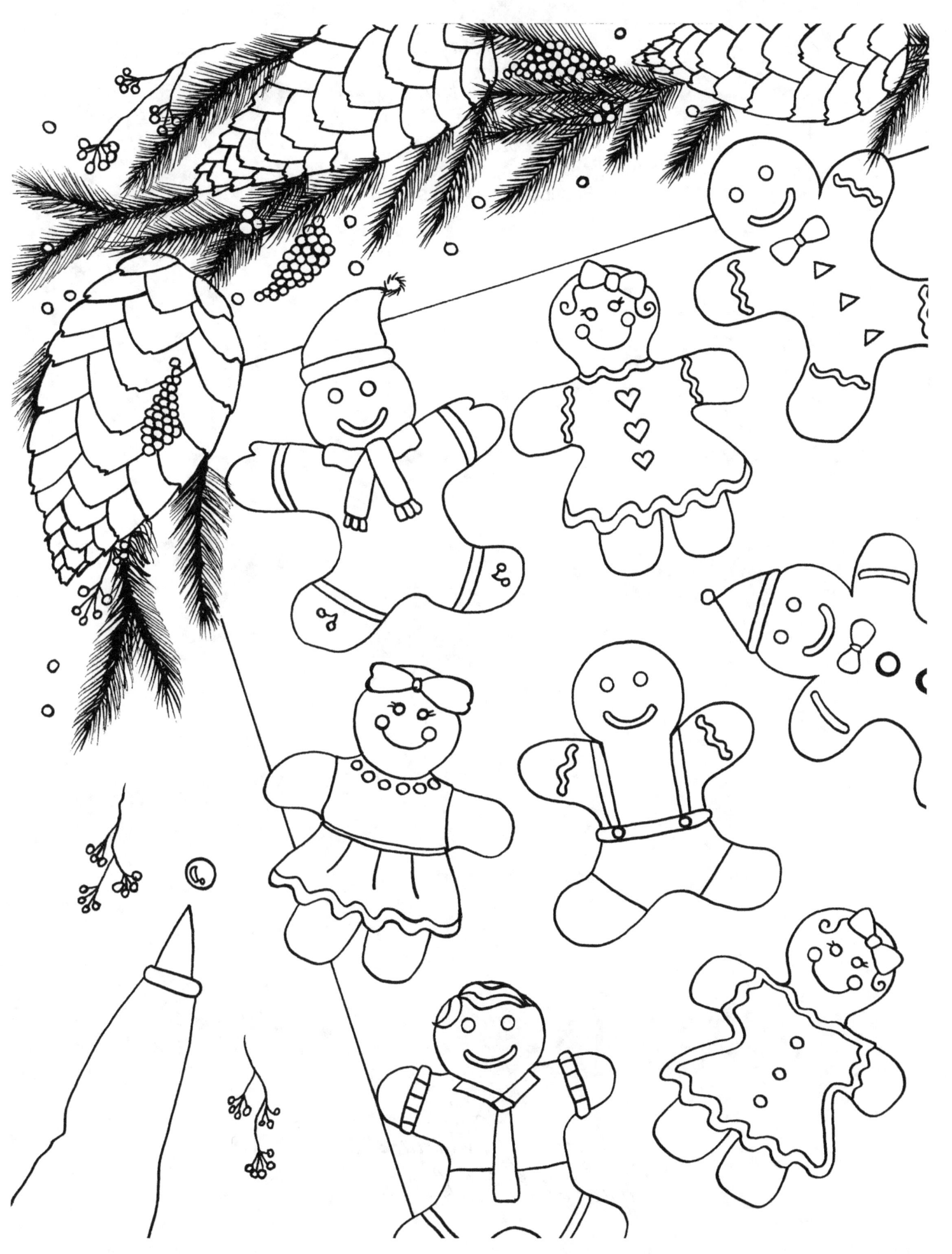

Contributing Artist
Alfred E. Villanueva
Philippines
Facebook : viworksart2015

Portrait of Maria Wedel
founder of Global Doodle Gems

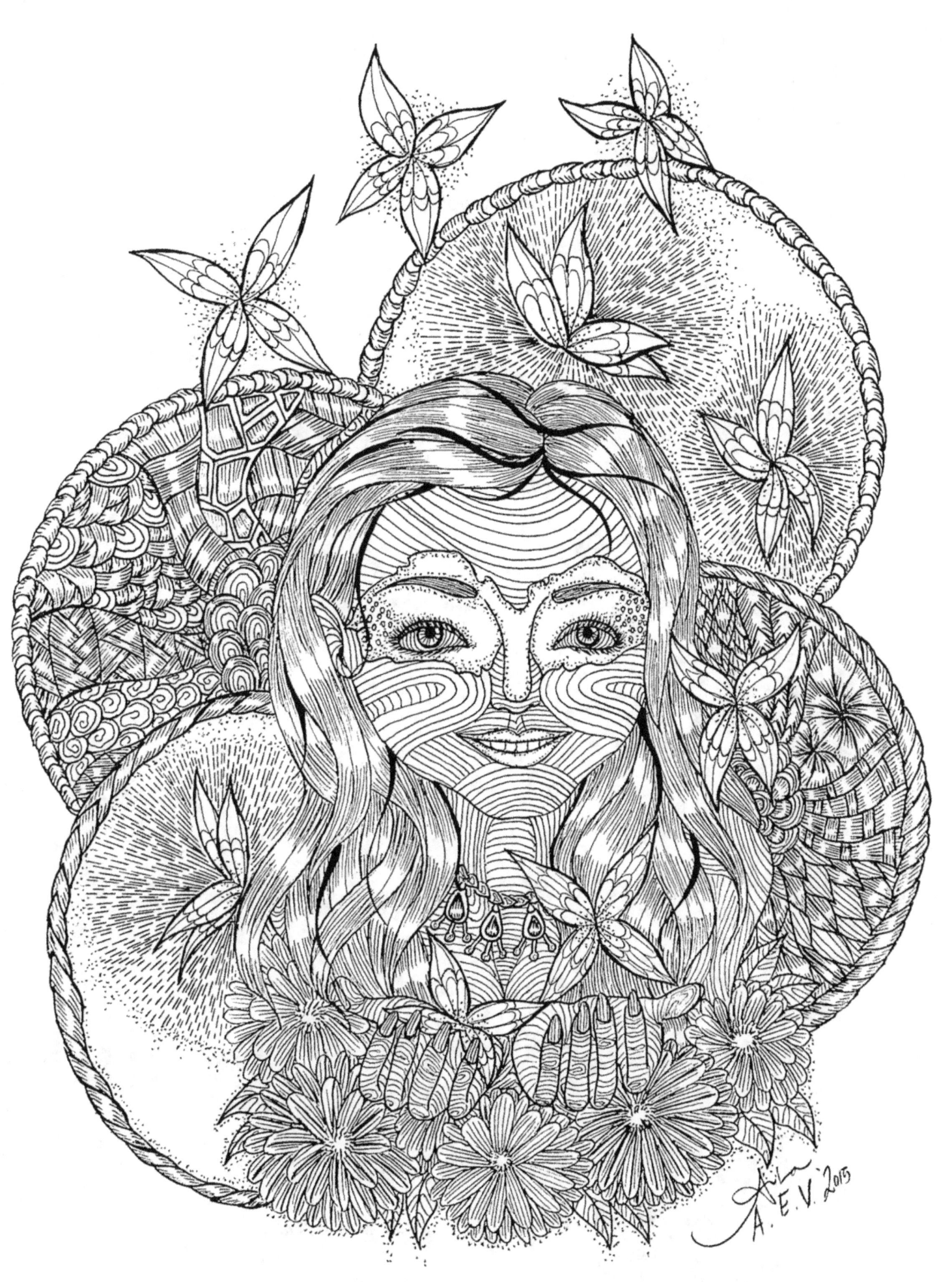

Contributing Artist
Alfred E. Villanueva
Philippines
Facebook : viworksart2015

Portrait of Johanna Ans
Blogger of Global Doodle Gems

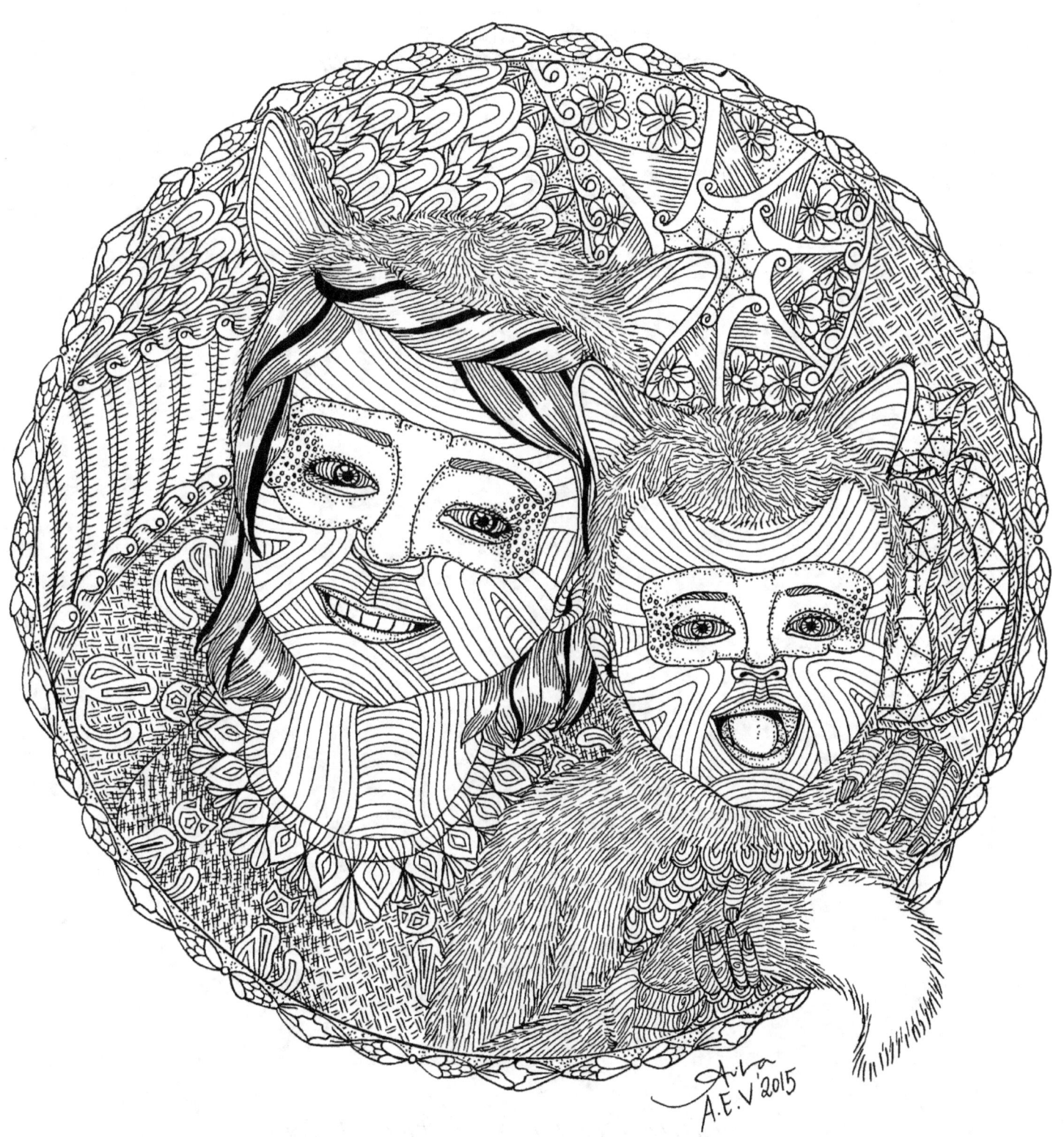

Contributing Artist
Maria Wedel
Denmark

Facebook : AMVWART
Facebook Group : ColorPagesOfAMVW/

The Little Big Book of Egg Designs

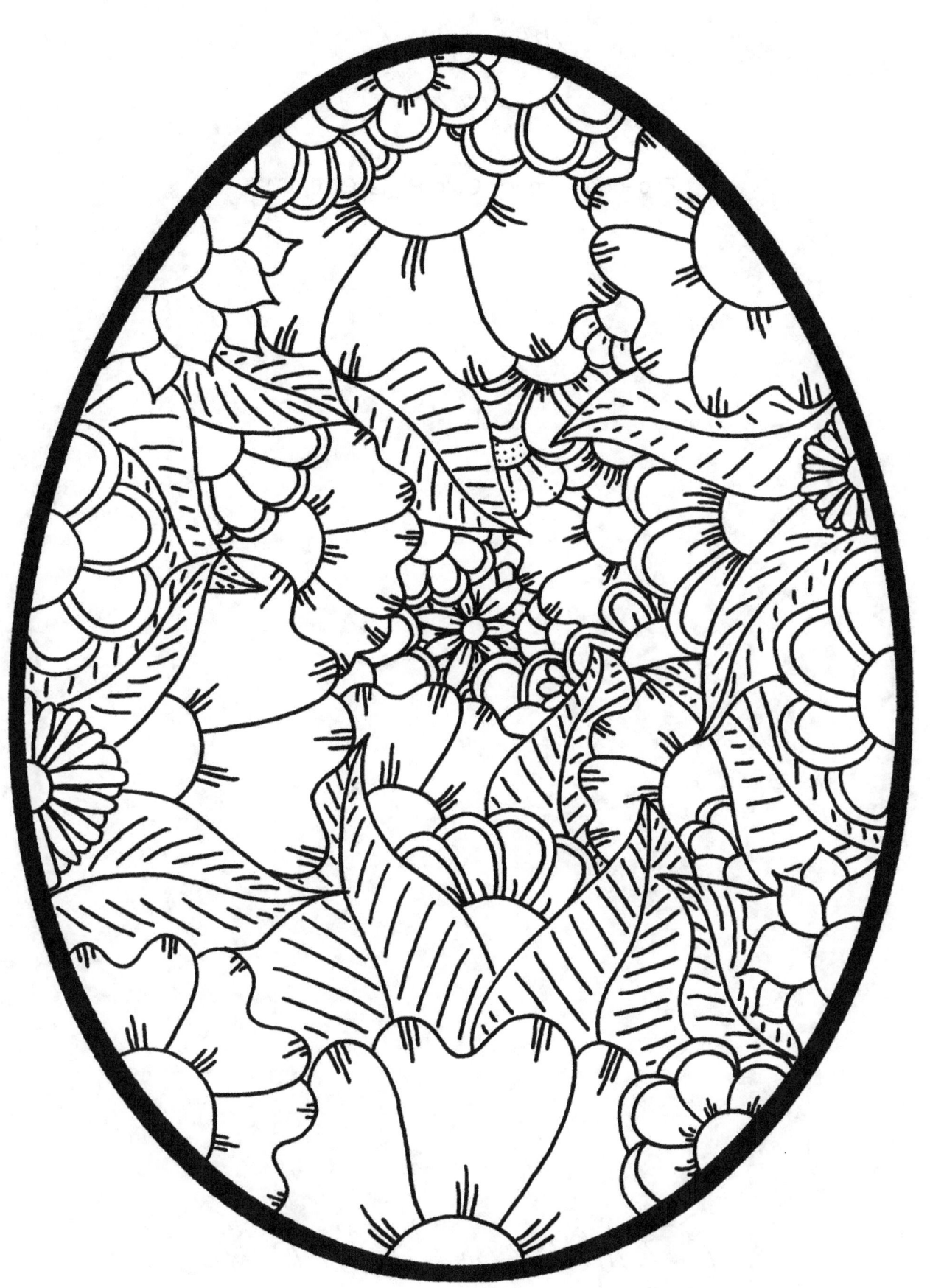

Contributing Artist
Maria Wedel
Denmark

Facebook : AMVWART
Facebook Group : ColorPagesOfAMVW/

The Little Big Book of Egg Designs

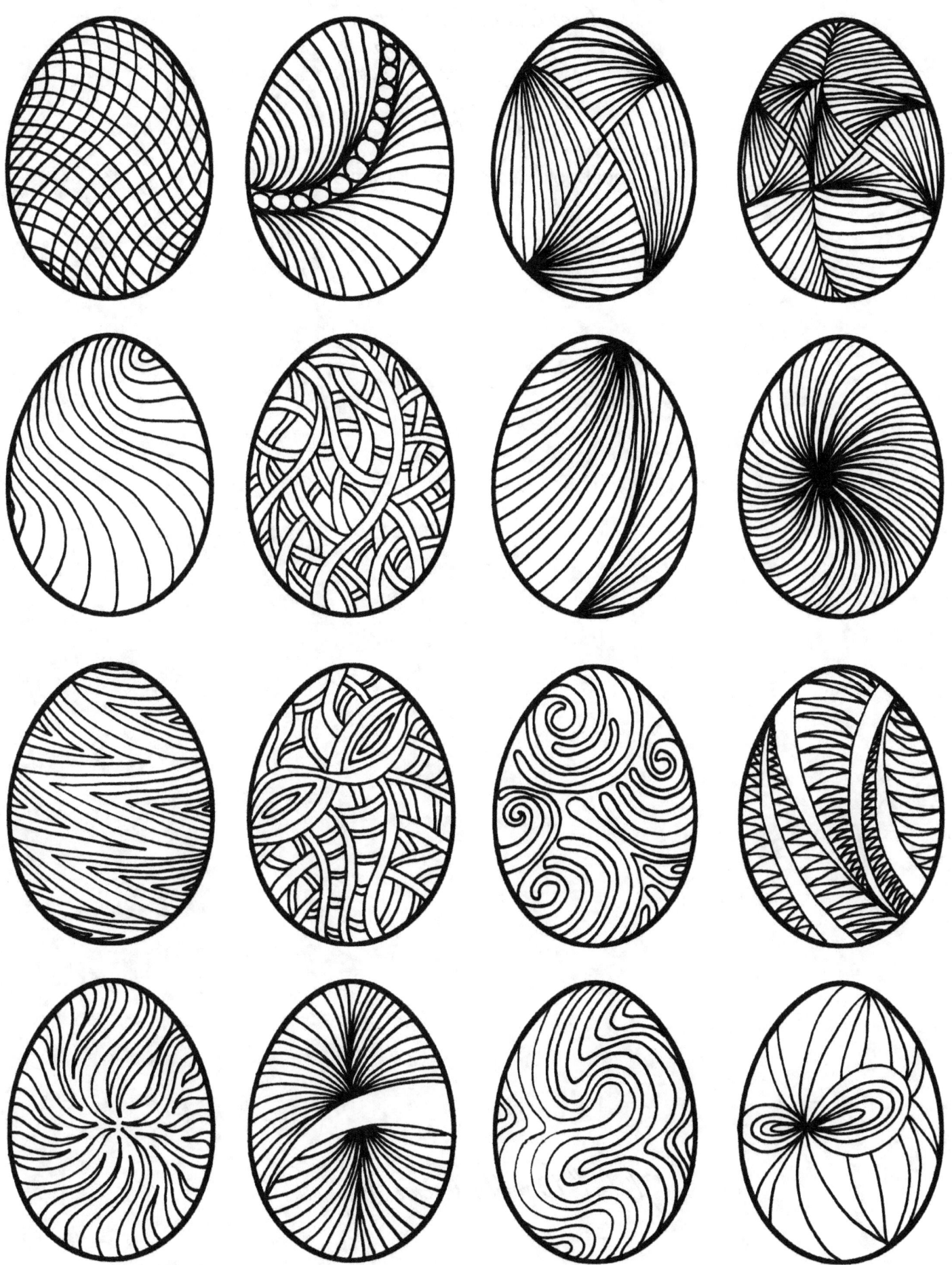

Contributing Artist
Marie-Eve Klein
Belgium

Facebook : lestraitsorsdemimieve

Global Doodle Gems Volume 8

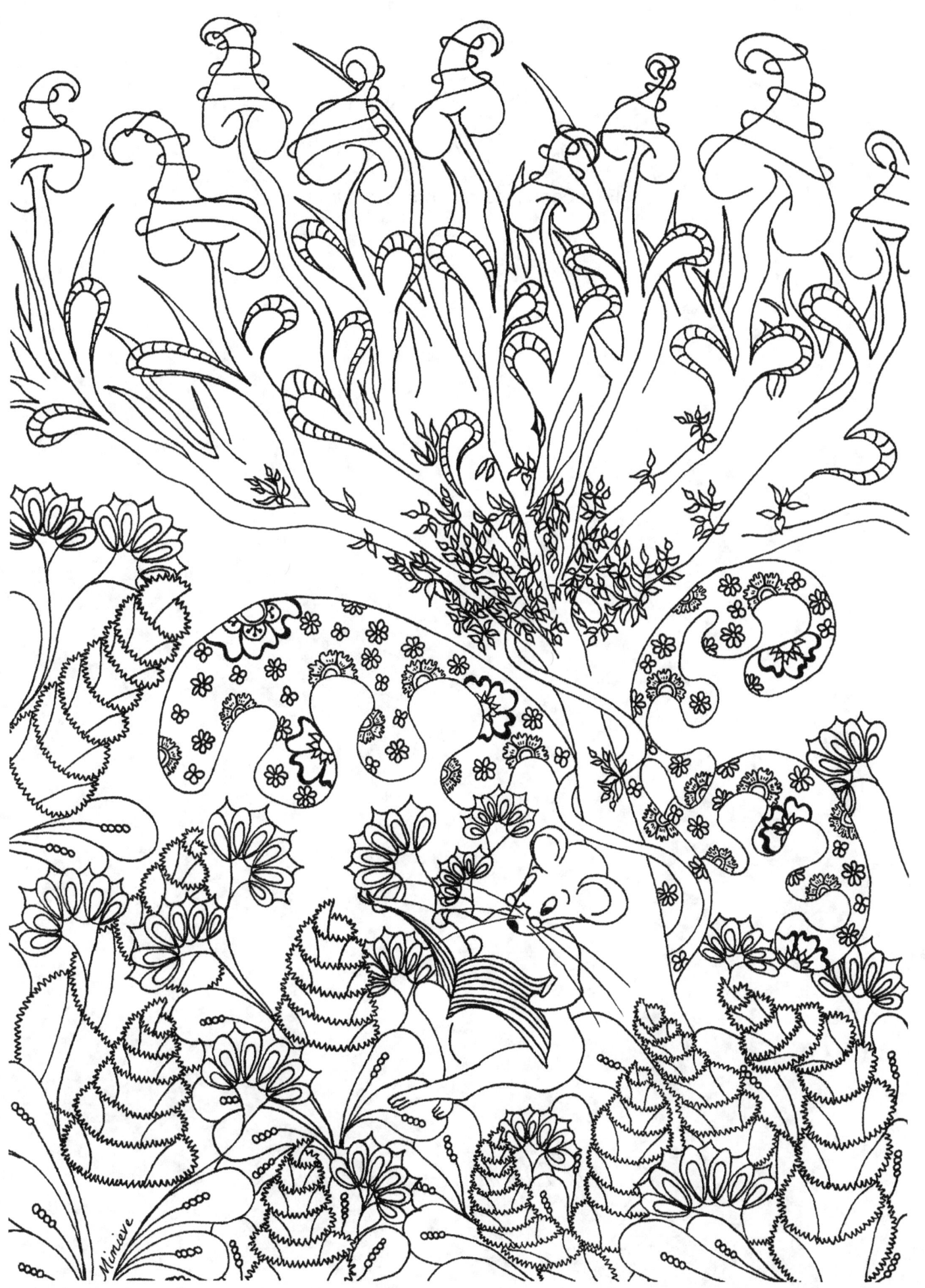

Contributing Artist
Marie-Eve Klein
Belgium
Facebook : lestraitsorsdemimieve

Global Doodle Gems Volume 8

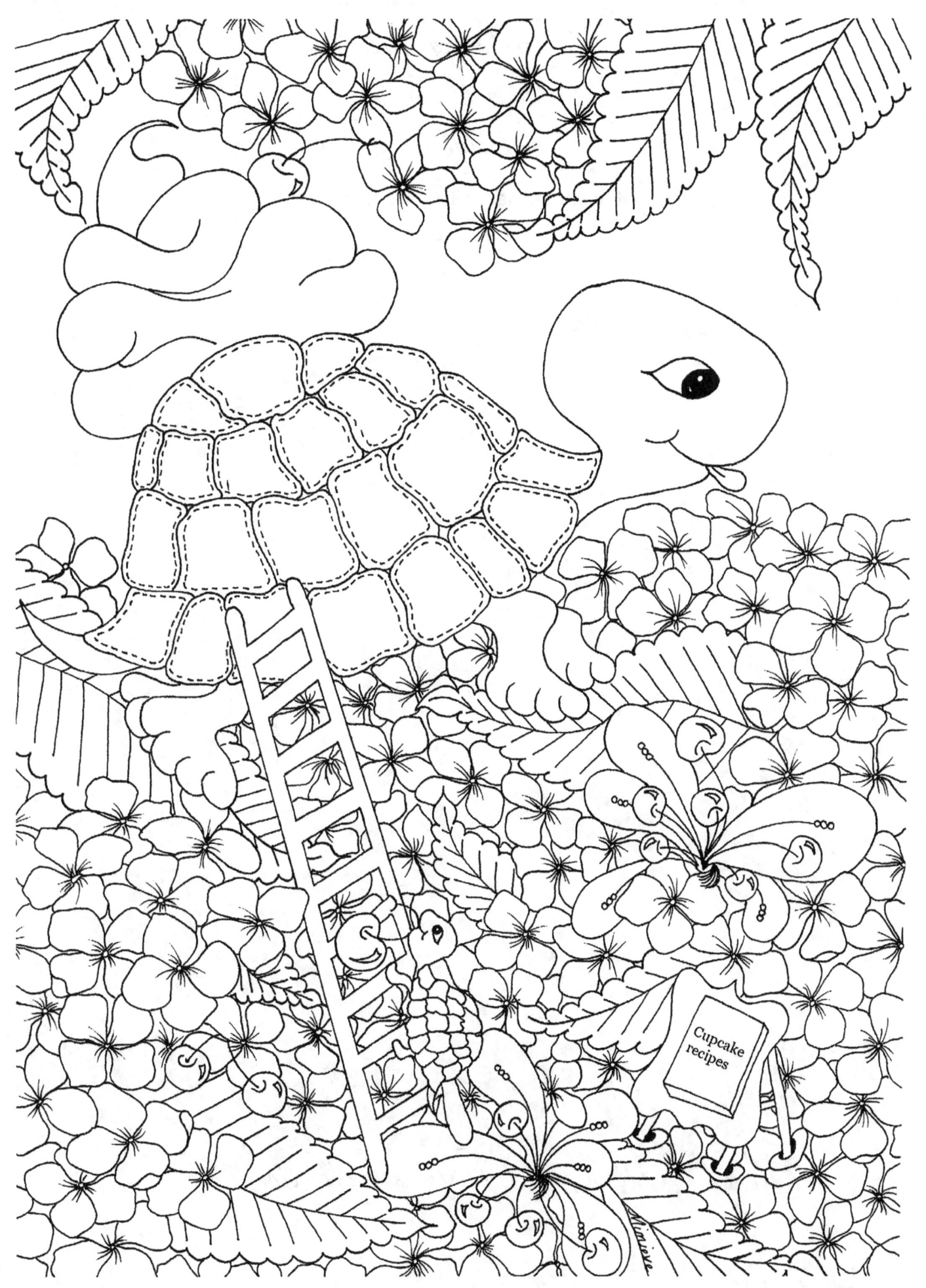

Contributing Artist
Marie-Eve Klein
Belgium

Facebook : lestraitsorsdemimieve

Global Doodle Gems Christmas Collection Volume 2

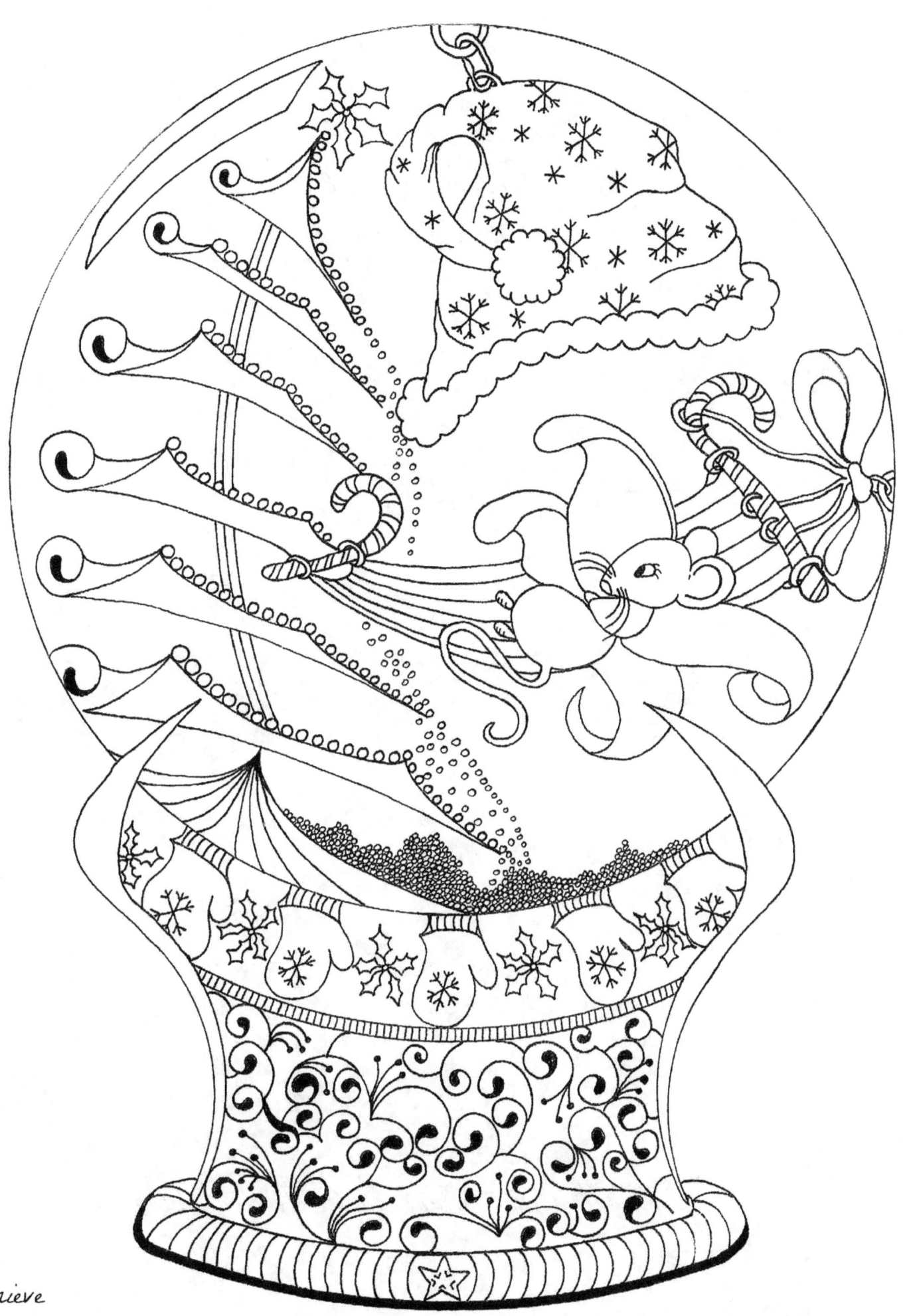

Contributing Artist

Marieke Raterman-Bos
Monnickendam, the Netherlands

www.monnickenwerken.nl
Facebook : Monnicken-Werken-by-Marieke-Raterman

Global Doodle Gems Mandala Collection Volume 1

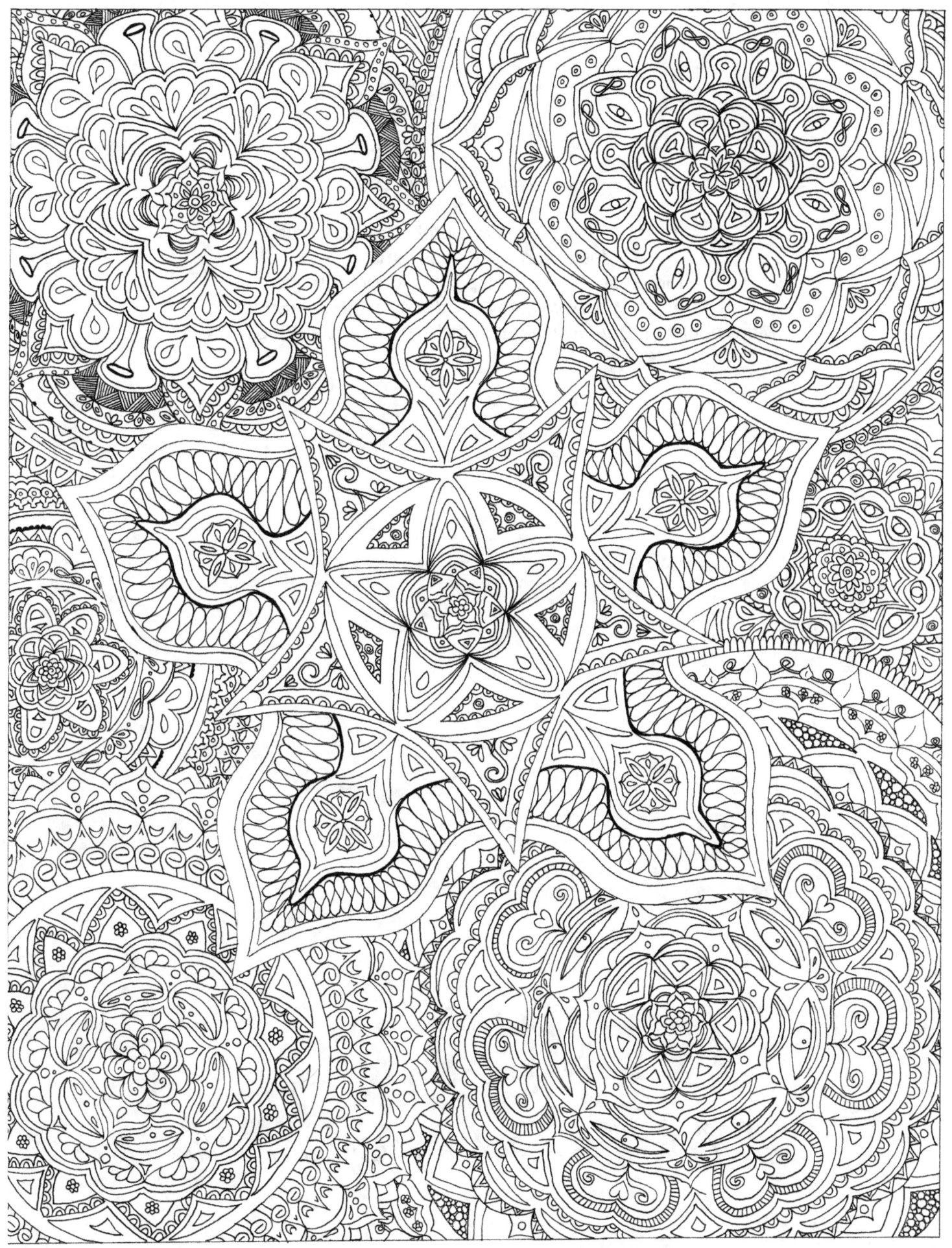

Contributing Artist
Maud Taron
France

Web : www.zendessin.com
Facebook : zendessin
YouTube : https://www.youtube.com/c/MaudT
Instagram : zendessin.maud
Pinterest : http://www.pinterest.com/taleque/
Shop : https://www.etsy.com/fr/shop/TalequeShop
More books : http://www.amazon.fr/Maud-Taron/e/B00QN8FGJS

Global Doodle Gems Valentines Collection Volume 1

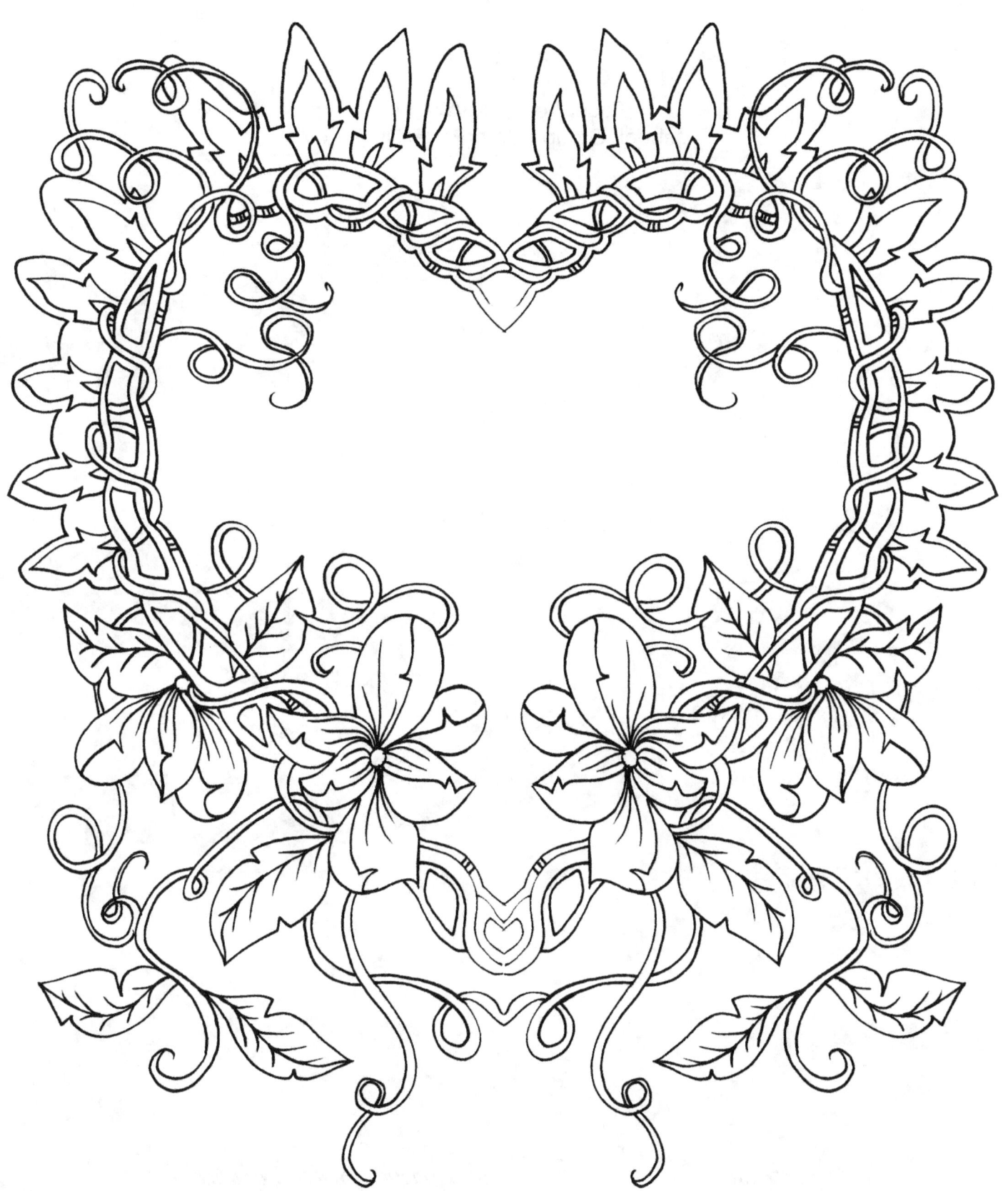

Contributing Artist
Maria Wedel
Denmark

Facebook : AMVWART
Facebook Group : ColorPagesOfAMVW/

Mephisto Coloring Therapy Bright Side Volume 1

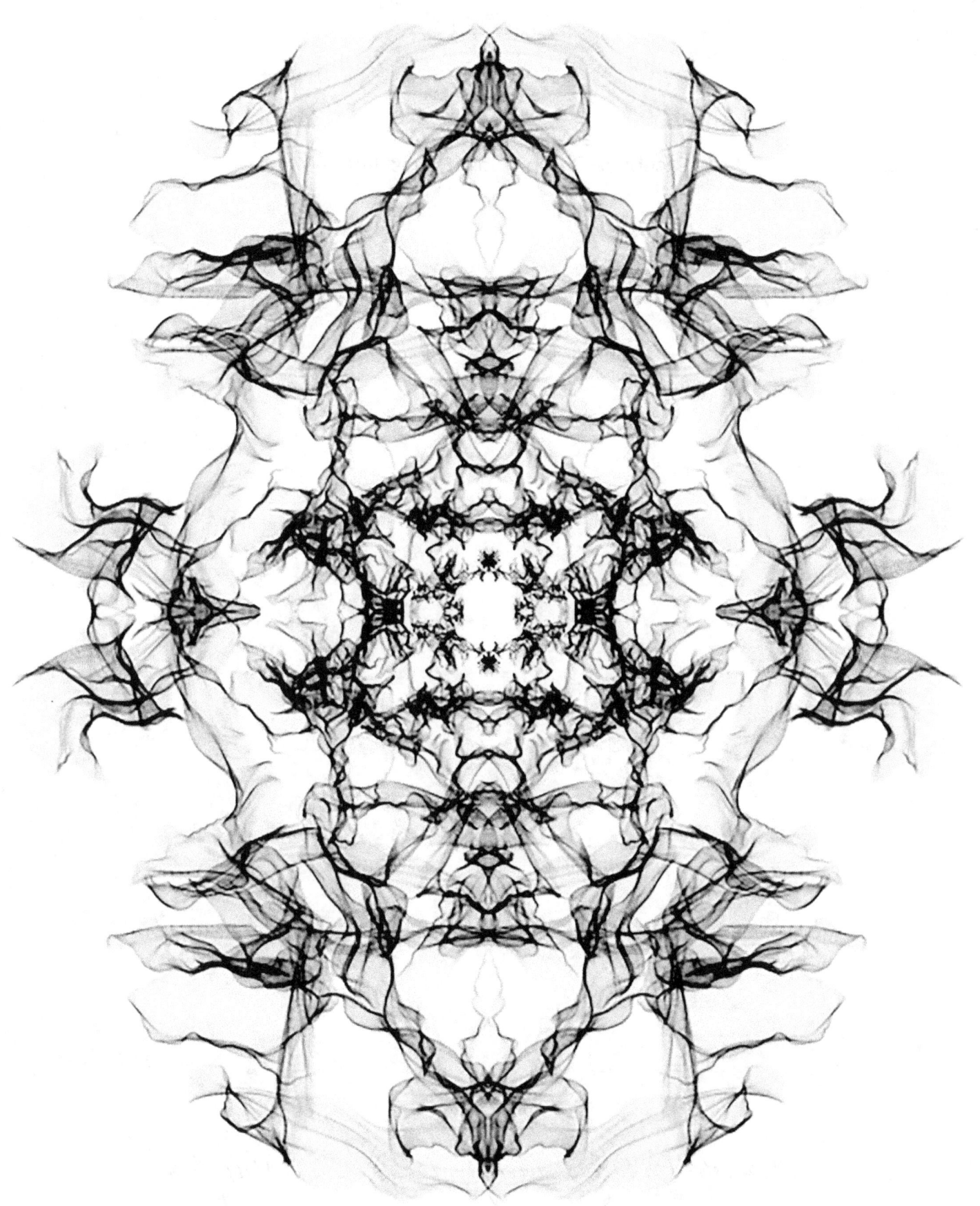

Contributing Artist
Maria Wedel
Denmark

Facebook : AMVWART
Facebook Group : ColorPagesOfAMVW/

Mephisto Coloring Therapy Bright Side Volume 1

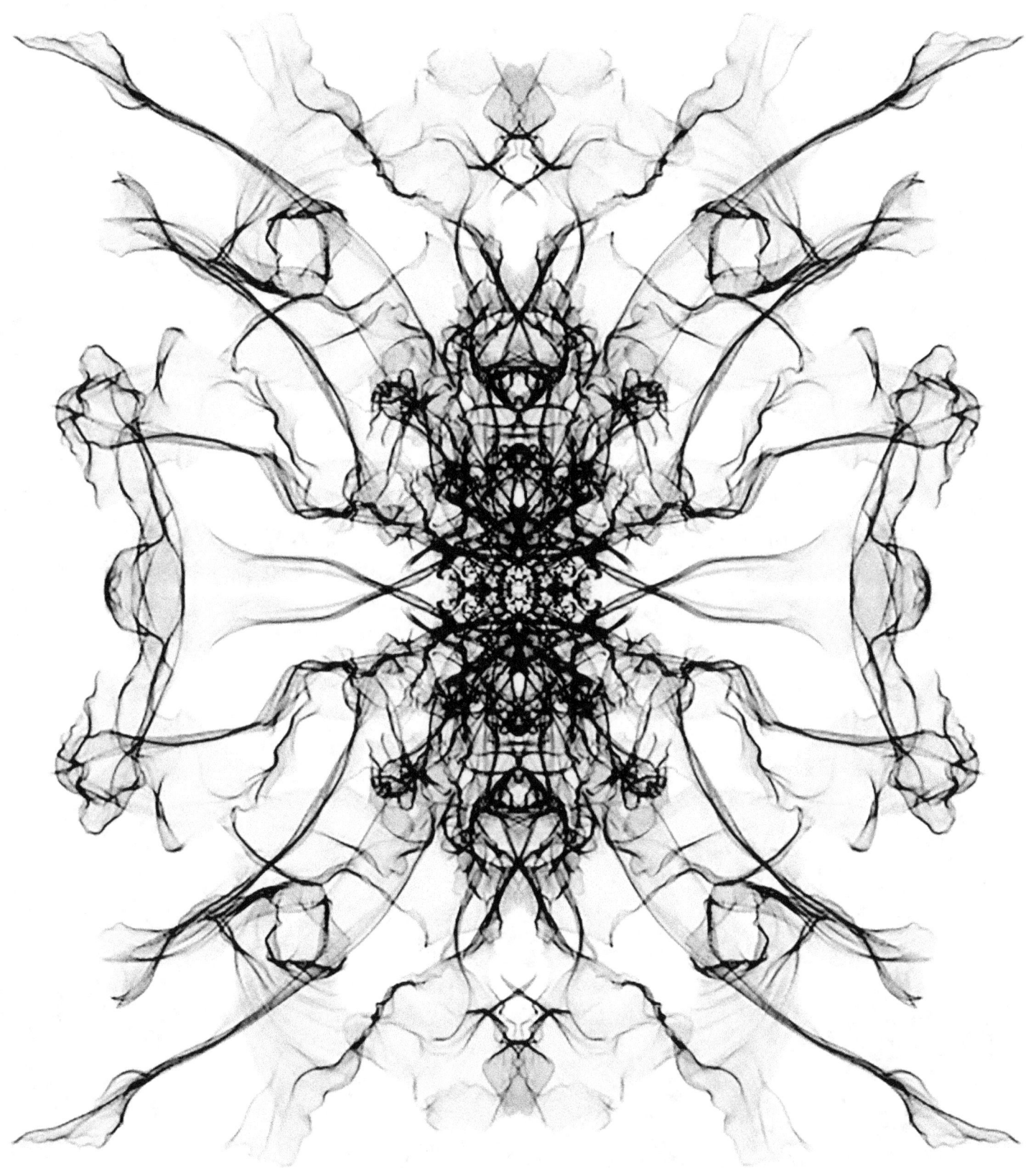

Contributing Artist
Maud Feral Chauveau
(MFC)
France

« MFC - Peinture, graphisme & illustration »

Global Doodle Gems Easter Collection Volume 1

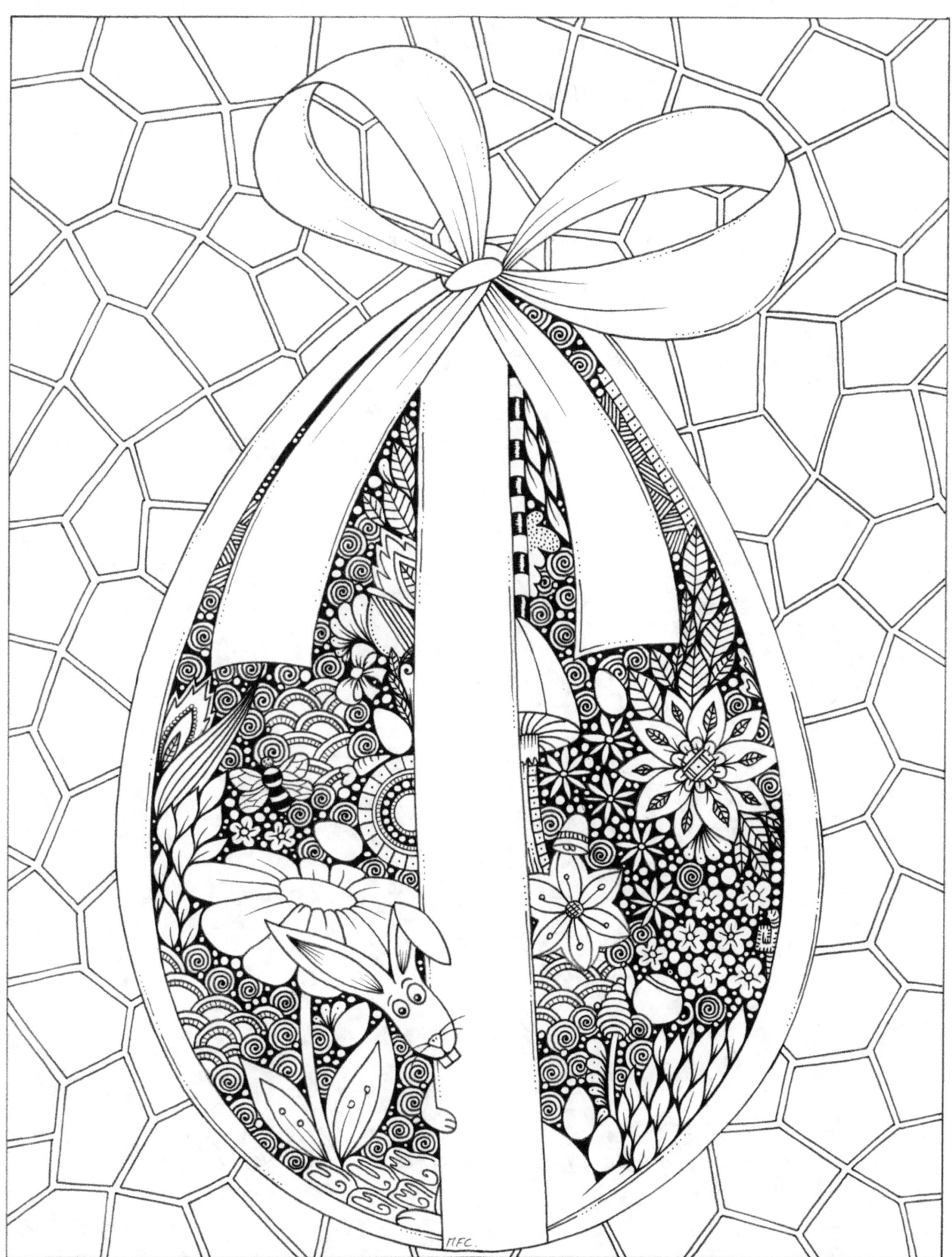

Contributing Artist
Maud Feral Chauveau
(MFC)
France

« MFC - Peinture, graphisme & illustration »

Global Doodle Gems Valentines Collection Volume 1

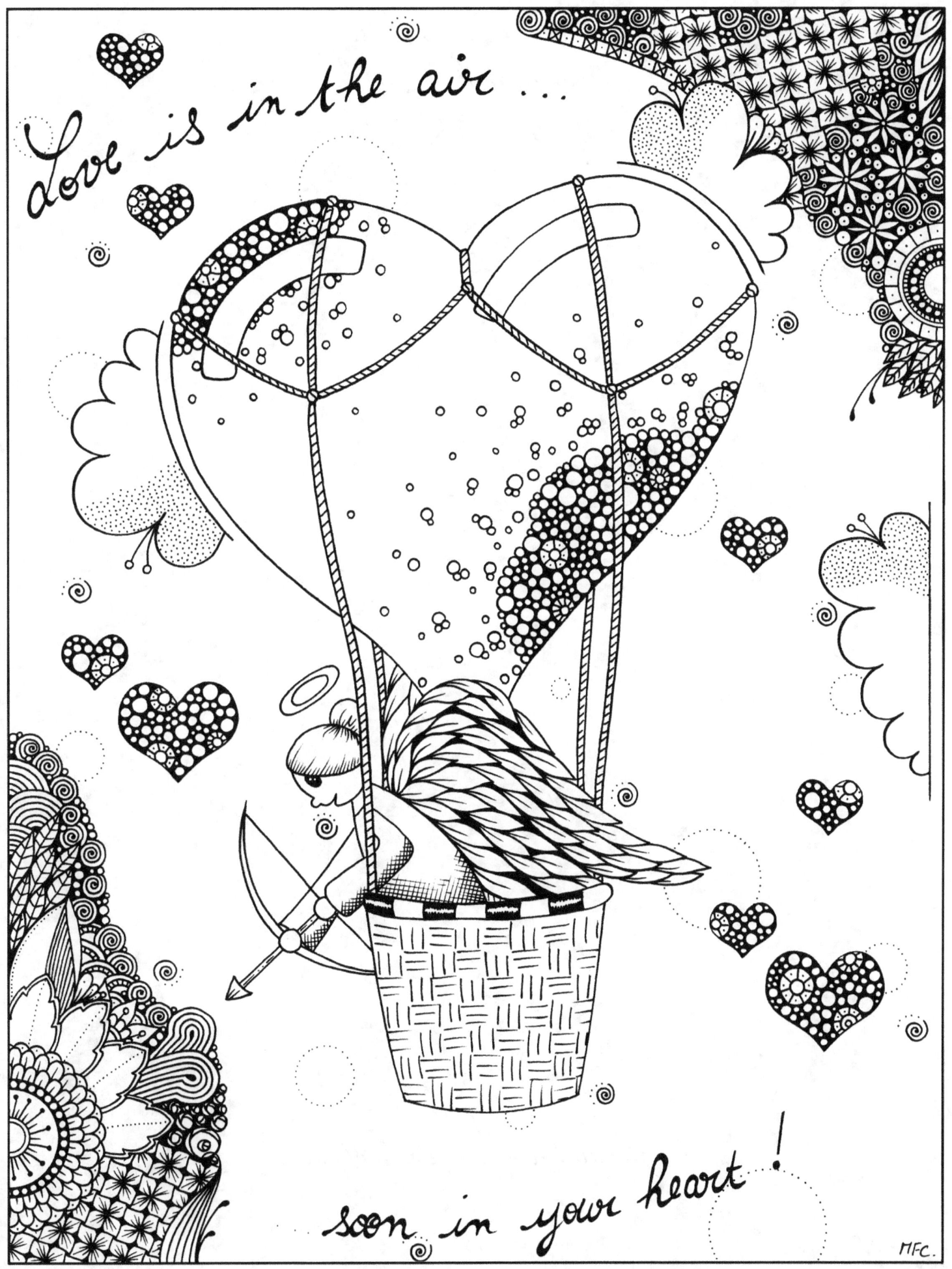

Contributing Artist
Mitchell Manuel
New Zealand AKA Aotearoa

Global Doodle Gems Volume 7

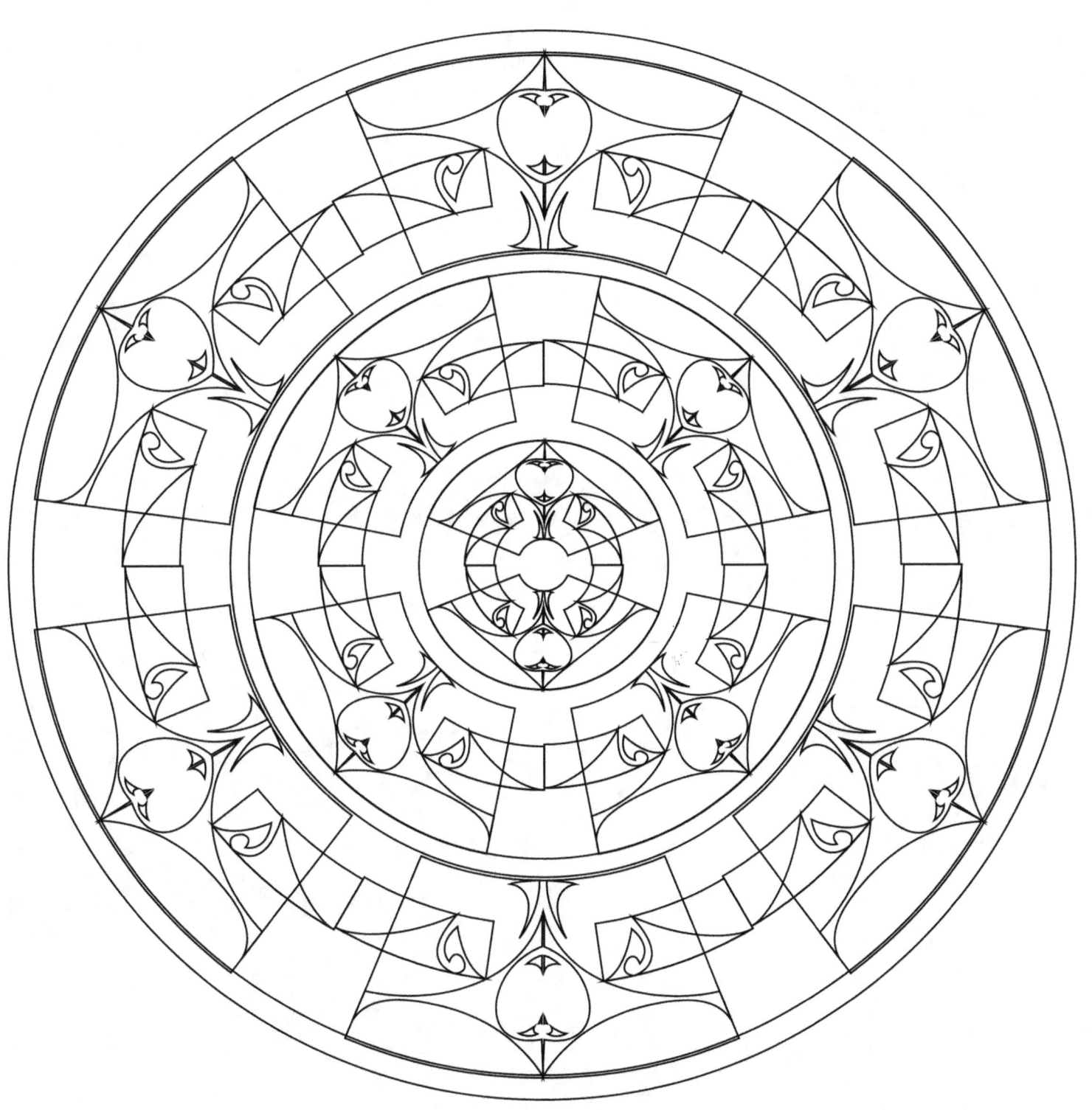

Contributing Artist
Mr. End
Taiwan

Facebook : Geometry-Flow

Geometry Flow

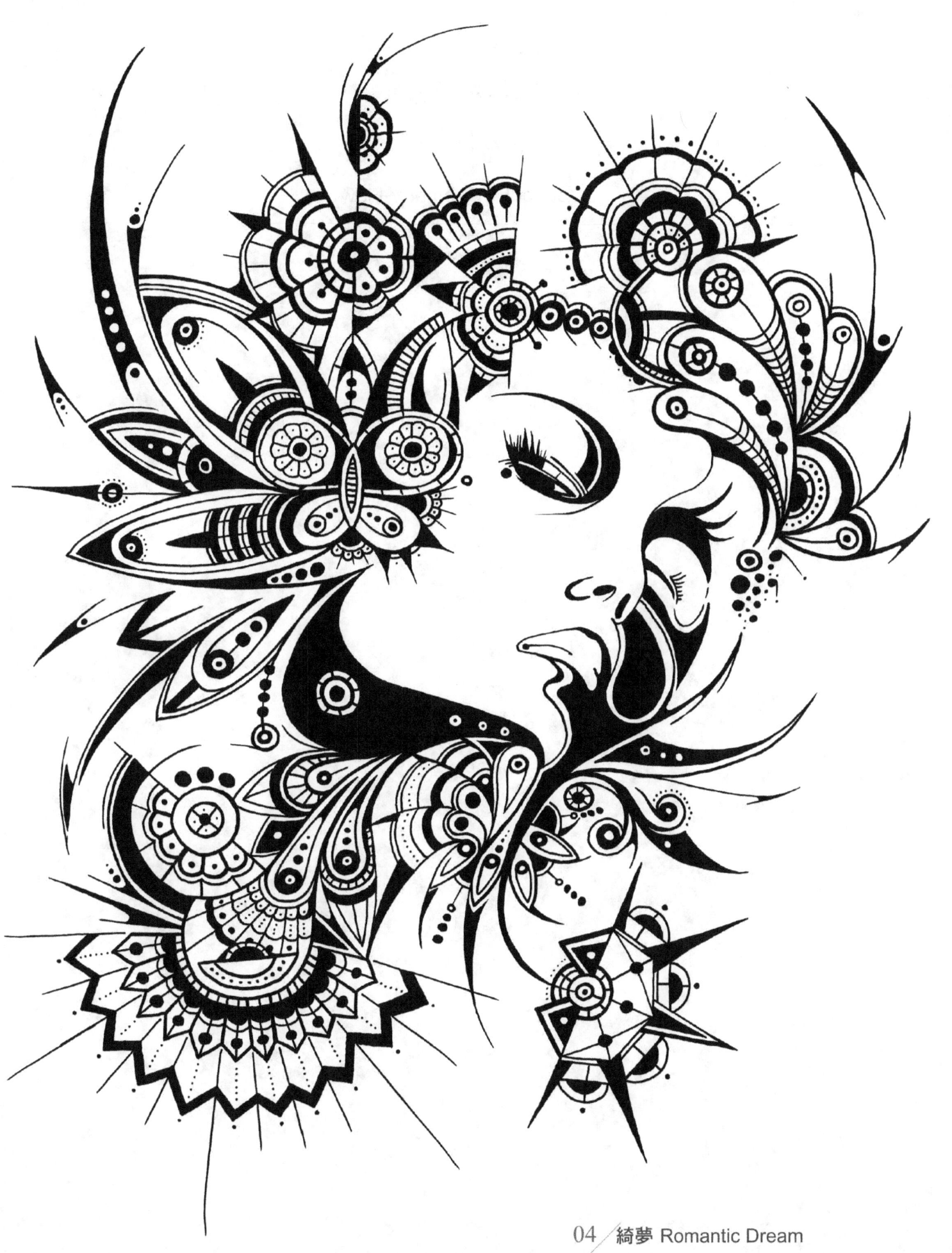
04 / 綺夢 Romantic Dream

Contributing Artist
Mr. End
Taiwan

Facebook : Geometry-Flow

Geometry Flow

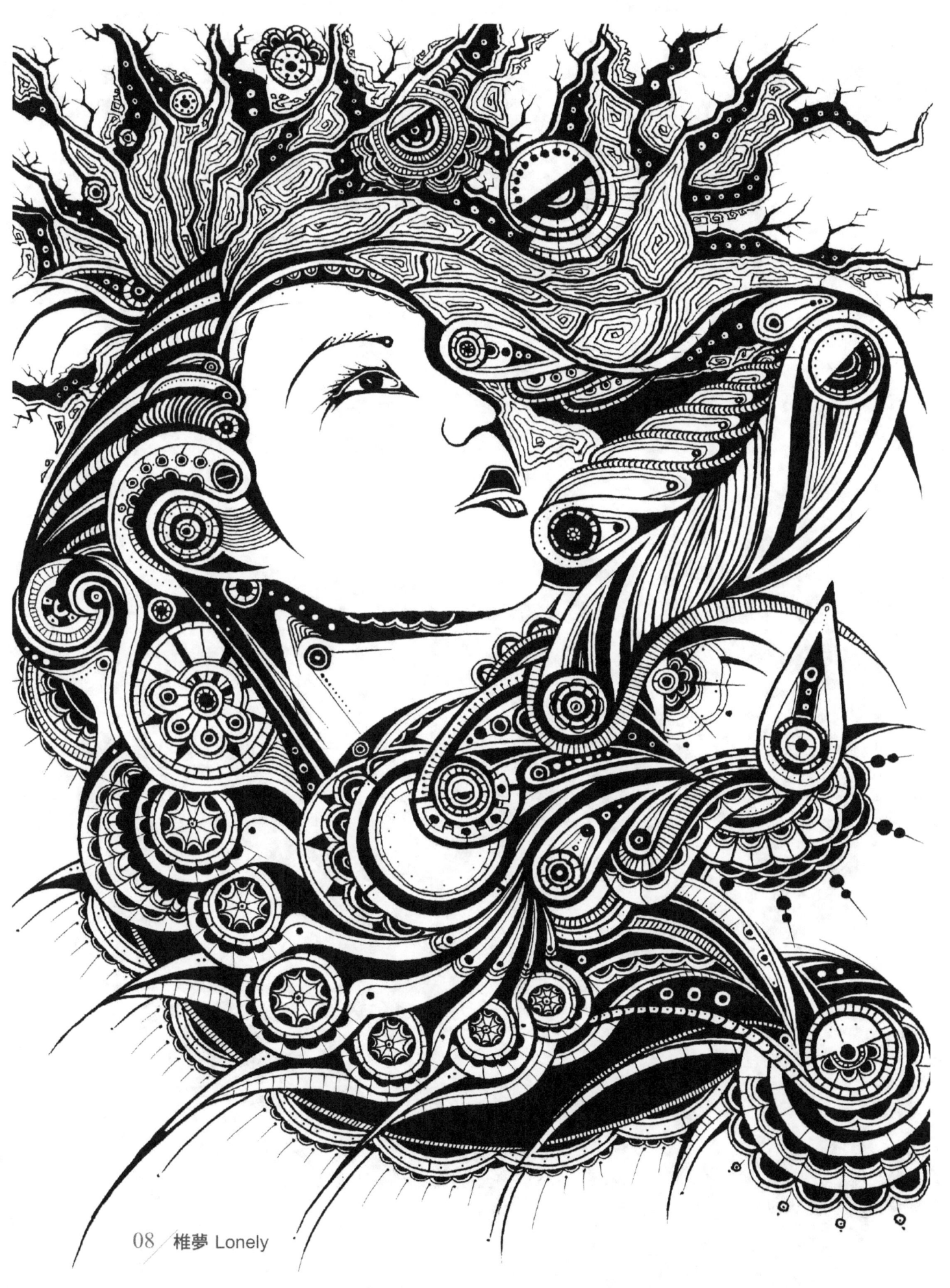

08 / 椎夢 Lonely

Contributing Artist
Mr. End
Taiwan

Facebook : Geometry-Flow

Geometry Flow

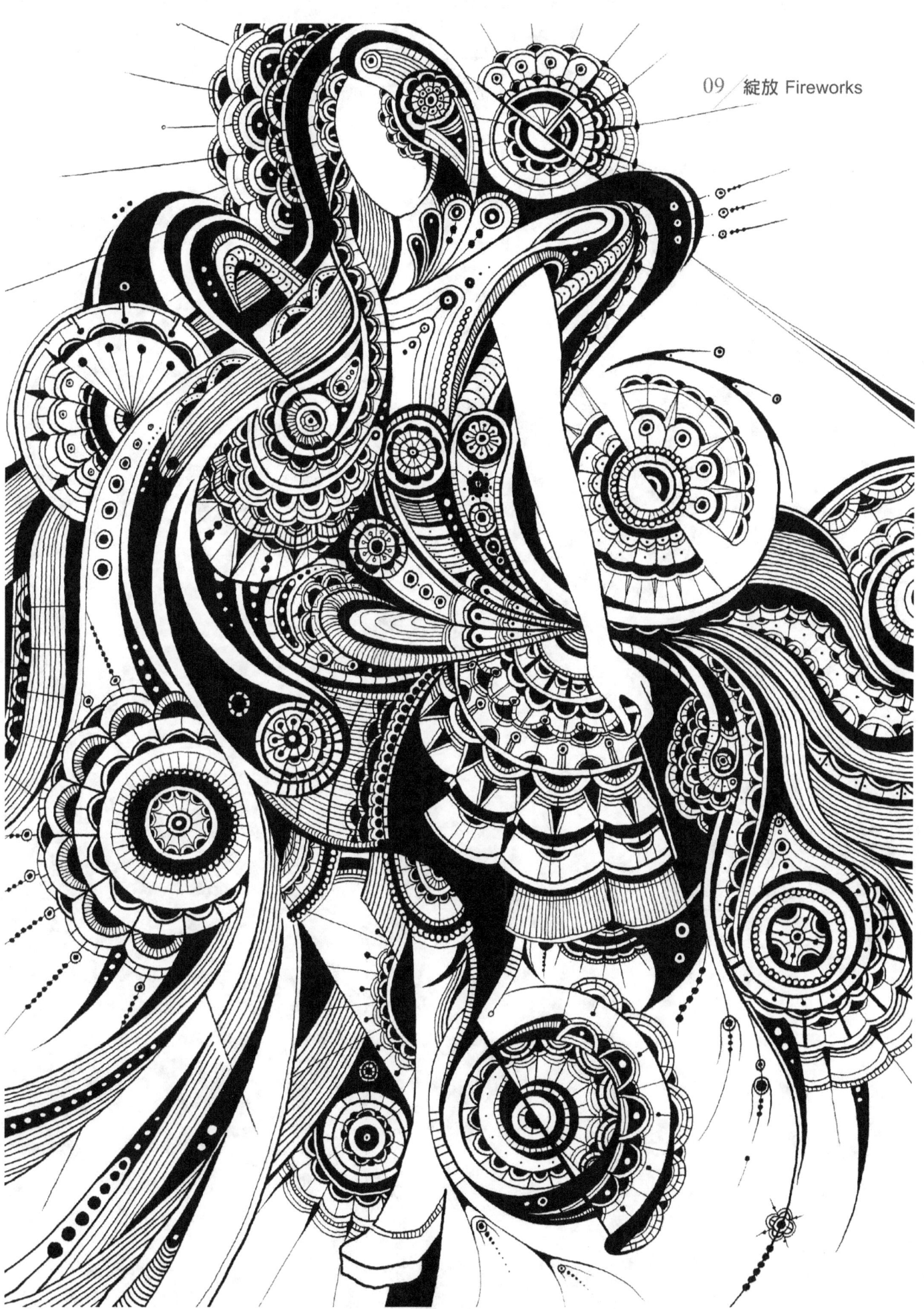

09 / 綻放 Fireworks

Contributing Artist
Mr. End
Taiwan

Facebook : Geometry-Flow

Geometry Flow

10 ／武妝 Tough

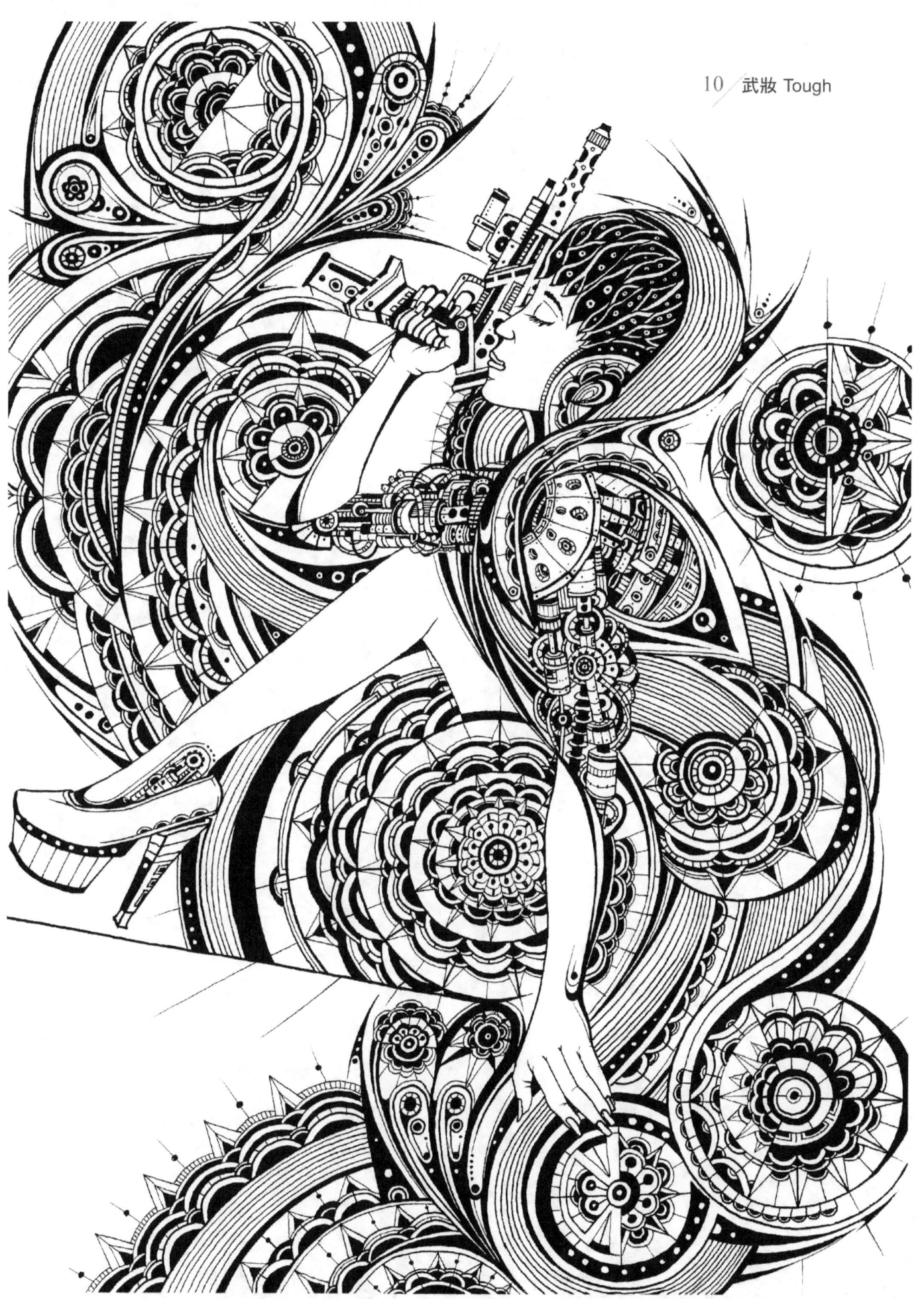

Contributing Artist
Maria Wedel
Denmark

Facebook : AMVWART
Facebook Group : ColorPagesOfAMVW/

Twist'A'Dala

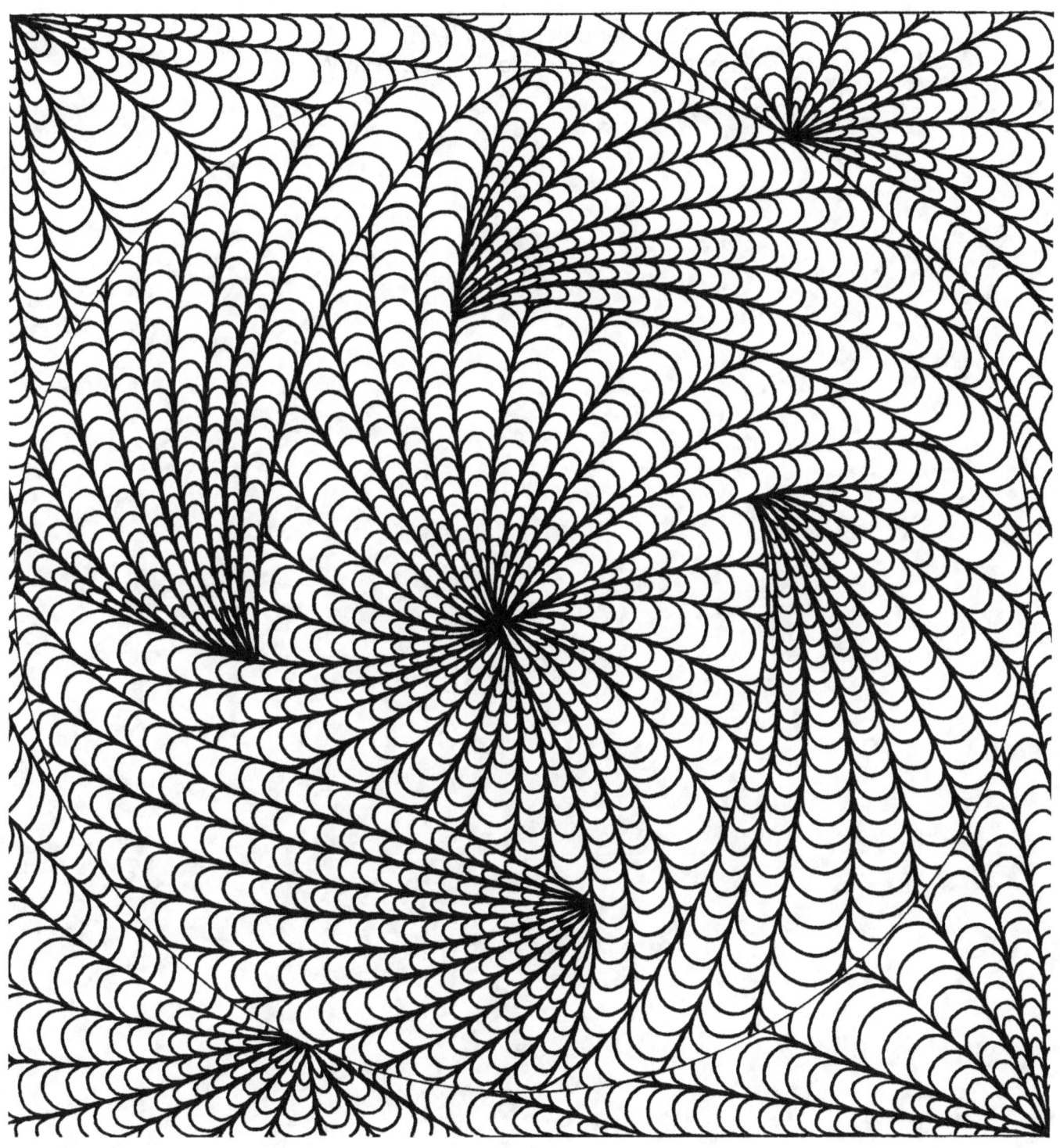

Contributing Artist
Maria Wedel
Denmark

Facebook : AMVWART
Facebook Group : ColorPagesOfAMVW/

The Twister Book Chill Pill Volume 1

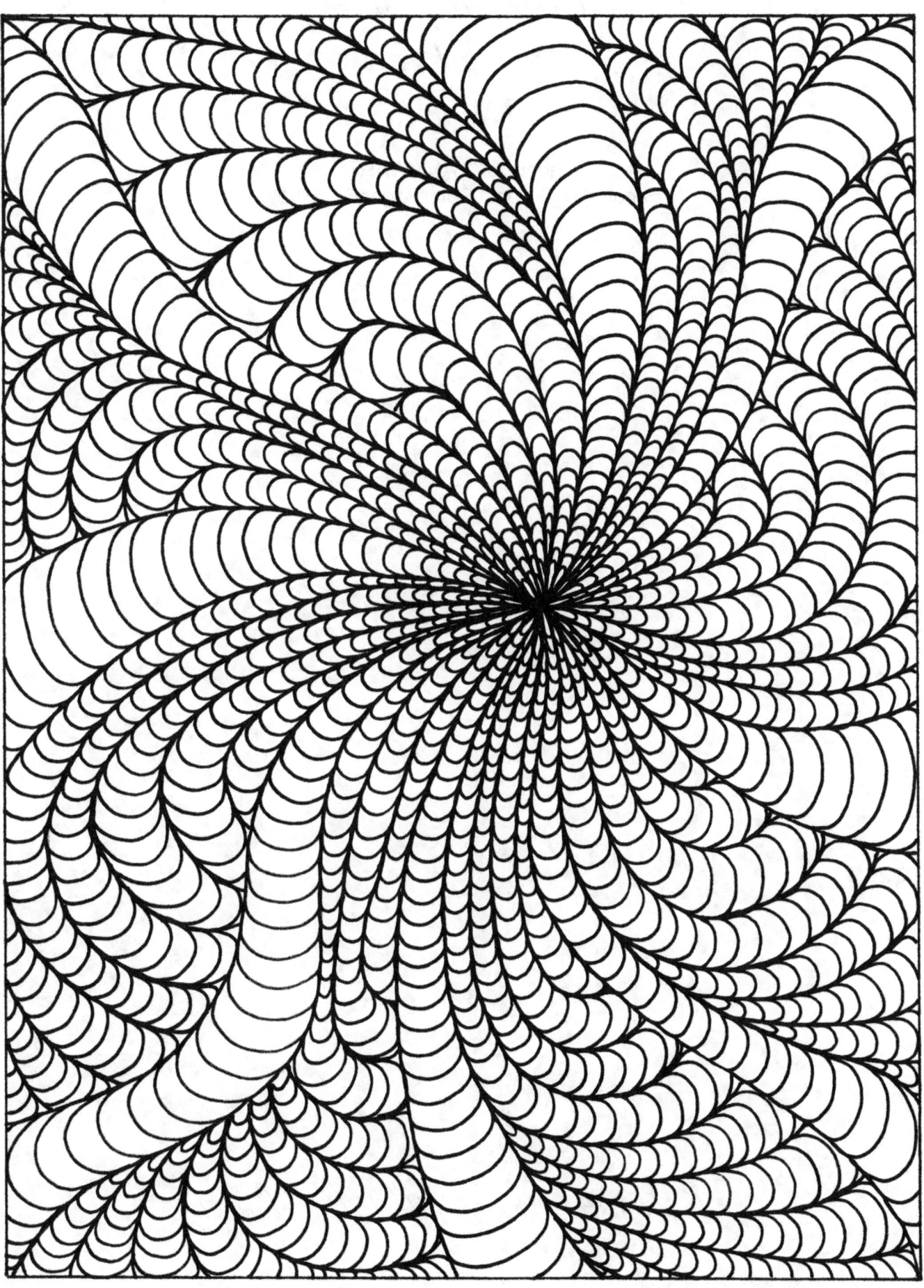

Contributing Artist
Maria Wedel
Denmark

Facebook : AMVWART
Facebook Group : ColorPagesOfAMVW/

The Twister Book Chill Pill Volume 1

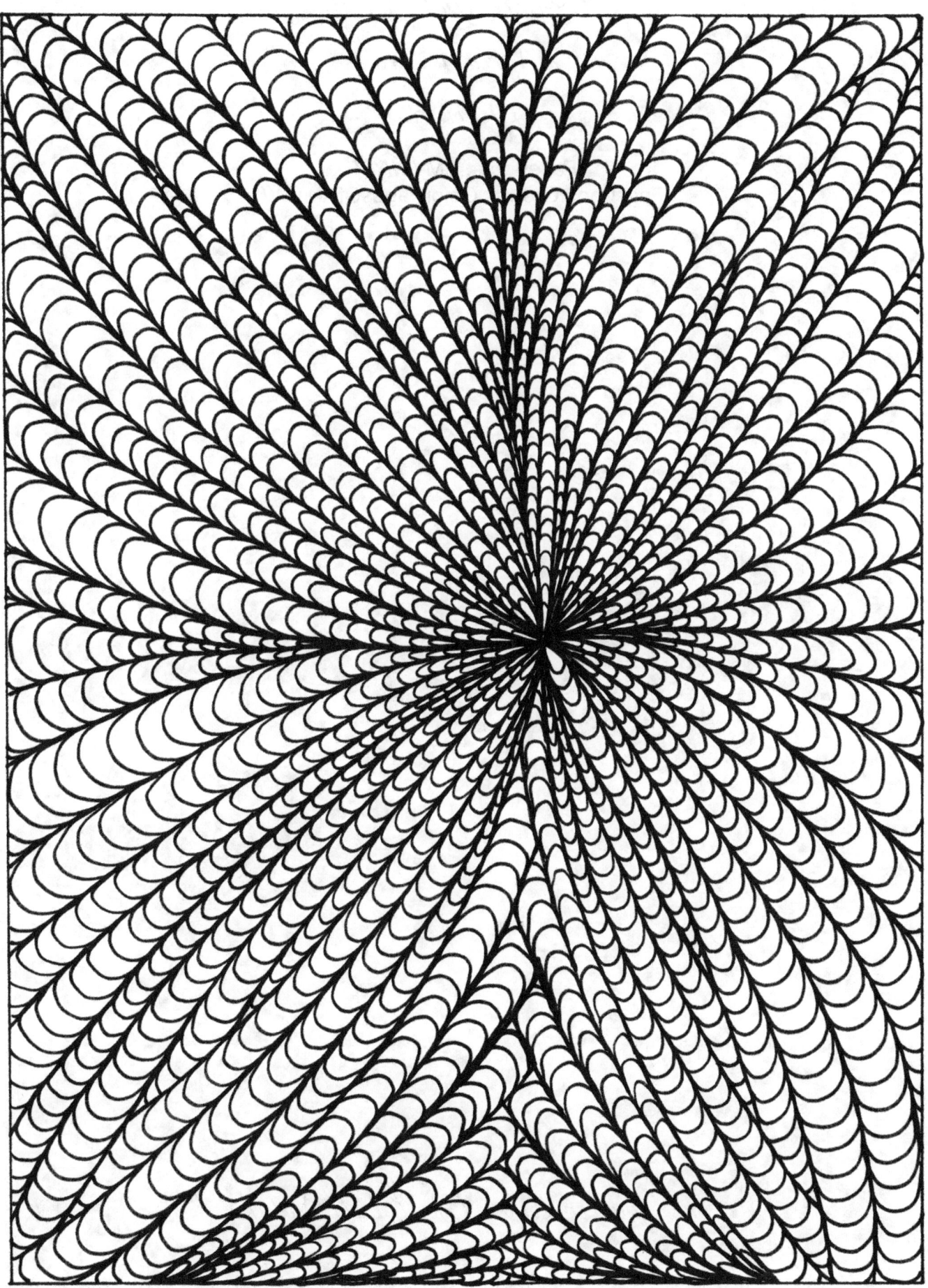

Contributing Artist
Maria Wedel
Denmark

Facebook : AMVWART
Facebook Group : ColorPagesOfAMVW/

The Twister Book Chill Pill Volume 1

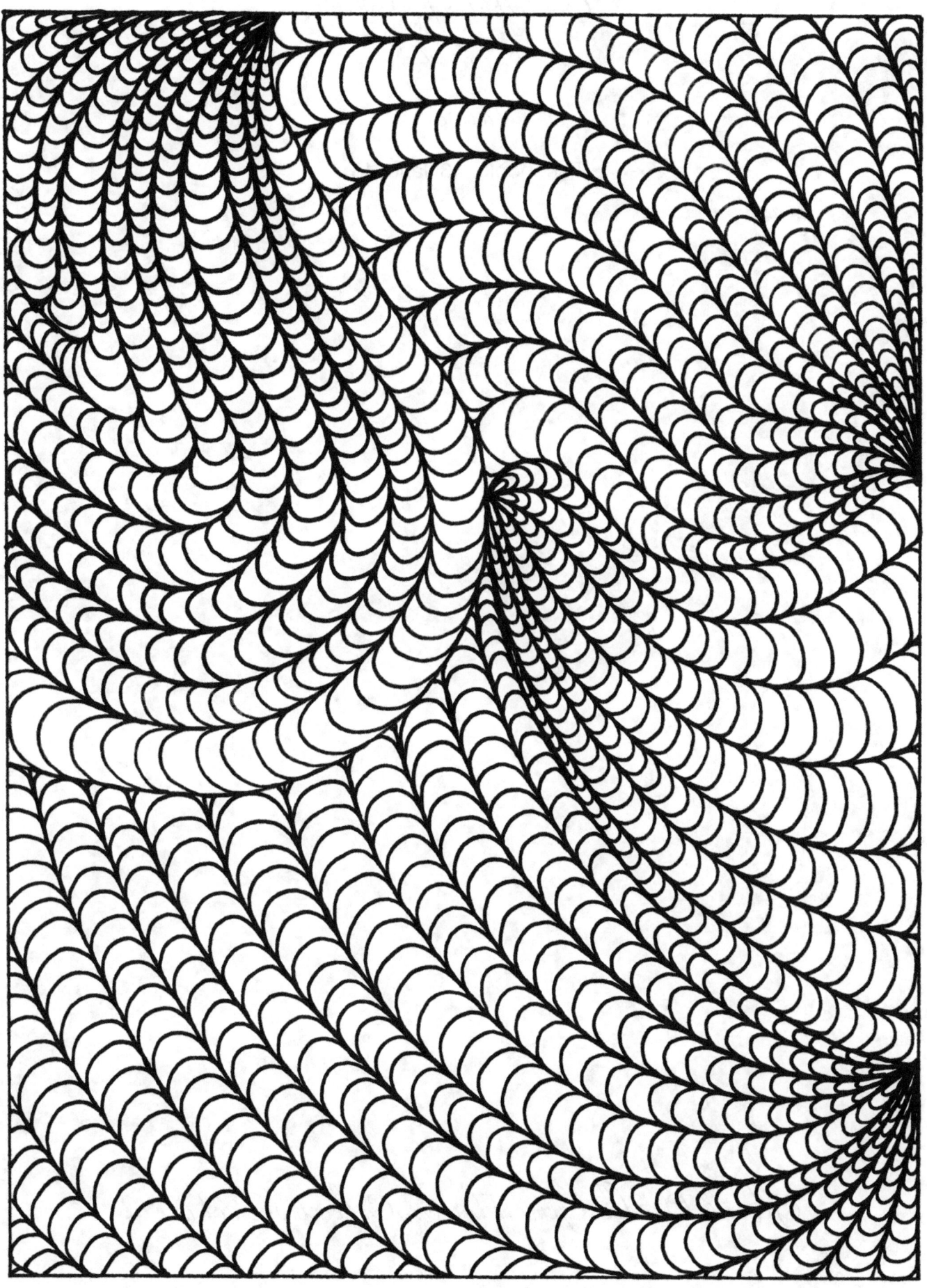

Contributing Artist
Nancy43
Taiwan

Facebook : 43Nancy43

Global Doodle Gems Flowers Collection Volume 2

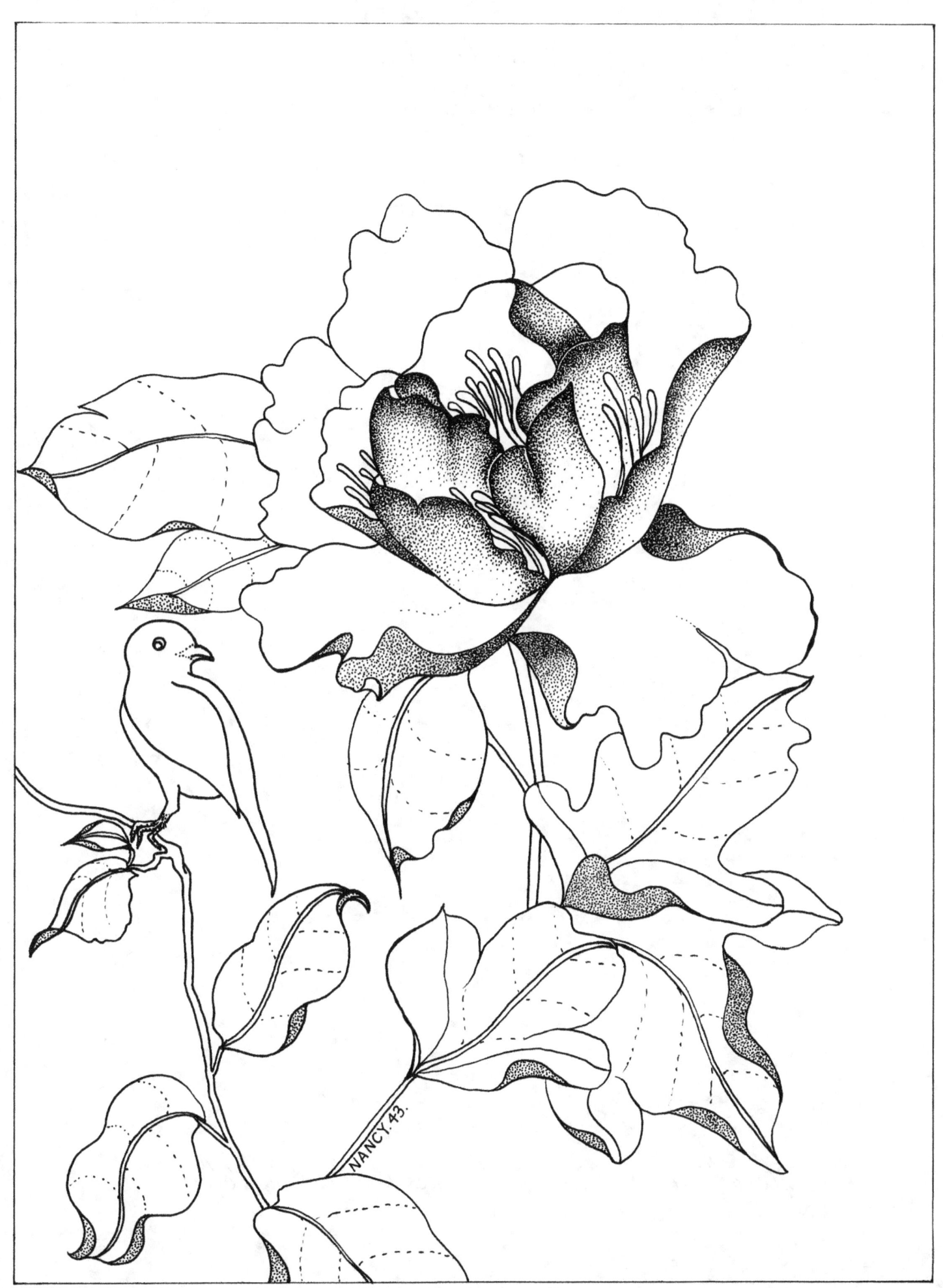

Contributing Artist
Neeti Goswami
Canada

www.artbyneeti.ca

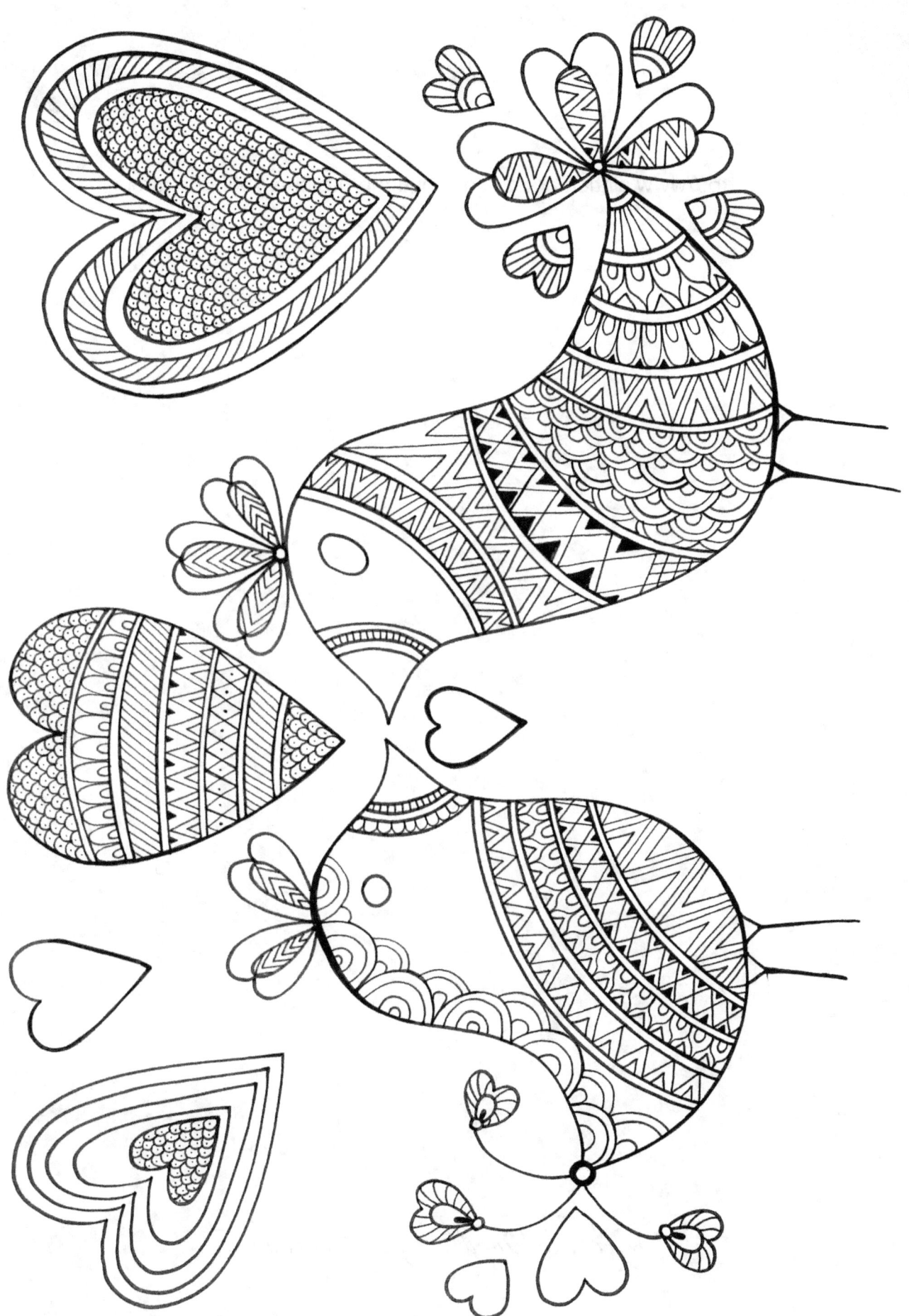

Contributing Artist
Orbleue's
France

http://www.alittlemarket.com/boutique/orbleue-1682885.html

Global Doodle Gems Volume 5

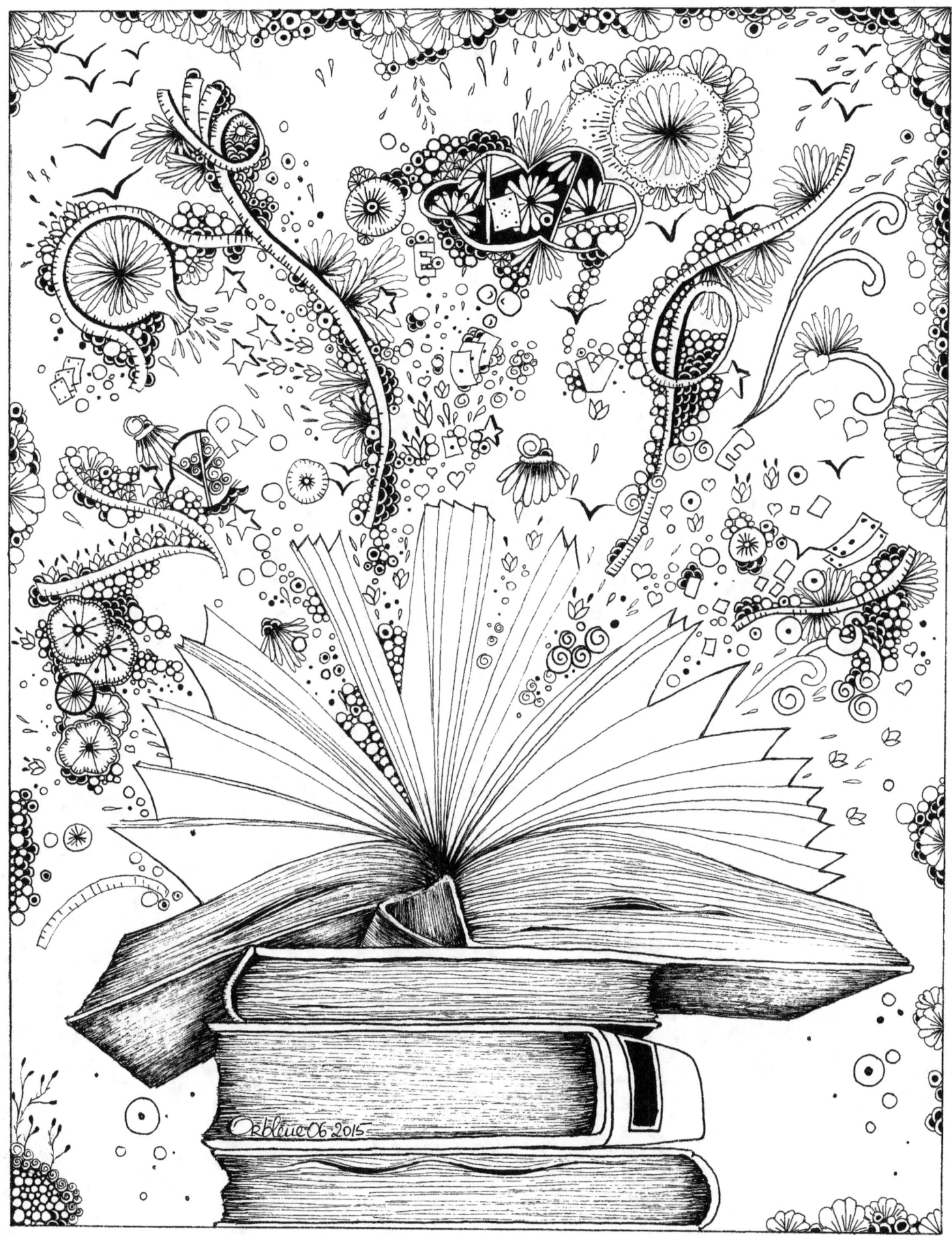

Contributing Artist
Orbleue's
France

http://www.alittlemarket.com/boutique/orbleue-1682885.html

Global Doodle Gems Volume 5

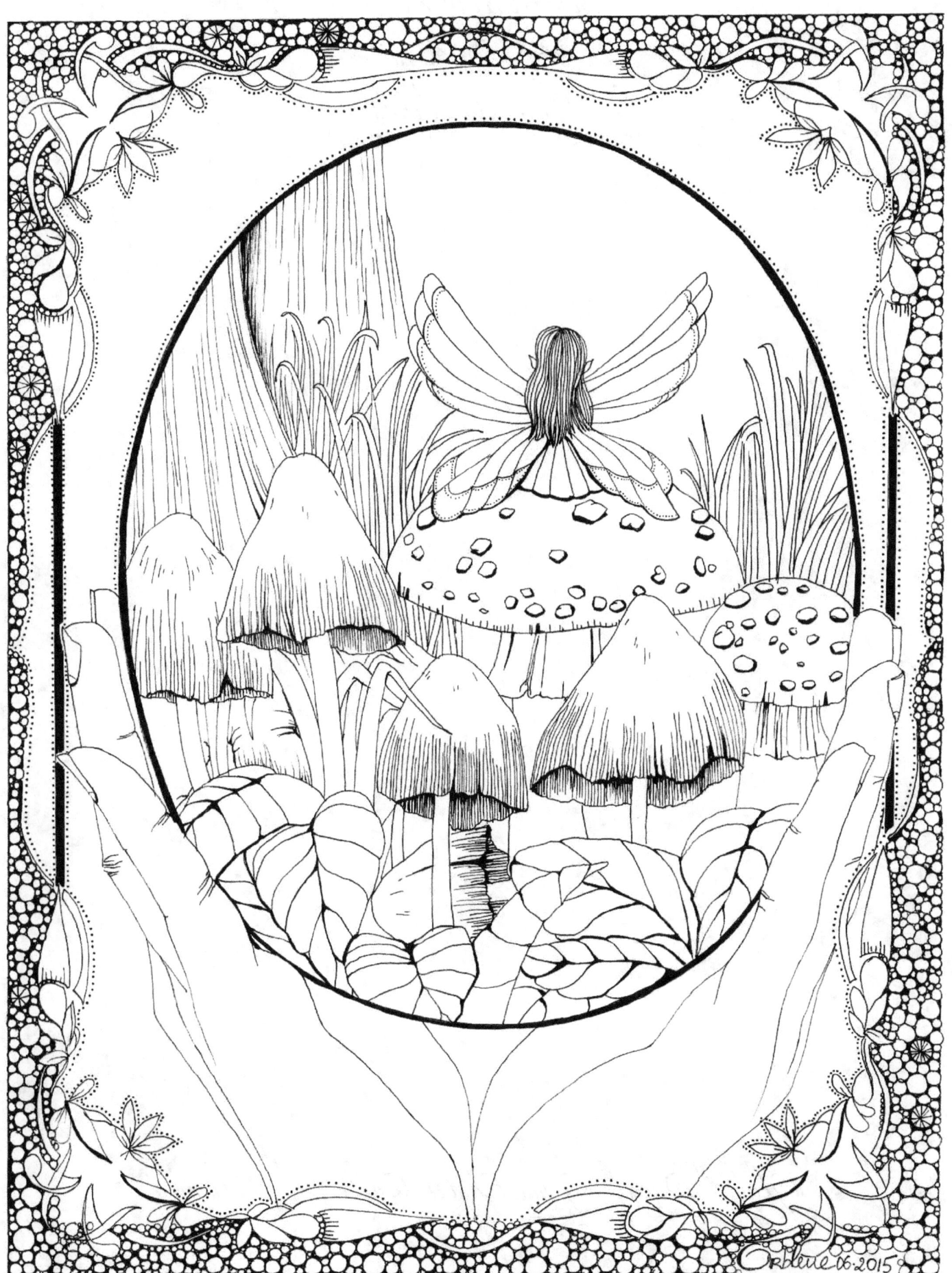

Contributing Artist
Peggy Sue's Artwork
The Netherlands
Facebook : Peggy-Sues-Artwork

Global Doodle Gems Easter Collection Volume 1

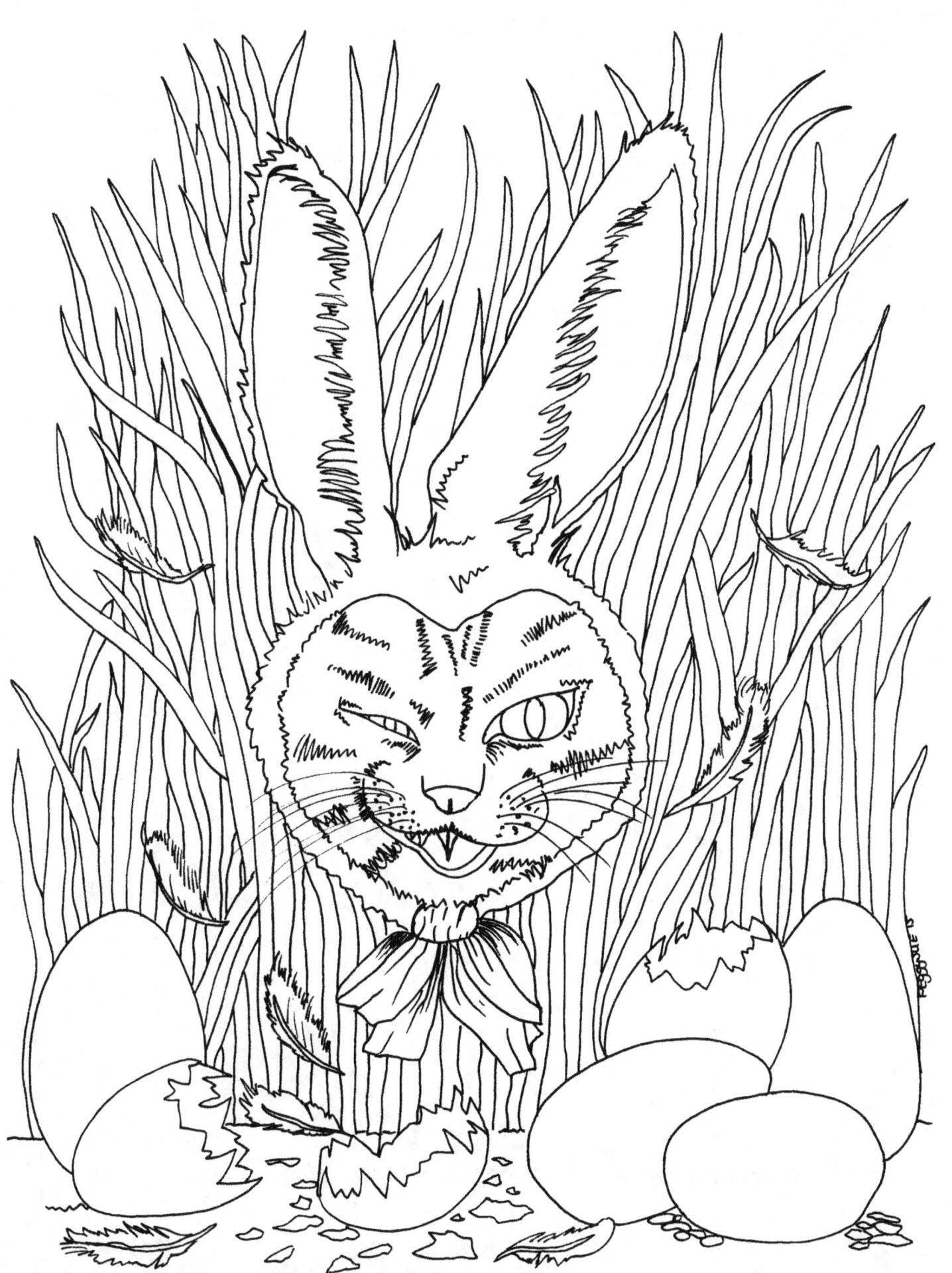

Contributing Artist
Peggy Sue's Artwork
The Netherlands
Facebook : Peggy-Sues-Artwork

Global Doodle Gems Flowers Collection Volume 1

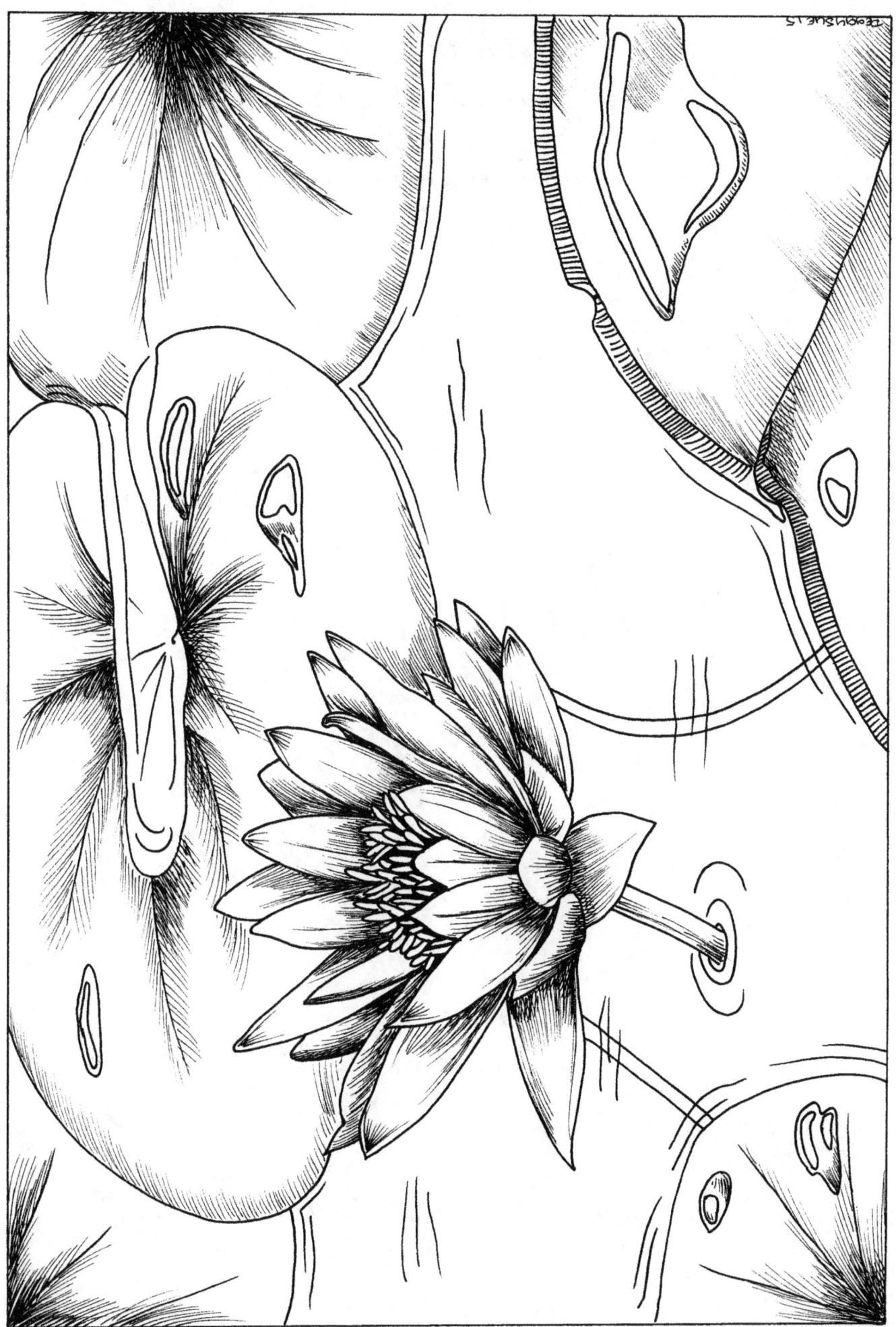

Contributing Artist
Peggy Sue's Artwork
The Netherlands
Facebook : Peggy-Sues-Artwork

Global Doodle Gems Oceania Collection Volume 2

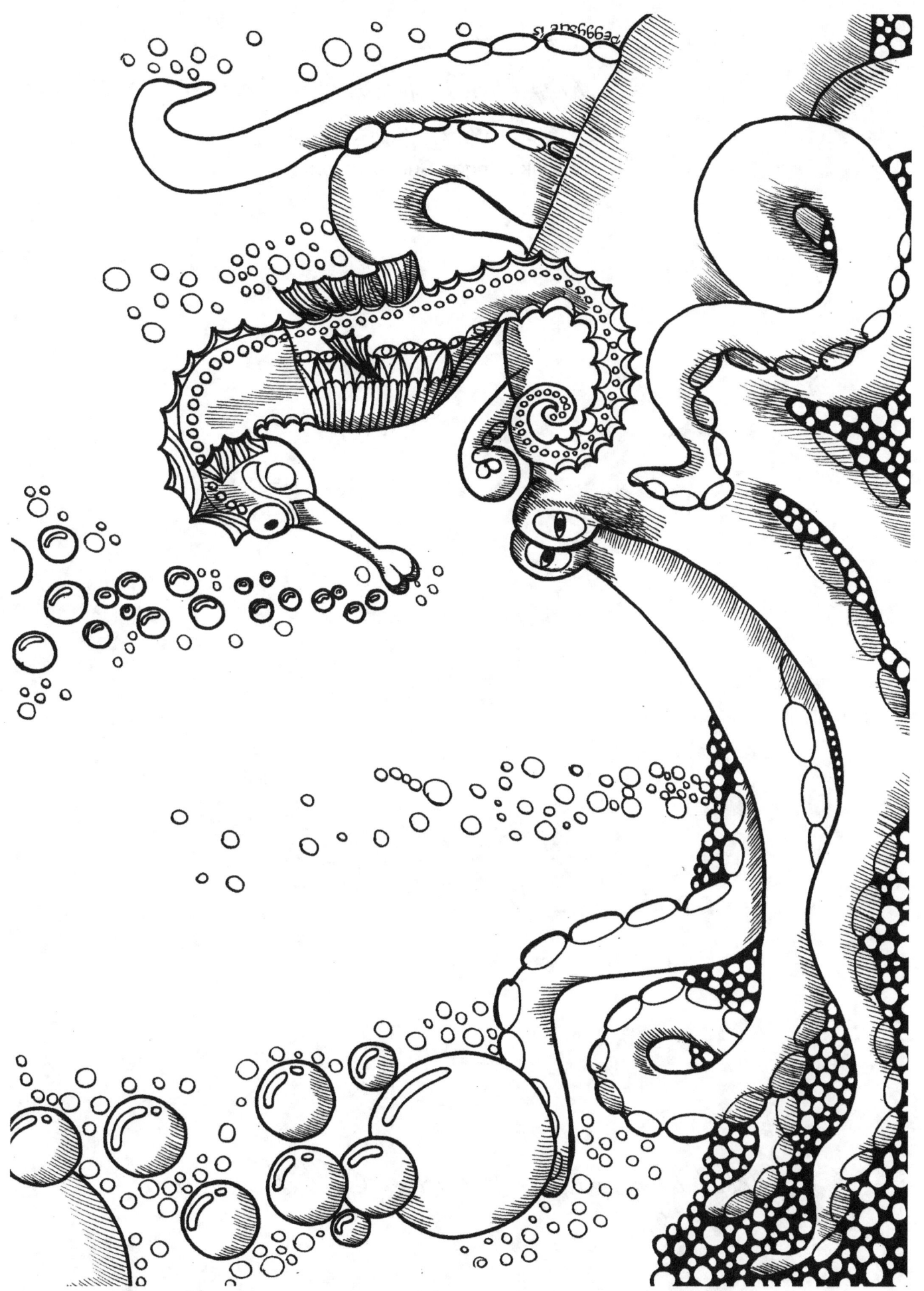

Contributing Artist
Peggy Sue's Artwork
The Netherlands
Facebook : Peggy-Sues-Artwork

Global Doodle Gems Valentines Collection Volume 1

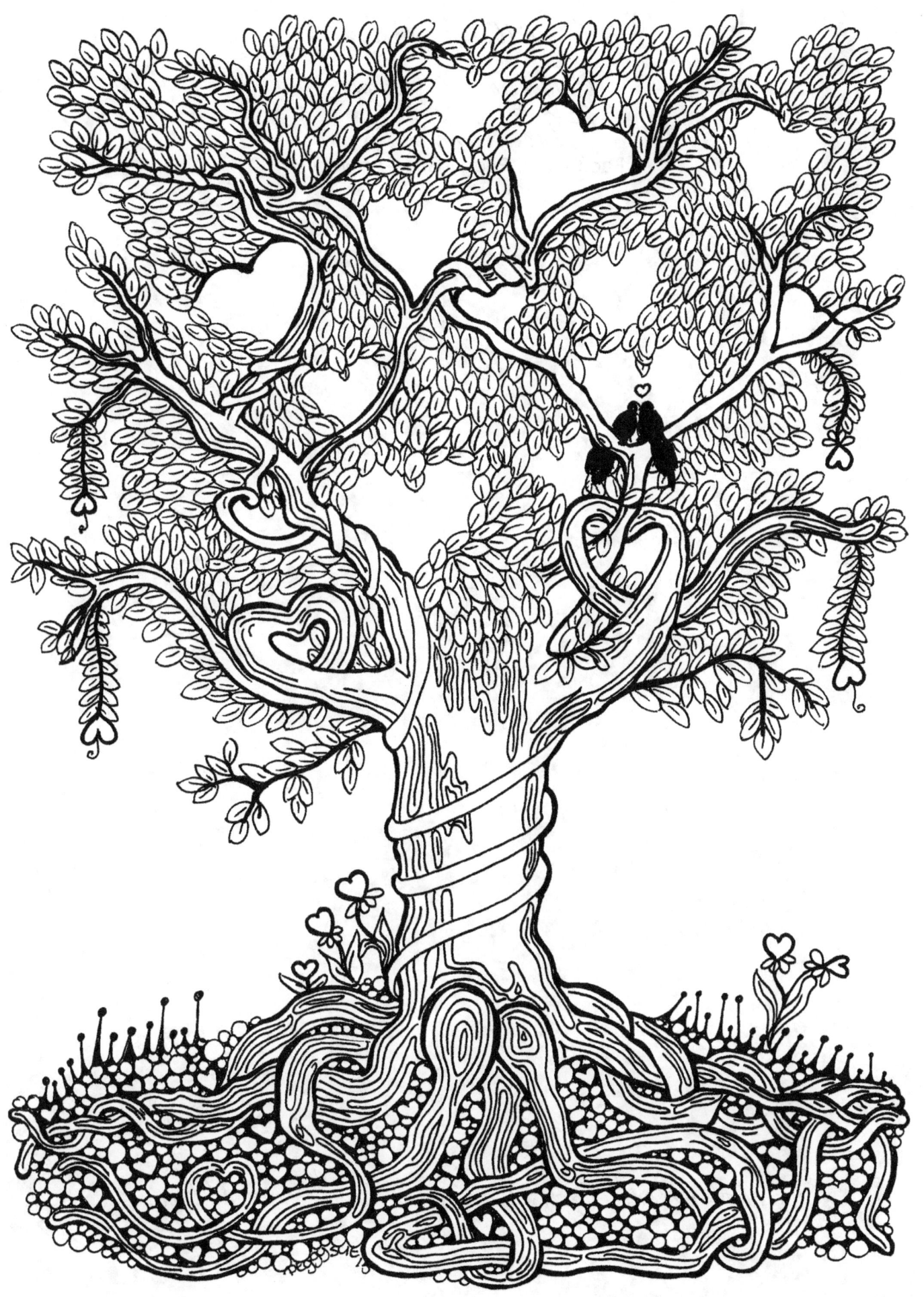

Contributing Artist
Peggy Sue's Artwork
The Netherlands
Facebook : Peggy-Sues-Artwork

Global Doodle Gems Christmas Collection Volume 2

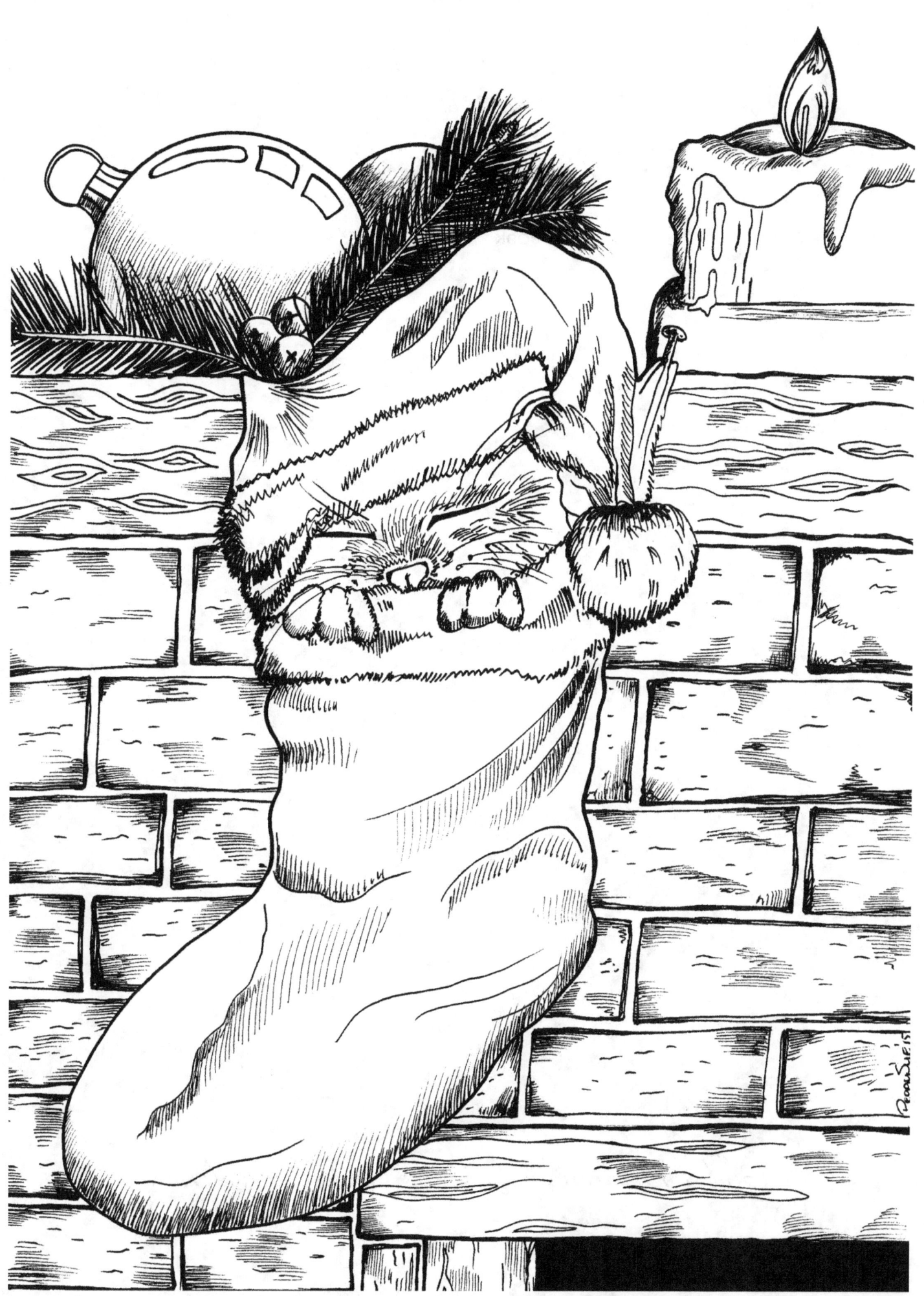

Contributing Artist
Pica Wu
Taiwan

Facebook : picapicadrow2

Global Doodle Gems Flowers Collection Volume 1

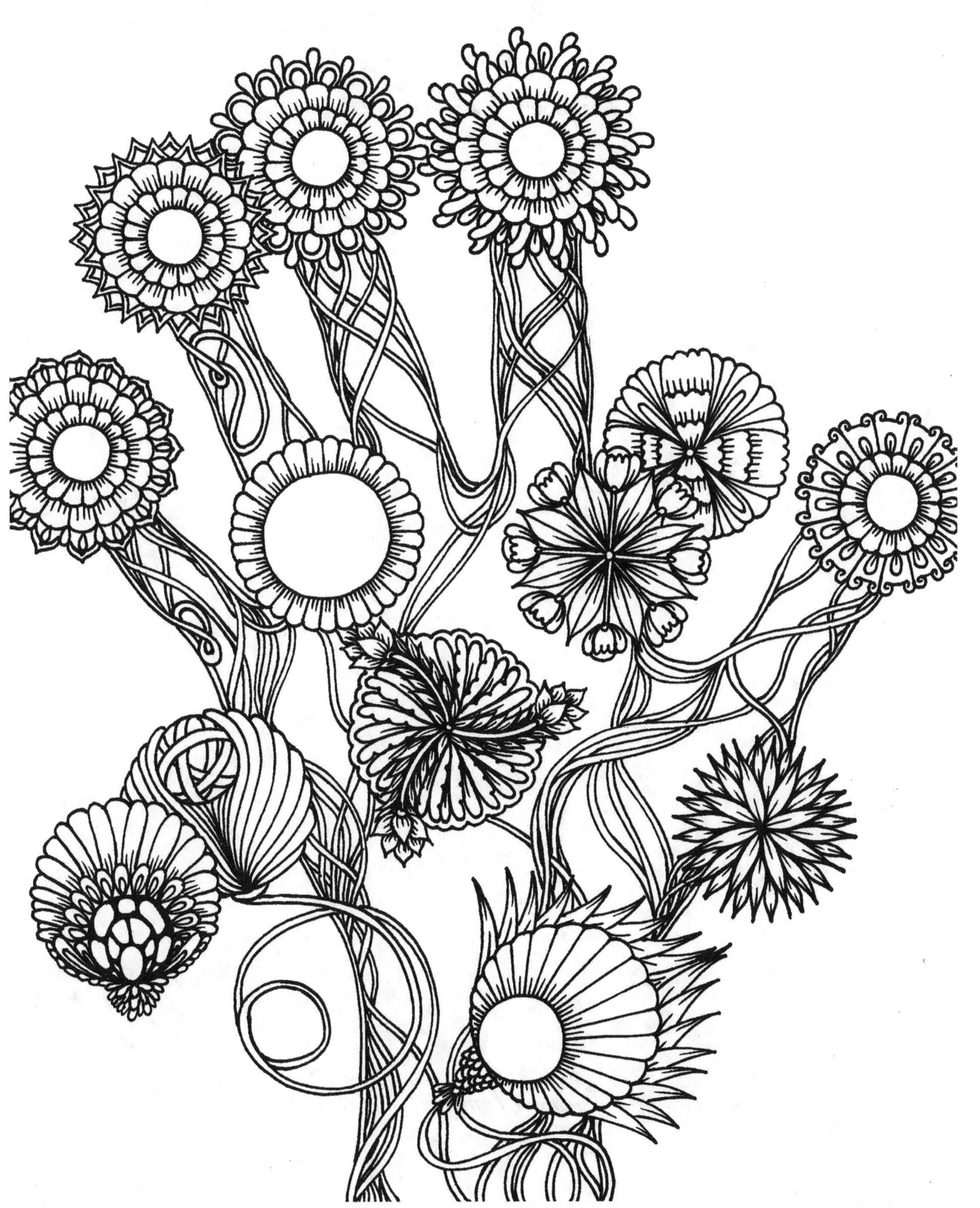

Contributing Artist
Rover Hsiao
Taiwan

Facebook : roverhsiao2015

*Contributing Artist
Rover Hsiao
Taiwan*

Facebook : roverhsiao2015

Global Doodle Gems Mini Collection Volume 4

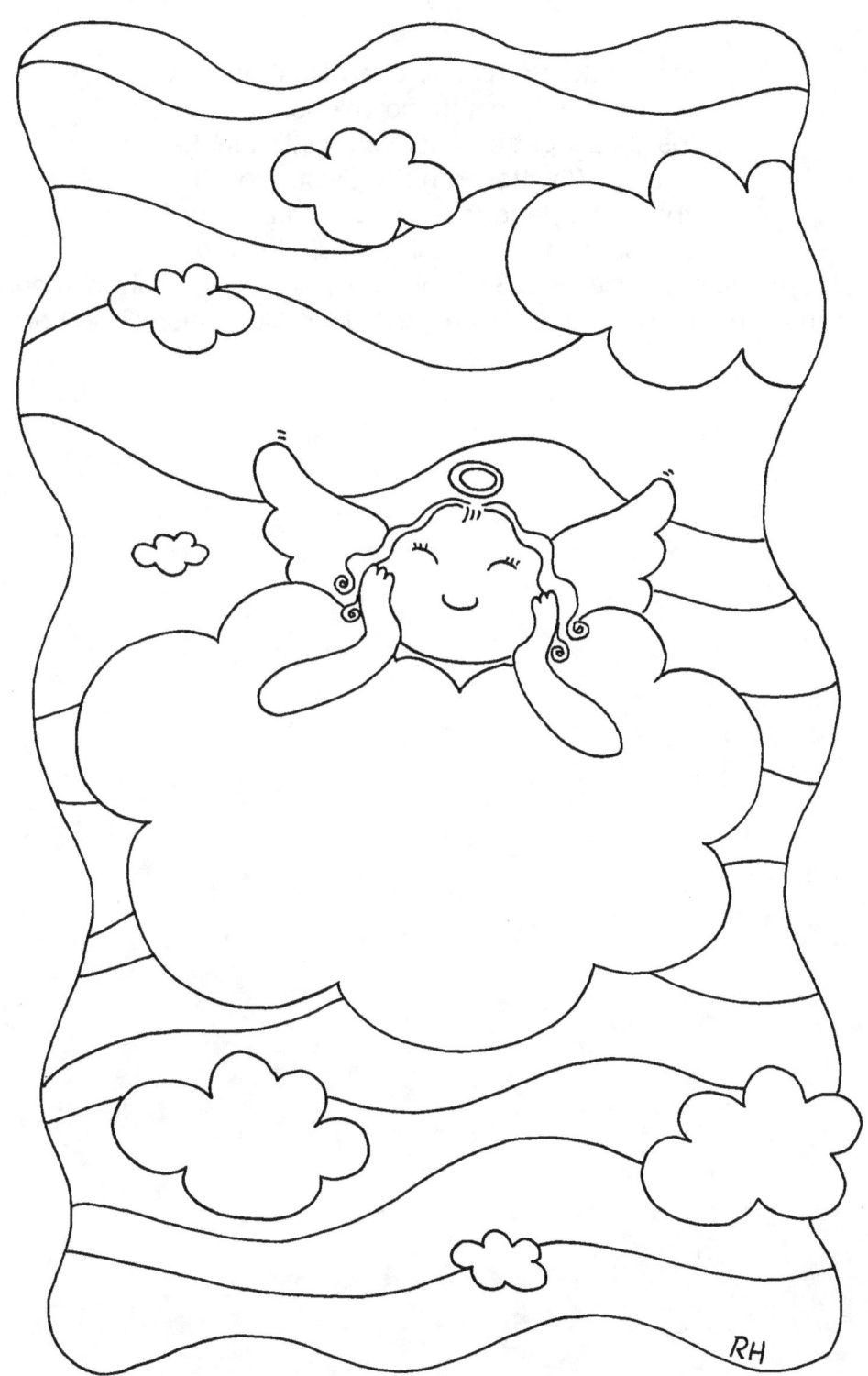

Contributing Artist
Samantha J. Decker
USA

Facebook : Samantha-Jean-Illustrations
www.samanthanowak.com
https://www.patreon.com/samanthadecker
https://twitter.com/SN_Illustration
http://gargoylegoddess21.deviantart.com/
https://www.pinterest.com/sj_illustrat/
https://www.etsy.com/shop/SamanthaJeanArt?ref=hdr_shop_menu
http://www.amazon.com/handmade/Samantha-Jean-Illustrations?ref=hnd_dp_smp

Global Doodle Gems Valentines Collection Volume 2

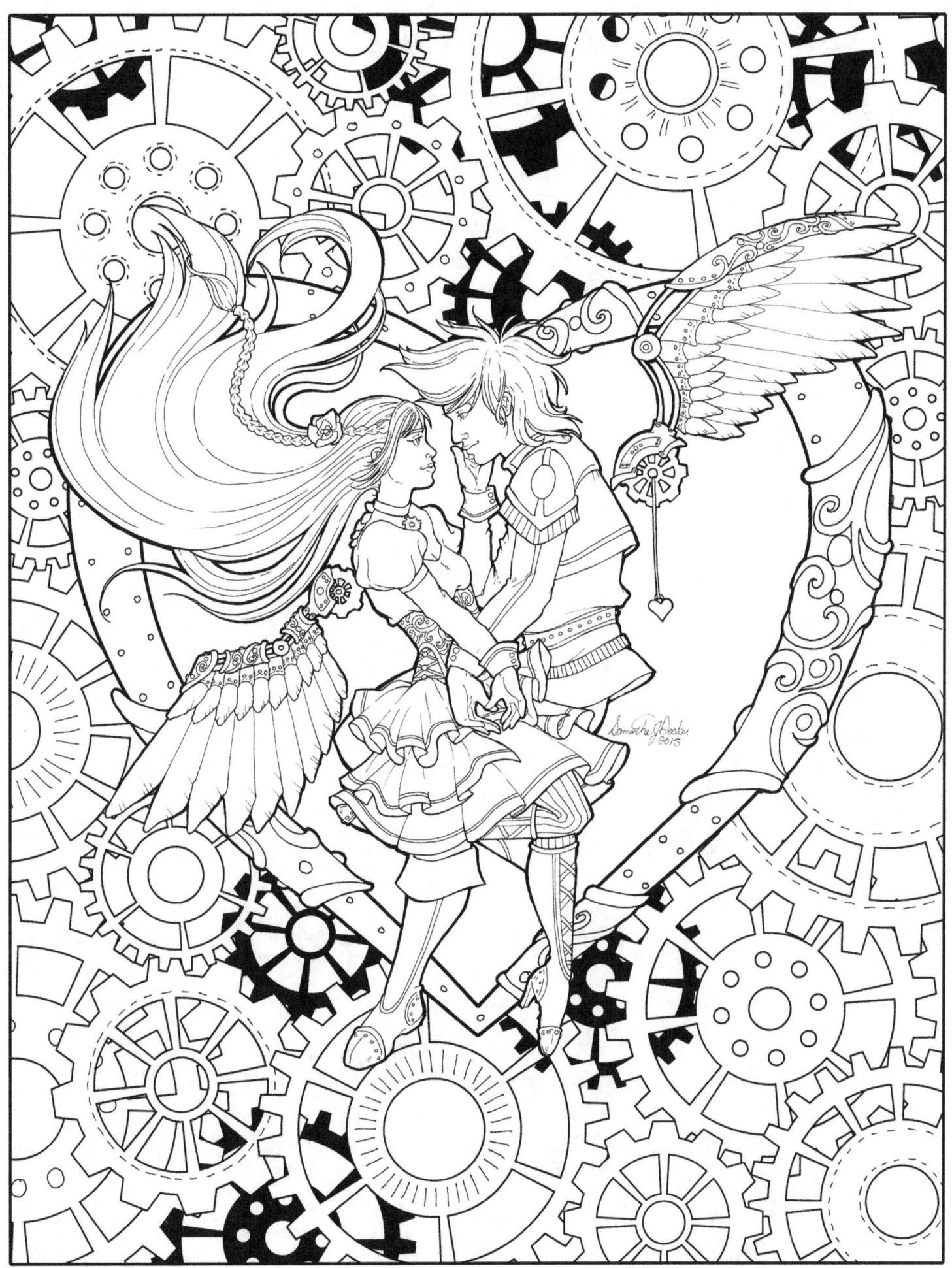

Contributing Artist
Les galaxies de 'Qi
France

Les galaxies de 'Qi

Global Doodle Gems Easter Collection Volume 1

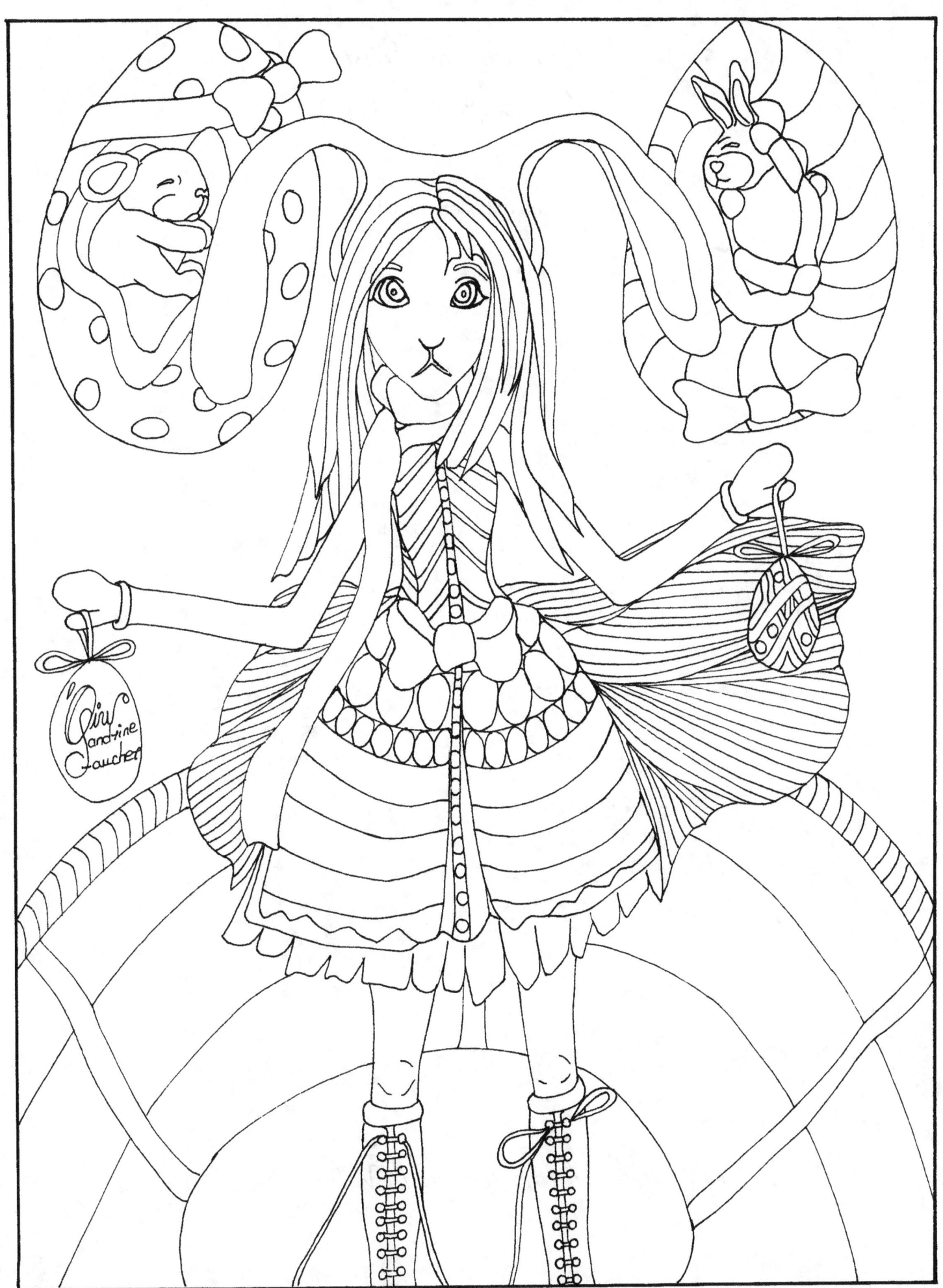

Contributing Artist
Les galaxies de 'Qi
France

Les galaxies de 'Qi

Global Doodle Gems Volume 8

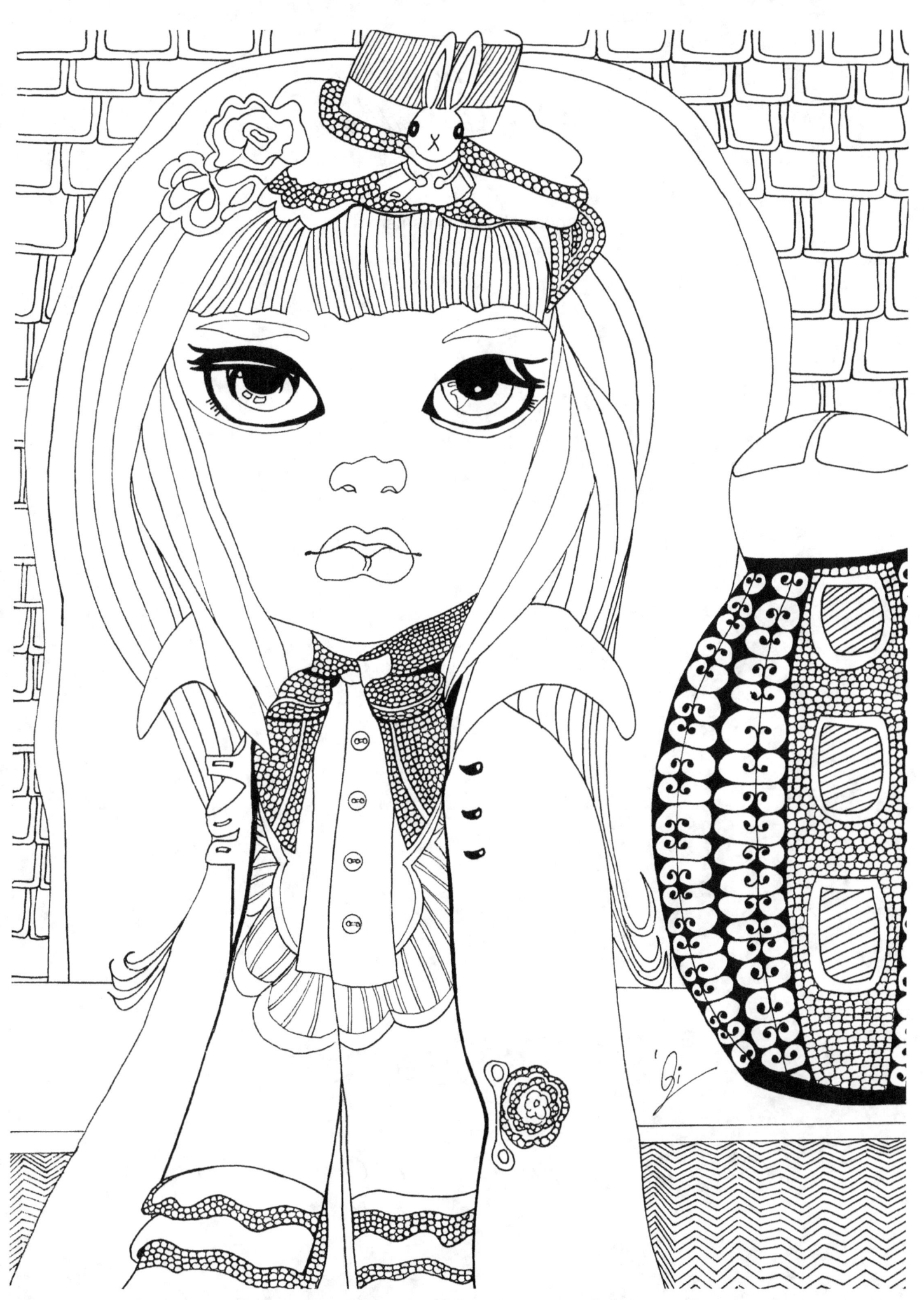

Contributing Artist
Wenyu Lin Small Fish
Taiwan

Facebook : smallfish.smallfish

Global Doodle Gems Christmas Collection Volume 3

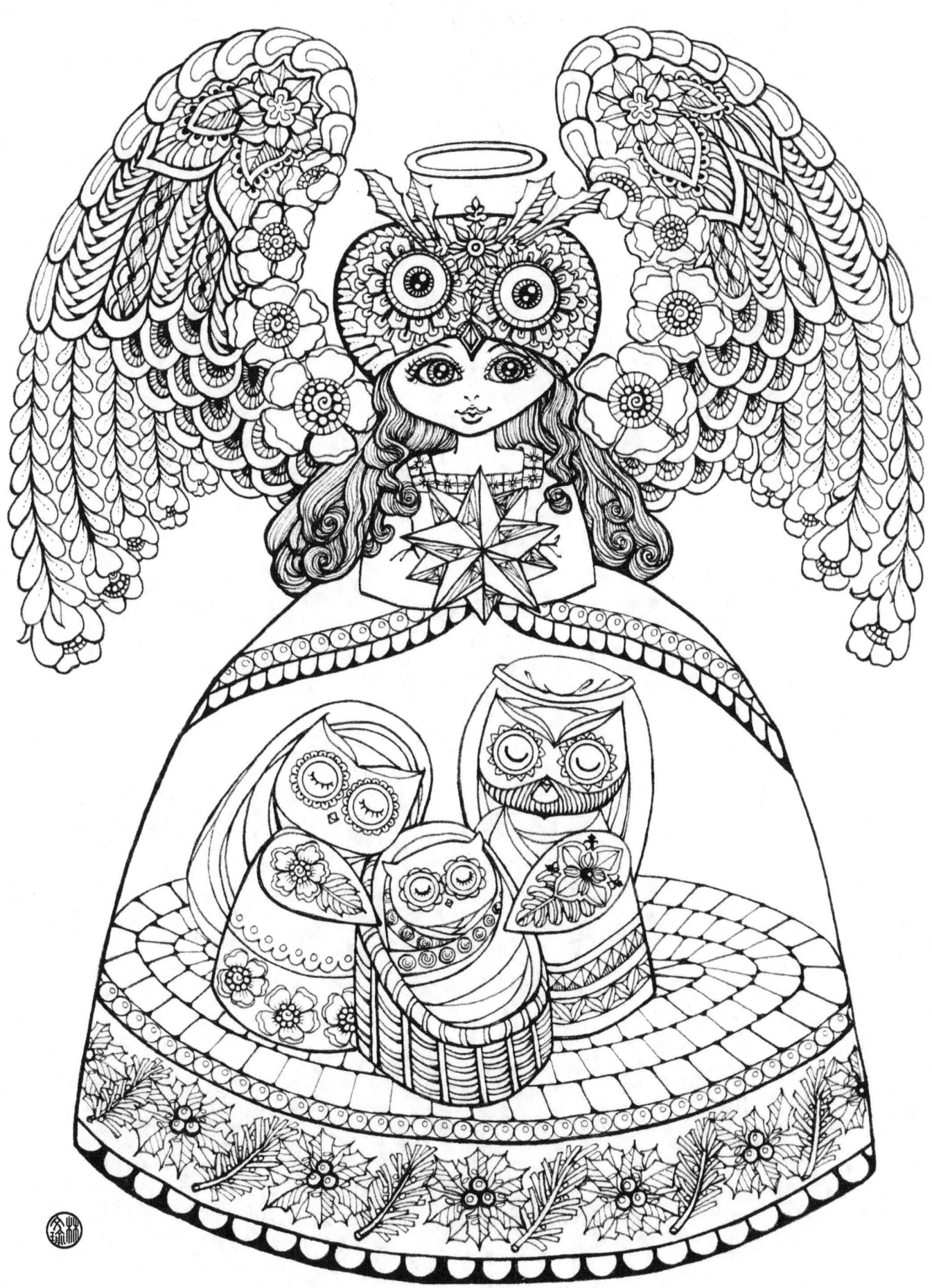

Contributing Artist
Takumi Nariyoshi
France

Facebook : takumidrawing

Art Coloring Book Day Version

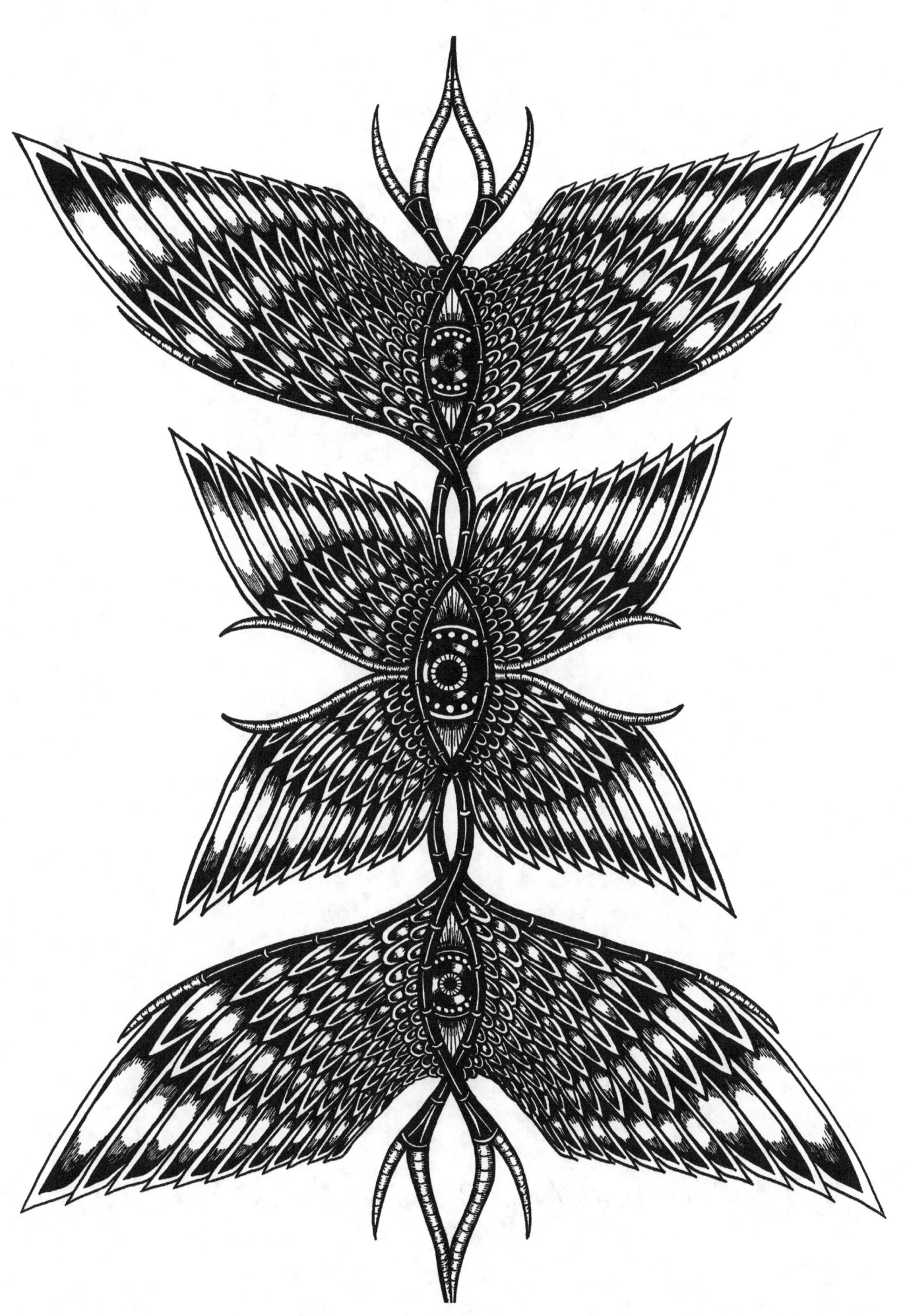

Contributing Artist
Takumi Nariyoshi
France

Facebook : takumidrawing

Art Coloring Book Day Version

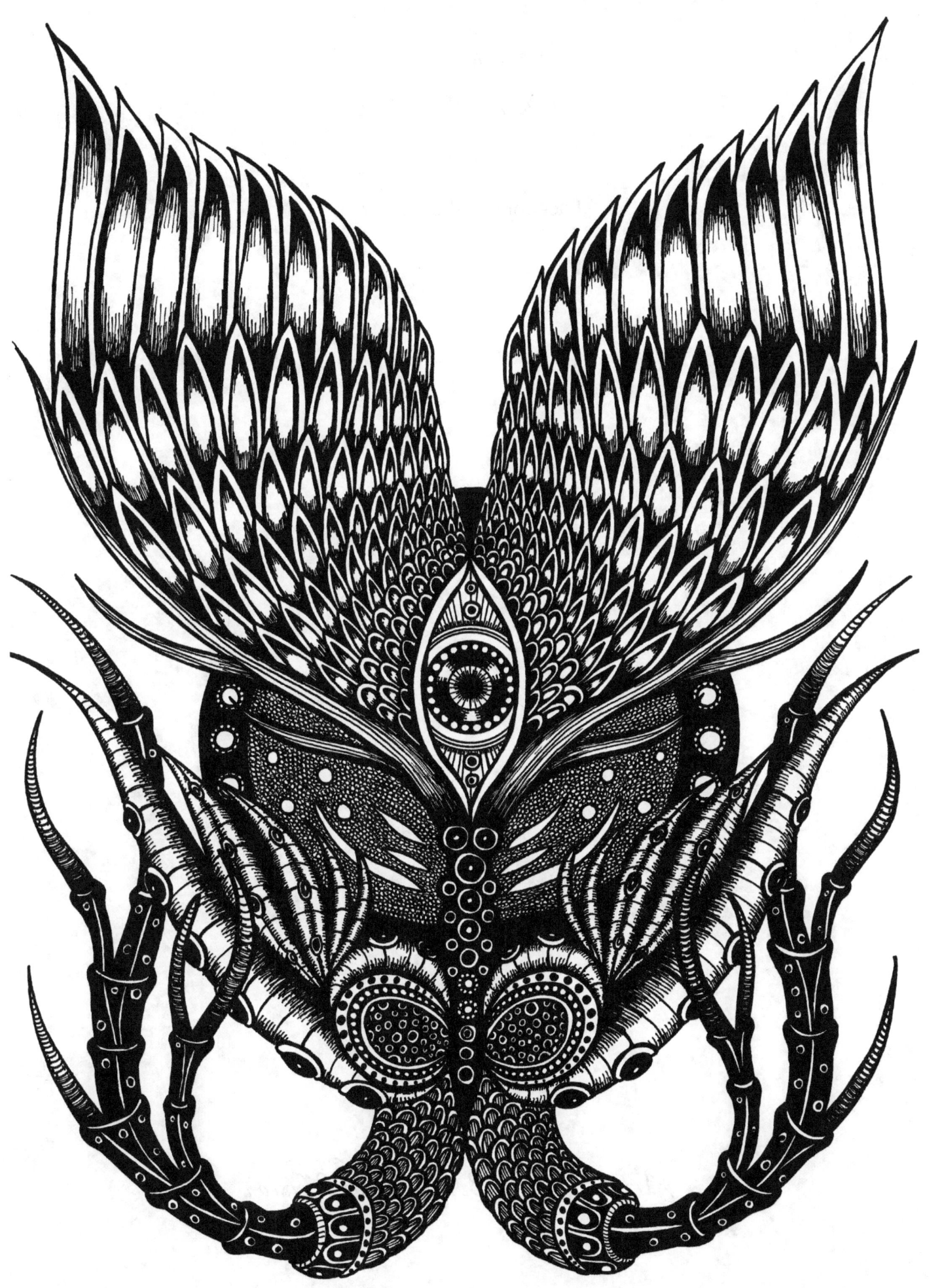

Contributing Artist
Takumi Nariyoshi
France

Facebook : takumidrawing

Art Coloring Book Night Version

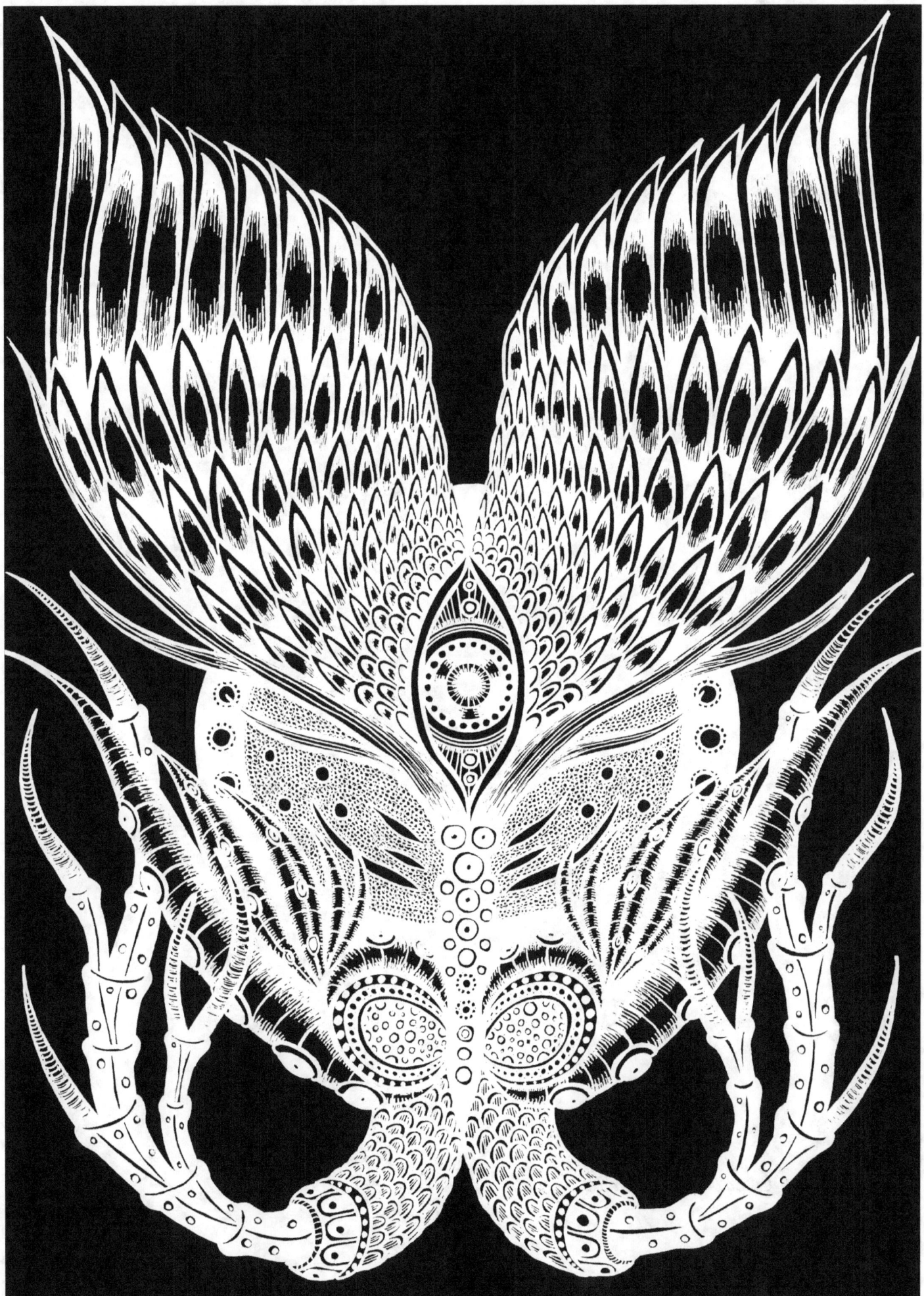

Contributing Artist
Velvet Comeau
Canada

Facebook : tranquilmoonart

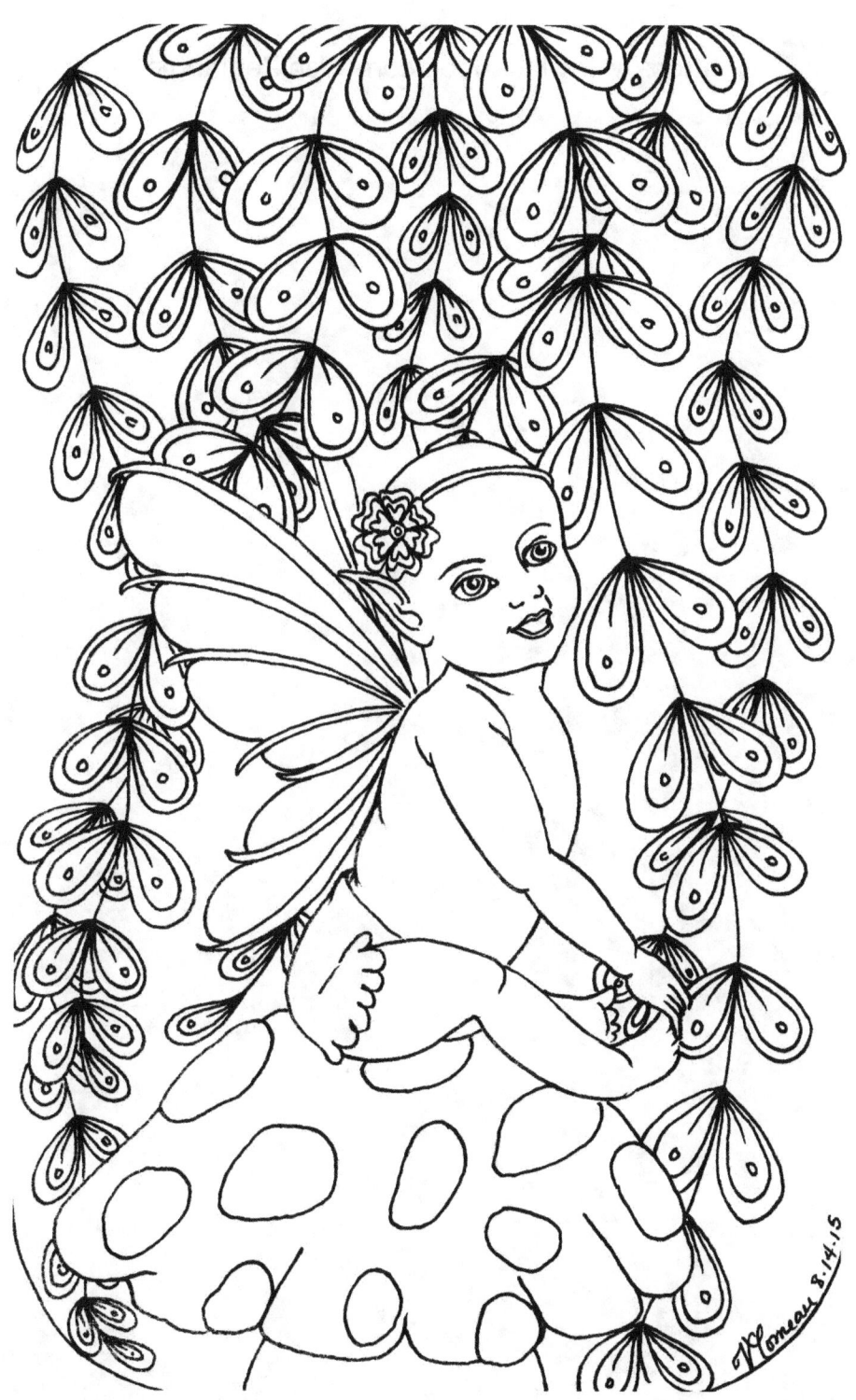

Contributing Artist
Wen Kung
Taiwan

https://www.facebook.com/Wen.Zentangle

Global Doodle Gems Christmas Collection Volume 3

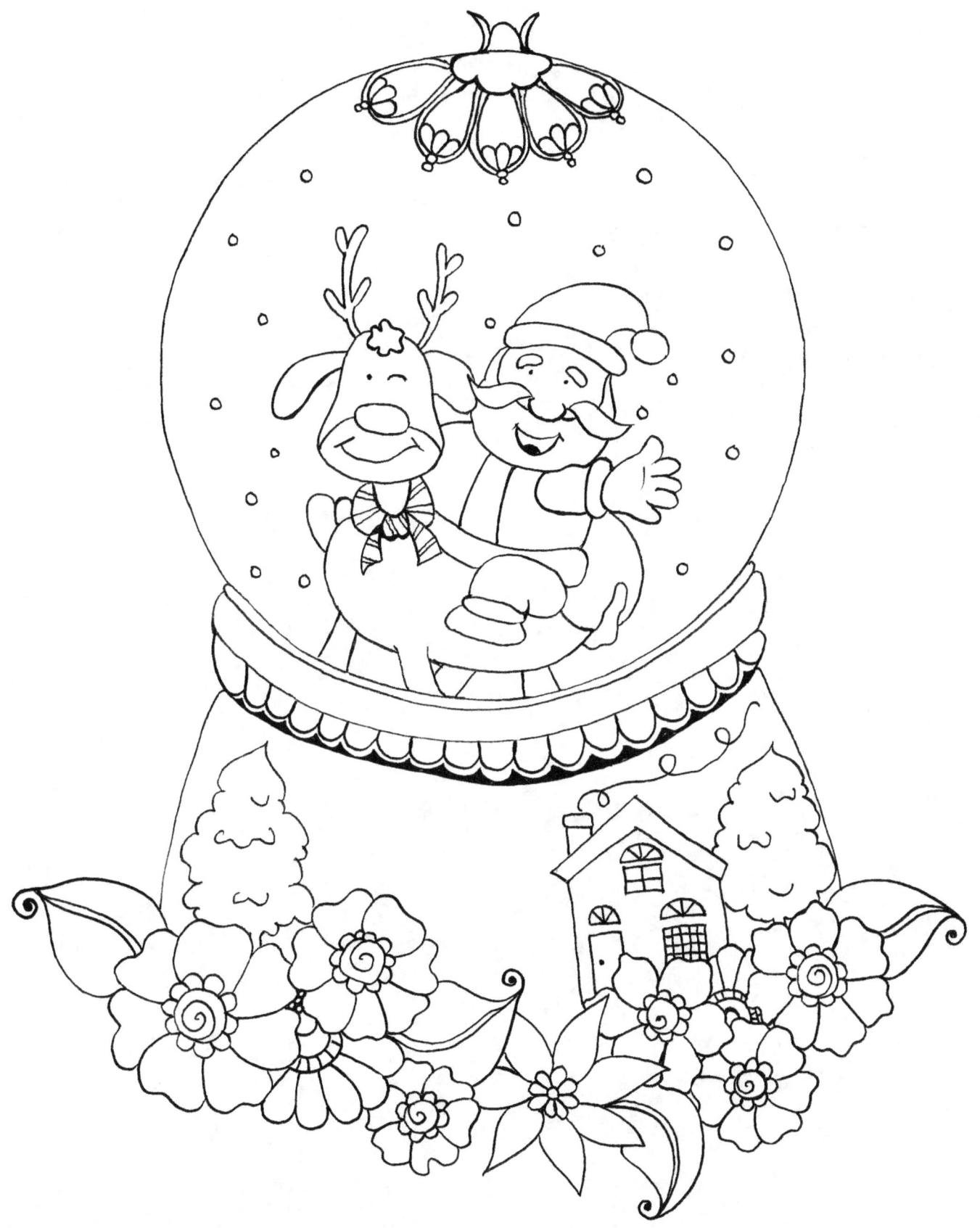

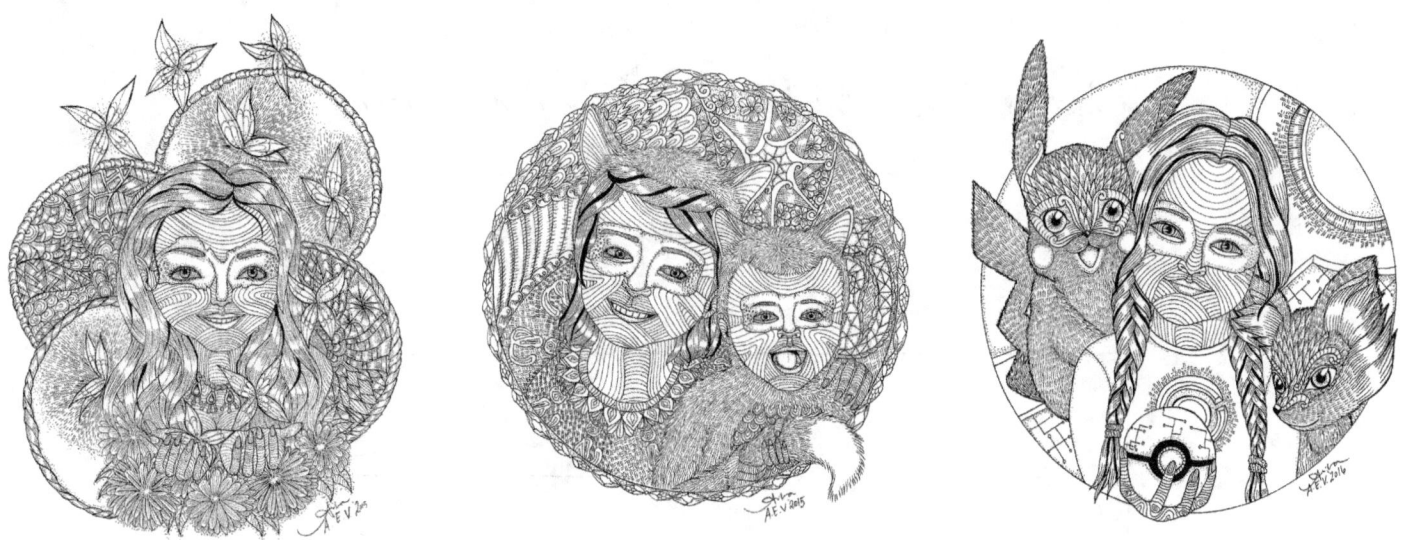

Interested in getting your own personal Coloring page ?

Digital Portrait commission by alfred
Size: 12"x18" in size
Format: high quality printable PDF files
Final pieces will be:
1 Black and white
1 colored piece in PDF formats
Both signed by the artist
Price: 40 dollars
Maximum 3 subjects on one commision piece
Inquiries just message on his Facebook page

Alfred E. Villanueva
Philippines

Facebook : viworksart2015

Test Your Colors here....
Charts from "My Pocket Color Companion"
and
" My Color Companion"

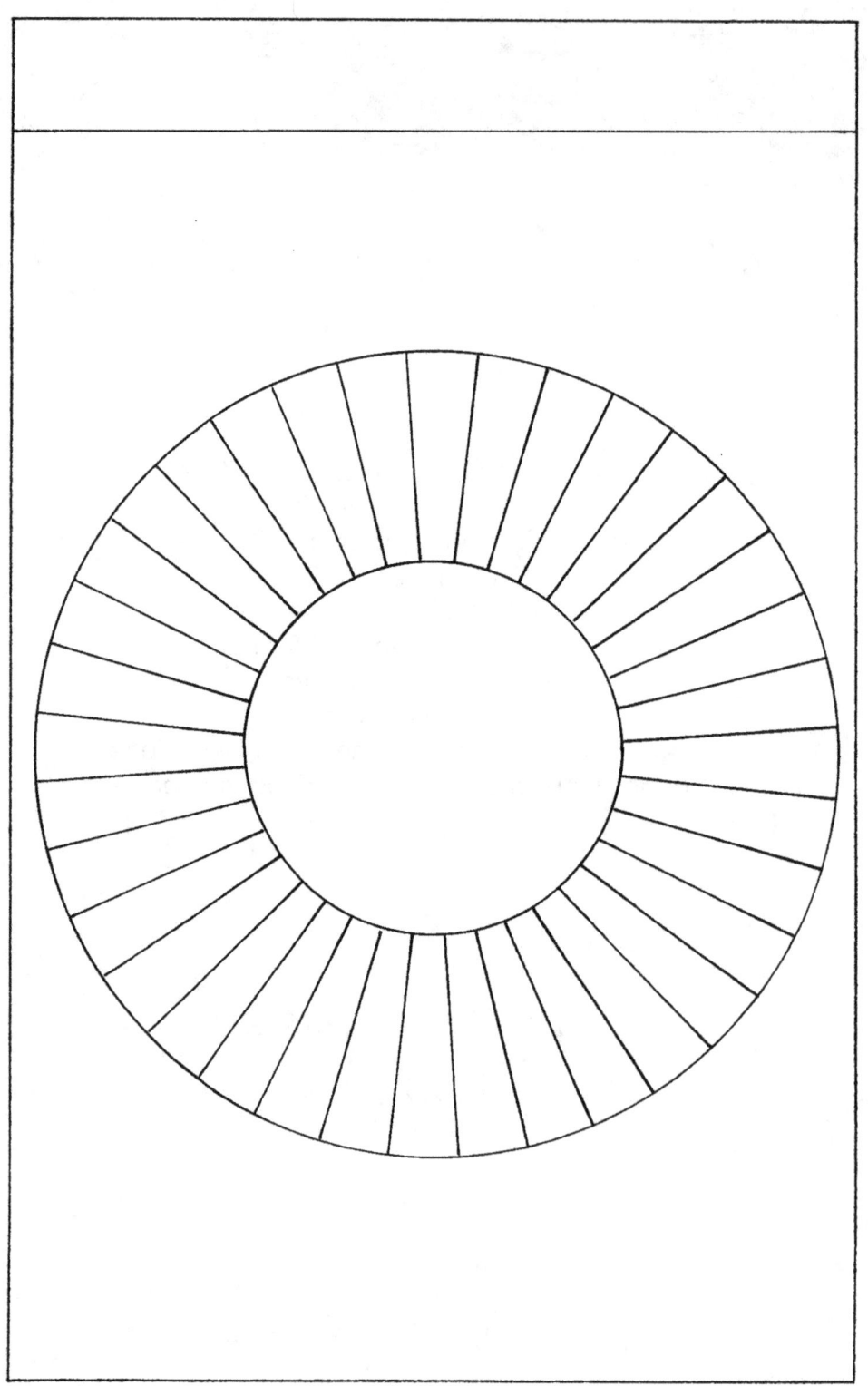

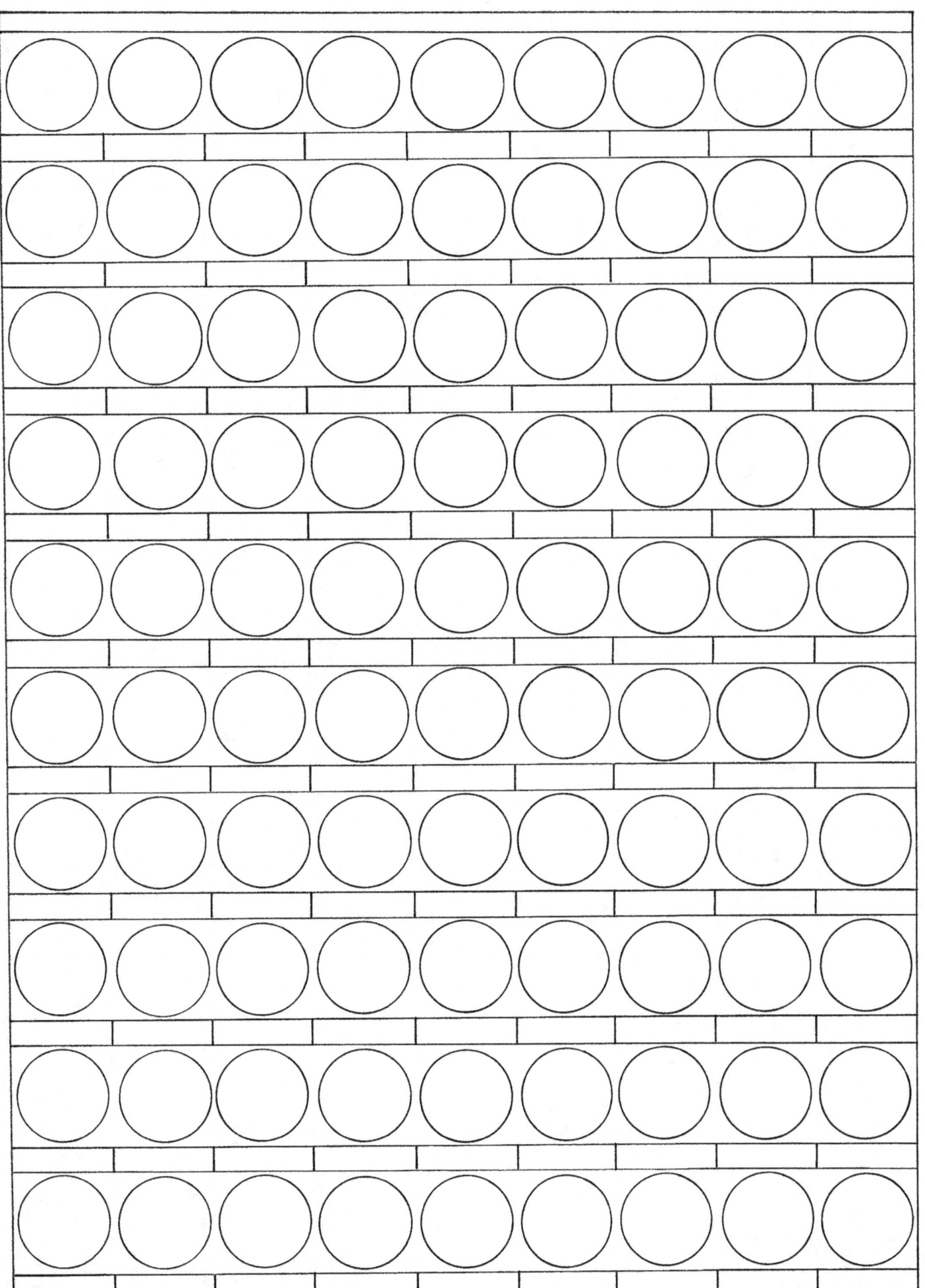

www.ingramcontent.com/pod-product-compliance
Lightning Source LLC
Chambersburg PA
CBHW082324220526
45470CB00008B/2398